THE SUNDAY TIMES
BOOK OF
DO-IT-YOURSELF

EDITED BY BILL CATER AND SHIRLEY CRABTREE

BOOK CLUB ASSOCIATES
LONDON

CONTRIBUTORS

Editors: Bill Cater and Shirley Crabtree.

Designer: Clive Crook

Main contributors: James S. Fardell, George A. Hedges, Kenneth Hensman, Arnold H. Masterman, Roy G. Payne and Henry Wyeth. Other contributors: John Houston, Alf Martensson, Charles Shea, Kenneth Unsworth.

Illustrations were by Alistair Campbell, Leslie Chapman, Bill Easter, Dan Fern, Alain le Garsmeur, Su Huntley, Barry Jackson, Richard Jacob, Ted Kinsey, Sally Launder, Ken Lewis, Osborn Marks, David Penney, Andrew Smee, Diane Tippell, David Worth.

The glossary was written by Shirley Crabtree and illustrated by Paul Marsh.

We would like to acknowledge the help of Berger Paints, the British Wood Preserving Association, Broads Builders' Merchants, Building Research Station, Crown Decorative Products, R. Durtnell & Sons, the Electricity Council, P.C. Henderson, Hire Association Europe, ICI Paints Division, London Brick Company, Marley, Nairn Floors, Rentokil, J.E. Sexton, and Walker Crossweller; and in particular the help made available by the School of Building, Vauxhall.

ISBN 0 904406 13 X
Copyright 1975 © Times Newspapers Ltd.

Published in 1976 by:

The Construction Press Ltd.,
Lunesdale House,
Hornby,
Lancaster, LA2 8NB.

Reprinted 1978 and 1979
Updated and reprinted 1980

Printed in Great Britain by
Redwood Burn Ltd., Trowbridge & Esher

CONTENTS

FOREWORD

by TONY WILKINS

Editor, Do it yourself magazine.

It has been my privilege, over a period of some 20 years, to watch the growth of the do-it-yourself movement in Britain. From very small beginnings it has developed into what has become for most of us an accepted part of everyday life. Its adherents are numbered in millions, and the industry which now backs them is estimated to be worth over £500 million a year!

Interest has grown steadily over the years, and so has the range of jobs the d-i-y enthusiast is willing to tackle, but the present economic climate has given the whole movement fresh impetus. Apart from rising material costs, labour charges have risen alarmingly — particularly in those areas concerned with getting faults diagnosed and repair work undertaken.

I am therefore pleased to have been asked to write a brief introduction to this book, for here, in easy to follow words and pictures, is a wealth of advice and instruction designed to teach you new skills, help with things that go wrong about the house, and perhaps improve your techniques in d-i-y jobs you have already tried. Apart from a real sense of achievement to be obtained, there is money to be saved, which on larger projects can amount to hundreds of pounds. Incidentally, prices (and savings) quoted in this book are already on the modest side, and you would be wise to check locally or with manufacturers before undertaking any projects.

I hope, too, this book will encourage the timid, for as you try your hand at some of the projects dealt with you will realise that the mystique which surrounds so many of the jobs once considered the cherished preserves of the tradesman is quite unfounded. With care and by following the instructions you'll find you too can produce work of the highest quality. True, you may take considerably longer than a professional to achieve the end result, but time is on your side.

Your home, however humble, represents a very considerable financial investment, and it makes good sense to keep it in first class condition. By doing much of the work on it yourself, you will find that some of the money you save will be free for spending on better quality decorating materials, fittings and fixtures. Thus, despite the economic situation, it is still possible to cut expenditure while at the same time improving the standard of décor and comfort in your home.

It is a wise investment to use some of the money which you save on d-i-y to buy good quality tools and accessories, gradually building up a comprehensive tool kit. This will help you to work efficiently and safely in any future jobs you tackle.

Here's wishing you success in all you undertake.

INTRODUCTION

TAKE A HOUSE LIKE THIS: THE SAVINGS YOU CAN MAKE

There are millions of houses like this, detached or paired, built 40 years ago and now beginning to need attention beyond normal redecoration and maintenance. We took such a house as our example to see what savings were possible to the householder willing to become his own painter, plumber, joiner, bricklayer. But the jobs this book will describe will apply equally to most other houses.

We asked our experts what it might cost to keep a house like this in good repair and to tackle some modernisation. They said it all depended on how well the house had been maintained, what standards the owner expected. But our electrical expert, for example, suggested that, spread over five years, the owner might need to renew all the aged lighting flexes and lampholders: a contractor would charge about £30; without him it would only cost £6·50. Rewiring the whole house - lighting, cooker and power circuits – would cost about £290 if a contractor tackled it: using the owner's labour the cost would be £95.

Our carpentry expert reckoned a householder could save £750 over five years carrying out loft-insulation, draught-sealing doors and windows, dealing with small amounts of dry rot and wood-worm, flush-panelling doors, maintaining locks and hinges and installing kitchen units.

The plumbing expert estimated £600 could be saved in five years; the 'trowel trades' expert – whose trade is heavy on labour costs but low on materials and so offers big savings for the self-reliant – anyone who tackled bricklaying, plastering and concreting could save up to £1000. Savings on decoration depends on how you want your house to look, and on whether you would normally hire a small decorating firm or a big contractor; but it couldn't, said our expert, be less than £70 a year and it could be £200 or more. To check on our experts' figures, we asked a master-builder for his estimates for the same jobs. Independently he quoted figures within 10 per cent. of these savings. How the savings break down job by job is shown on the right. Plainly few of us have time to tackle every job and some are better left to experts. But all the tasks we shall describe are within the capacity of the amateur

Replace slipped, broken tiles: materials £2.00, ladder hire £5.25, total £7.25; builder's bill £26.25-£43.75. Save **£19-£36.50**

Replacing all gutters: materials £46, hire of ladders and scaffold £23, total £69; builder's bill £175-260. Save **£106-£191**

Insulate loft: materials £28; builder's bill £52. Save **£24**

Broken window: cost of glass and putty £4.25; builder's bill £13 or more. Save **£8.75**

Exterior painting: materials and ladder hire £87; builder's bill £350-£438. Save **£263-£351**

Paint and paper dining and sitting rooms: materials £87.50; builder's bill £350-£700. Save **£262.50-£612.50**

Drawing by Ken Lewis

Fitting draught seals to all windows and doors: materials £17.50; builder's bill £43.75. Save **£26.25**

Redecorating kitchen: materials £13; builder's bill £43.75–£78.75. Save **£30.75–£65.75**

Replace broken bathroom basin: materials £12; builder's bill £35–£52.50. Save **£23–£40.50**

Fit porch light, garage power point: materials £11.50; builder's bill £52.50. Save **£41**

NOW TAKE A LOOK INSIDE ▶▶

INSIDE YOUR HIDDEN HOUSE

When the architect Le Corbusier declared that a house was a machine for living in, he was offering a reminder to architects – and not to builders, who knew it all along. How complex and efficient a machine it is can be hard to remember when brick and plaster cover most of the mechanism and while the machine goes on working – the electricity and water arriving when they are wanted, the drains silently taking the waste away, the shapes and materials evolved over centuries keeping weather out. This house, opened up from foundations to rafters, shows the constructional details present in almost every house. Keep the picture in mind; as we deal with repair jobs from room to room you will be able to match up the details and see where pipes and wires, disappearing into walls and beneath floors, go to; which are the vital supporting walls and which are merely partitions whose positions can be altered; where a wire can be run easily and where it will meet obstacles

Staircase *treads* and *risers* slot into sloping *string*; wedges should prevent creaks. Space used as cupboard is *spandrel*

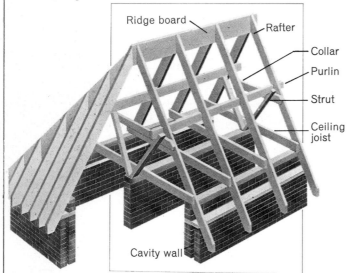

Weight of roof presses down and out; weight is carried by *rafters* on to wooden *wall plate* set into *loadbearing walls* at edges, by *struts* to loadbearing wall in middle. Outward push is held by *collar* and by *joists* resting on the *wall plates*

Water supply (pale blue) passes one, sometimes two, *stopcocks* before entering house to become *rising main*. Hot water system shown in orange

Sometimes bricks are carried up between rafters

Electric supply in armoured cable runs into house emerging at company fuse box

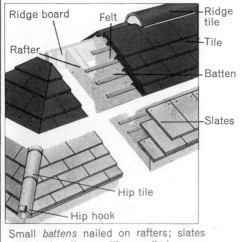

Small *battens* nailed on rafters; slates nailed to them; tiles nailed every third row, others hung by small *nibs*

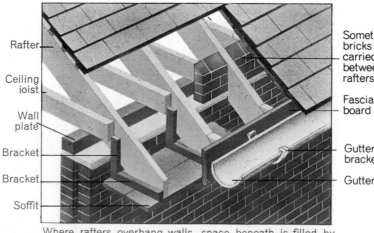

Where rafters overhang walls, space beneath is filled by horizontal *soffit board*, and the front is fitted with a vertical *fascia board* to which gutter is held by brackets

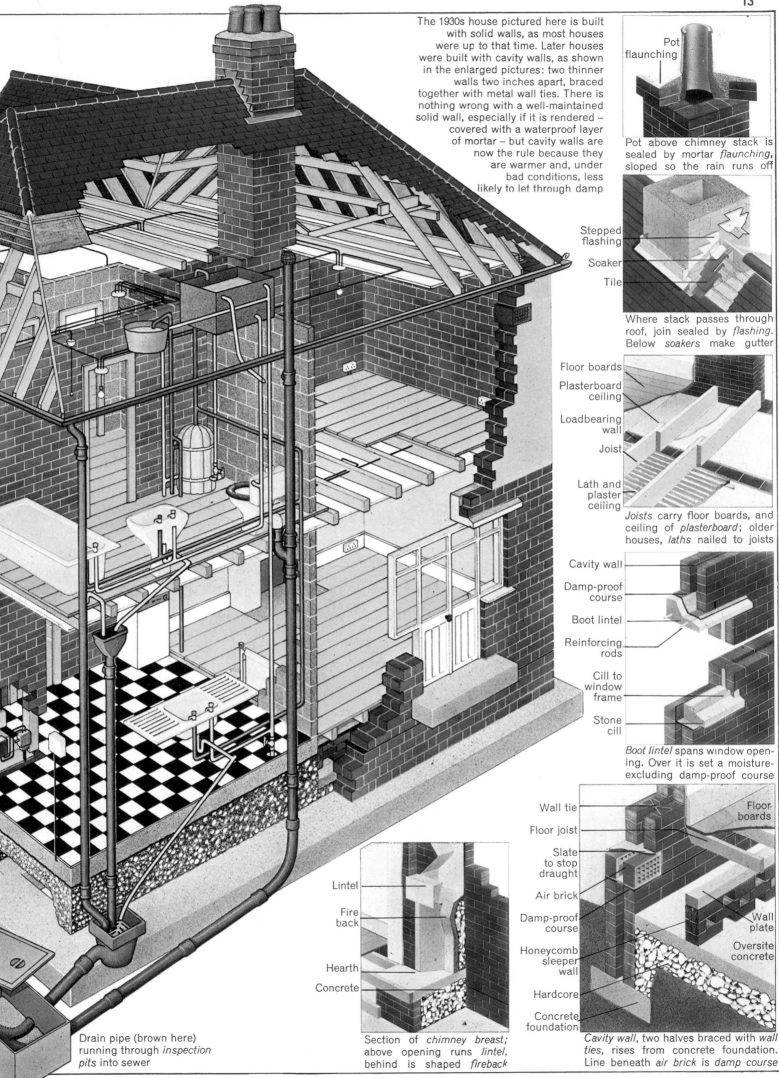

The 1930s house pictured here is built with solid walls, as most houses were up to that time. Later houses were built with cavity walls, as shown in the enlarged pictures: two thinner walls two inches apart, braced together with metal wall ties. There is nothing wrong with a well-maintained solid wall, especially if it is rendered – covered with a waterproof layer of mortar – but cavity walls are now the rule because they are warmer and, under bad conditions, less likely to let through damp

Pot flaunching

Pot above chimney stack is sealed by mortar *flaunching*, sloped so the rain runs off

Stepped flashing

Soaker

Tile

Where stack passes through roof, join sealed by *flashing*. Below *soakers* make gutter

Floor boards

Plasterboard ceiling

Loadbearing wall

Joist

Lath and plaster ceiling

Joists carry floor boards, and ceiling of *plasterboard*; older houses, *laths* nailed to joists

Cavity wall

Damp-proof course

Boot lintel

Reinforcing rods

Cill to window frame

Stone cill

Boot lintel spans window opening. Over it is set a moisture-excluding damp-proof course

Wall tie

Floor joist

Floor boards

Slate to stop draught

Air brick

Damp-proof course

Honeycomb sleeper wall

Wall plate

Oversite concrete

Hardcore

Concrete foundation

Cavity wall, two halves braced with *wall ties*, rises from concrete foundation. Line beneath *air brick* is *damp course*

Lintel

Fire back

Hearth

Concrete

Section of *chimney breast*; above opening runs *lintel*, behind is shaped *fireback*

Drain pipe (brown here) running through *inspection pits* into sewer

BUILDING RULES: CHECK BEFORE YOU LAY A BRICK

Every now and again somebody hits the headlines by building something his local council doesn't like and, after a long legal struggle, being ordered to knock it down again. Prudent householders will avoid such confrontations, if only because lawyers cost even more than builders; but if you are self-sufficient as well as prudent you *must* check carefully before you begin putting brick on brick, and even sometimes before dipping brush into paint pot.

There are two departments most likely to be concerned. One is the Building Inspector's office (in London the District Surveyor) and the other is the Planning Office.

The Building Inspector enforces a local authority's rules designed to see that our houses are healthy (no leaking drains) and safe (no walls collapsing, no unnecessary fire risks). There have been rules like this since 1189 (walls between houses should be stone, three feet thick).

It is the Building Inspector who, when you want to knock down a wall between two rooms, makes sure that you do it in such a way that the bedrooms don't fall into your new through-lounge while you're sitting watching television (it has happened). He will insist that your new extension is built of such materials that if it catches fire you'll have time to get out of bed before the whole house goes up. You will find your inspector through the town hall; you should tell him about any solid building (or demolition) you plan to do, and if it comes under his rules he will check your plans and tell you what alterations in them may be necessary. Take him seriously; it is for your own good, and anyway, he will call round while the work is going on to see that you are doing it properly. He is usually helpful to amateurs, and even builders have been known to speak highly of him.

Less happily placed is the Planning Officer who has to administer the Town and Country Planning rules. He is usually over-worked so that the decisions he is supposed to make within two months may not be dealt with for six or more. The jungle of regulations does not ease his task. He doesn't guard you against your house falling down (though he does guard you against having a glue factory built next door). Often lampooned as the typical obstructive bureaucrat, he runs an office that safeguards our towns from being more hideous and our countryside more despoiled than it is at present.

There are one or two clearings in the planning jungle: the Town and Country Planning General Development Order, 1973, maps some of them. You can enlarge your house (which includes building a garage) by a tenth without planning consent, provided that the enlargement does not stick up above the top of the roof, or stick out in front (it can stick out at the back). Beware, though; that tenth includes any previous extensions, so if you or the previous owner of your house has already built a garage or an extension you may not be able to build another one.

High walls beside road: permission needed

Swimming pool: permission to fill it

Greenhouse, henhouse: not more than half garden

Roof room: front no, back yes

Drawings by Diane Tippell

To get clearance under this one-tenth rule there was an architect who had to include the volume of the chimneys.

You can erect garden sheds, greenhouses and "any building or enclosure (other than a dwelling, garage, stable, loose box or

Garden shed: not more than 4 metres high

coach house) required for a purpose incidental to the enjoyment of the dwelling-house as such, including the keeping of poultry, bees, pet animals, birds or other livestock for the domestic needs or personal enjoyment of the occupants of the dwellinghouse". These buildings also must not stick out beyond the front of the house, and they must not be more than four metres high with a ridge roof or three metres with other kinds of roof; and they must not cover more than half the garden. If you do have a half-acre garden that could let you build a pretty big henhouse, but beware: it's for personal enjoyment, and if you sell the eggs you could be in trouble. And beware again: if you put your shed or henhouse close to a fence, planning and fire rules could be broken. And beware again: do not build over the drainage system.

Garden pond: no problems

And beware yet again: though planning rules may let you put up a henhouse, there may be local by-laws that restrict you. Prudent householders ring the town hall first, and check.

You can put up gates, fences and walls – provided they are not more than a metre high where the garden flanks a road, or two metres elsewhere. You

Flagpoles: hoist away

can lay a drive – but only if it leads into a minor road. If it leads into a main road, you will need planning consent. You can build a porch provided it is not more than two square metres floor area – say 3ft. 3in. by 6ft. 6in. – not more than three metres high, and at least two metres from your boundary.

You can dazzle the neighbours by building a swimming pool and the Planning Officer cannot stop you – until you come to fill it with water. Then you'll probably have to have planning consent. (Fish have an unfair advantage: there is no restriction on ponds.) You can set up a flagpole though probably not if you hoist on it a flag

Extension: not more than a tenth of whole

which says "Buy at Snooks". Advertising needs consent.

Statues are permissible, provided they do not get out of hand. Nobody can object to plaster gnomes: but a man who put up an equestrian statue of the Duke of Wellington in his back garden ran into trouble because the statue was so big and the garden so small that the horse was peering into his neighbour's window. You can paint your house, without hindrance, unless it's in a conservation area, when you may well have to conform with the style that makes the area worth conserving; you will not be able to repaint your 17th-century black-and-white house purple, and if you live in a historic Listed Building you'll hardly be able to lay a finger on it. As a rule the Planning Officer is helpful. Most things a self-sufficient householder wants to do won't concern him: but ring to check.

Porch: yes – if you keep it small

PAINTING
and
DECORATING

DECORATION: 1 preparing for work

Main difference between amateur and professional decorators is that the professional knows what the amateur learns only by bitter experience – that the work you do before you start painting matters more than the painting itself. A thin film of paint or a thin sheet of wallpaper, come to that – won't hide faults in the surface underneath; and no paint can last longer than the surface underneath. So force yourself to take time over preparing for paint and paper. In following pages we will explain the experts' way for you to paint and paper the room you've prepared.

The right tools

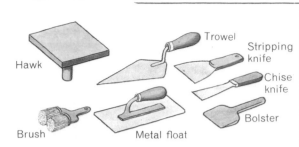

Hawk
Trowel
Stripping knife
Chise knife
Brush
Metal float
Bolster

Small cracks in plaster can be filled with patent fillers, following the packet directions. Bigger damage – it often occurs round door frames or on corners – needs a more professional approach and the right tools are worth while. A *hawk* you can make yourself: a 9in. square of ply or even hardboard nailed or screwed to a short piece of broomhandle. A *pointing trowel* is needed – and it will be useful for other jobs later; an old paint-brush, a *flat stripper* (you'll use that for stripping paint, too) and possibly a *chisel knife* (a narrower version of the stripper; a broken kitchen knife will do); if you've a large area to repair, a *metal float*; and for hacking away loose or cracked plaster, a *bolster* – a broad-bladed chisel; and a small bag of plaster – tell the builder's merchant what it is for and he'll supply the right kind. Most amateur problems with plaster are through not knowing the right consistency: put a small mound of plaster on your hawk, make a hole in the middle, add water and mix: the plaster should be as stiff as possible while still being workable. A good test: when you tip the hawk sideways the plaster should not ooze off

Repairing plaster cracks

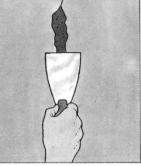

With any plaster repair, hack away loose or damaged material with bolster and hammer, brush away dust, damp broken surfaces. Pick up plaster on under-side of trowel and press into hole, adding more until not quite level with surrounding good plaster. Leave to harden, scratching lines to make key for top layer. This is best put on with flat surface of stripping knife, finishing by smoothing with the knife wet; plaster will stick to a dry blade

Edge of stripping knife can clean out cracks. All loose dust must be removed; then damp

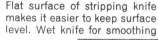

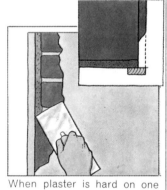

Plaster is scooped up on back of trowel. Use point to pack in to corners. Press plaster in hard

Flat surface of stripping knife makes it easier to keep surface level. Wet knife for smoothing

Matching damaged edges and corners

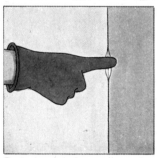

Easiest repair to small cracks or holes on internal corners is to press plaster in with finger, smooth with wetted rubber glove, sand when dry with sandpaper wrapped round a block of wood

Most easily damaged plaster is on external corners. If more than small area damaged, problem is to match level of surrounding plaster with only one edge to rely on. Answer is a batten longer than damaged area nailed top and bottom so edge just lines up with plaster; plaster up to it; when hard remove batten carefully, hold on other edge of corner and fill in remaining plaster. Smooth off sharp edge slightly with your hand in wet rubber glove

Large area of metal float makes it easier to maintain line of the plaster on external corner

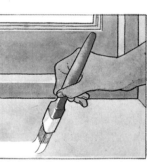

When plaster is hard on one side, hold – don't nail – batten over it and plaster the other

Making ready for the gloss paint

Wash down walls with decorator's soap, rinse clean; roughen gloss paint with sandpaper so the new paint can grip. Sound paint on woodwork need only be roughened; fill small holes and cracks with putty or patent filler. Bad paintwork should be stripped with chemical stripper or gas blowlamp and knife. Work upwards, keep lamp upright, tackle awkward bits first, go gently to avoid charring. Keep flame from glass; strip windows with chemical stripper

Narrow flexible blade – old kitchen knife will do – will fill cracks in woodwork before painting

Square blade helps fill cracks at corners; smooth off before filler hardens to save work later

For even, easy sanding wrap sandpaper round block of wood. Clean all the dust away

Paint won't stick on resinous knots; if you uncover any, brush with knotting fluid to seal

Preparing metal frames

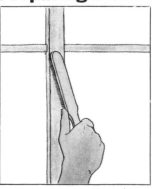

Metal windows to be repainted should be rubbed down with a wire brush, any lumps sanded off, and any rust spots sanded down and treated with one of the jelly-type rust cures. Don't paint over rust; it will spread and force the paint off from underneath. Loose putty should be cleaned out, and new putty put in so that it is level with the metal; gaps left here will mean moisture from condensation getting in, spoiling the paint and possibly, starting more rust

Stripping old distemper

Most tiresome job for self-sufficient householders decorating an old house is stripping off layers of distemper, especially from ceilings. Some distempers will wash off with warm water – add a squirt of washing-up liquid to a bucket of water; work a small patch at a time, sponge in one hand, stripping knife in the other (careful you don't scratch the plaster). Cover the floor; the old distemper makes a lot of mess. When finished, wash ceiling over with clean water. Oil-bound distempers won't come off so easily. If you must get them off, and they don't

respond to prolonged soaking, consider hiring a steam stripper from one of the tool-hire depots. Steam strippers cost about £3 a day to hire, and are useful for getting off obstinately stuck wallpapers, too. The hire depot will explain how they work. As a rule, if the oil-bound distemper is not loose and flaking, it can be washed over, left for paint or emulsion. Sharp edges of flaked patches can be sanded so that they don't show under the paint, especially if matt

DECORATION: Painting without pain

In the highly-competitive paint business there are bargains – end-of-range colours, for example – but as a rule you get what you pay for. We'll take a detailed look at paint types in a later section. Gloss lasts longer, though with better paints and more frequent redecoration that isn't everything. Matt finishes help to hide faults – both in the under-surface and in the painter's skill – which gloss reveals mercilessly. Bare

wood must be painted first with primer and then, if you are using conventional paints, one or two layers of undercoat, before the top coat goes on. (Non-technically you might say undercoats are lots of pigment, little varnish; topcoats little pigment, lots of varnish.) Let each coat dry well, and sand between coats with wet-and-dry paper to remove small imperfections. If the old paint is sound you can simply clean and roughen it before putting on a new topcoat of the same colour. If you want a different colour you will need at least one undercoat to stop the old colour grinning through. Among the new paints one-pack polyurethanes stand up well against hard wear and water; thixotropic (gel) paints save splashes and allow thicker coats without running. Water-thinnable acrylic paints are quick-drying and brushes wash under the tap.

How to build the versatile trestle

You can paint ceilings from a step-ladder, but for safe, fast work follow the experts and use trestles and planks: with this easily made design, you've a pasting table and sawbench as well. You'll need 10 2ft. pieces and eight 3ft. pieces of 3in. by 1in. (75mm. x 25mm.) planed timber; two planks 1¼in. thick, 8in. wide and about 6ft. long (30mm. x 200mm., 1·8 metres long); 40 1¾in. No 10 screws, four 2in. backflap hinges with screws to fit, a couple of yards of sashcord some PVA glue.
.Each trestle is 2ft. wide; glue and screw (two screws to each joint) a 2ft. crosspiece level with the top of the 3ft. legs and another about 6in. from the bottom; hinges are screwed to top crosspieces and sashcord between bottom crosspieces holds legs of each trestle about 2ft. apart. As a staging for ceiling work the planks rest on a further crosspiece on each trestle. Measure the height from the top of your head to the ceiling and subtract 7in.;

Trestle ready for painting ceiling

Hardboard in position for pasting table

that's the height the top of these crosspieces should be from the ground. When the planks are on the crosspieces and you are on the planks, your head will be 6in. below the ceiling, the most comfortable working height. To use as a pasting table, set the planks on top of the trestles and cover

them with a sheet of hardboard the width of the wallpaper (21in. for most papers). To saw hardboard, leave a narrow gap between planks for the saw, so that the hardboard is supported both sides.

The painter's tools

Radiator/ flag brush

Cutting-in brush   Paint pad

Foam rollers are cheap – some have use-and-throw-away sleeves – but need care if they are not to distort and scatter paint. Synthetic fur is better – long pile for rough surface, short for smooth: you can buy frames with interchangeable pile sleeves. For many smooth surfaces pads are even better. For heavy paints and smaller areas you still can't beat brushes. Buy the best. Shaped cutting-in brush is useful for windowframes, radiator brush is useful for awkward corners.

Finding your way round the room

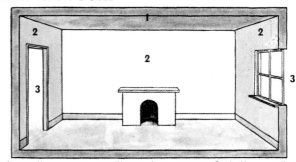

Decorator's dictionary: there's more to walls, especially old-fashioned walls, than you think

In decorating a room, ceilings always come first, then walls (if they are to be painted), then woodwork. If walls are to be papered then they come last, after all the paintwork is completely dry

Tricks of the trade – learning from the professional

Experience has taught experts the easiest way, so follow them. You hardly ever see a professional painting straight from the tin: he uses a paint kettle – any container with a handle (pint enamel mugs are good) which can be cleaned out every night. He strains his paint into the kettle through an old stocking so dust and bits of paint-skin never spoil his work. When he stops for tea he keeps his brushes from drying by suspending them in the paint by a wire through a hole in the handle or wrapping them in a plastic bag. At night he washes them thoroughly, first in thinners, then in water, flicks water out and hangs them up to dry. He always wipes his brush on the same side of the kettle, so the other stays clean and so does the brush-handle; and he keeps an old knife by him to scoop up any paint that accidentally gets in the wrong place. Remember that it is an idea to run-in new brushes. Always wash new brushes before use, and use them first for primer and undercoat painting.

Metal shield or masking tape makes windows easier, but nothing can beat a steady hand

If you paint sash windows in this order you won't find yourself trying to move sash with only wet-painted bits to hold it by. Be frugal with paint around the sliding parts or they may stick

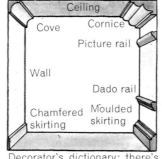

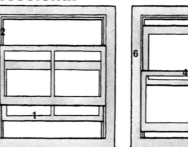

Paint tread over carpet line to ensure neat finish

For stairs, casement windows and doors the same principle applies; work from top down and tackle awkward bits first. It's on narrow, complicated sections that paint is most likely to run down; as you finish and go on to surrounding plain sections you can mop up these tears before they dry completely

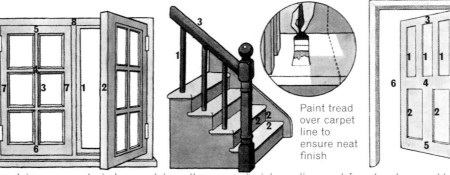

Smooth finish

Paint large areas a bit at a time, vertical stripes first, then cross-strokes to join them without putting more paint on brush, then laying-off – smoothing gently – back into painted piece. Limit yourself to an area small enough not to be dry before adjacent squares are started, or you'll get a hard line showing between sections. The faster paint dries, the smaller such sections should be. Remember, timber is best finished in same direction as grain.

First find a spell of fine weather

For painting gutters, bituminous paint is best unless you want light colours; then you'll have to use high gloss. Wire-brush off rust; prime with red lead primer

Gutters may not stand weight of ladder – plastic ones won't. Check; if in doubt use ladder-stay

Smooth-rendered or pebble-dashed walls should be dusted down with a brush, hosed and scrubbed if very dirty. Repair cracks and undercoat before repainting

If you need to stand on asbestos roof use crawling boards to spread weight

Pay special attention to the end-grain of wood and to joints, and to any nail holes and crevices where weather penetrates most easily

Where paint has flaked off and the timber become 'dead', the woolly surface should be scraped off. Coat any knots with knotting

DECORATION: Tackling the outside

Aluminium surfaces – use zinc chromate primer. For zinc (galvanised metal windows) use calcium plumbate primers

For fences, creosote is cheapest and best protection, unless you want to preserve colour of new wood, when a clear wood preservative should be used

Don't try burning off paint near glass: use solvent stripper or rub away with sandpaper

Dingy brickwork can be improved by sweeping down, or wire brushing. Drastic treatment: scrub with dilute acid

Easily-forgotten edges of window-frames, exposed when windows are opened, should be painted – and don't forget the top and bottom edges

If cracks have opened round door joints, don't putty them up without first tightening joints by drilling and dowelling

Bare wood must be primed – pink wood primer for soft woods, aluminium wood primer for resinous woods (it stops the resin bleeding through), calcium plumbate primer for hard woods

Up the wall: the height of safety

Exterior decoration means working at a height, even if your house is a bungalow, so follow the professionals and take care; it will save time. Five minutes spent in making sure that a ladder is secure will not only keep you safe (and few things delay redecorating more than a broken leg) but, because you can work more easily from a secure footing, will get the job completed more quickly. Step-ladders should be fully open – if the rope tie is slack the steps can jump, throwing the painter off and often tipping paint down the wall.
Make sure that bigger ladders are really big enough. You can hire a 22ft. ladder for about £2·50 a week, a 36ft. ladder for £4 or £5.
A ladder stay to hold the head of the ladder clear of the wall (useful when painting gutters and fascia boards) will cost another £1 a week. If you are not used to ladder work pace yourself; you'll be using un-familiar muscles and will ache all over next morning. Don't stretch and lean from ladders

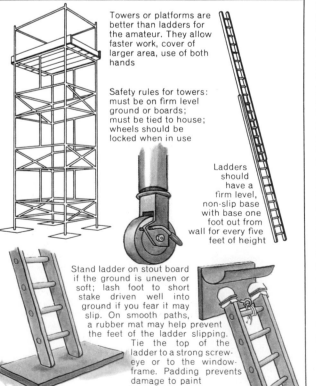

Towers or platforms are better than ladders for the amateur. They allow faster work, cover of larger area, use of both hands

Safety rules for towers: must be on firm level ground or boards; must be tied to house; wheels should be locked when in use

Ladders should have a firm level, non-slip base with base one foot out from wall for every five feet of height

Stand ladder on stout board if the ground is uneven or soft; lash foot to short stake driven well into ground if you fear it may slip. On smooth paths, a rubber mat may help prevent the feet of the ladder slipping. Tie the top of the ladder to a strong screw-eye or to the window-frame. Padding prevents damage to paint

as the experts do – they've had a lot of practice (and they still fall off now and then). To work over the roof, use proper roof ladders, securely tied.
Better than ladders for the amateur are towers; working platforms anything from 4ft. by 2ft. to 6ft. by 4ft., at heights of up to 30ft. Reassuring if you've a poor head for heights, the big platform with its guard rails enables you to work faster, cover a wider area without climbing down, and use both hands easily. Hire costs range from about £3 to £12 a week according to size. (Delivery of all hire equipment is extra; worth checking.)
Houses need exterior decora-tion roughly every five years and, appearance apart, the more carefully the job is done, especially *before* you begin painting, the longer it will last. Late summer or early autumn is the best time, when the weather seems settled for a good dry spell and any exposed timber has had a chance to dry. Paint-ing in damp weather is a waste of time and money. Start early

in the morning, as soon as the dew has dried; stop early enough for paint to be dry before dewfall. You'll need a lot of paint, so shop around. Supermarkets buying in bulk can sometimes undercut builders' merchants, but if in doubt buy the best paint you can afford, from a reputable firm. Some job-lot paints are no bargain. Use the right paint for the job, including primers (listed above); once you've painted your house you want to forget all about it for five years or more.
The general rule for exterior decoration is: start at the top and work down with each pro-cess (cleaning, repair, under-coat, top coat). Do one side of the house at a time (it's less strain than very long spells on a ladder). Treat gutters first, then walls, then woodwork.
If you need to burn off defective paint, have some water handy when you do so; more than one house has been set on fire by over-enthusiastic burn-ing-off, and not only by ama-teurs. Dry birds'-nests in the eaves are a particular peril.

Preparing and repairing the outside walls

Rendered walls have a layer of cement-sand mortar on top of the structural brick or blocks, rather as interior walls have a layer of plaster. Except in rare cases where they have already been painted with gloss paint (when you will be able to clean down and put on another coat) they are usually decorated with a cement-based paint, a paint containing sand to give texture, or with emulsion paint – which is cheap and holds well to masonry surfaces even out of doors. Before starting work tie back any wall plants (careful gardeners wrap them in plastic sheets). Scrape off any loose or flaking paint.

Small cracks in rendering can be treated like plaster cracks indoors (see details on page 18) except that the filler must be one prepared specially for outdoor use. Larger areas of rendering that have failed should be hacked out until a firm edge is reached and then filled with a not-too-wet mixture of one part masonry cement to five parts soft sand.

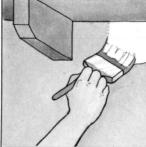

Where textured rendering is patched, float or brush is used to match new surface to the old

This is put on with a steel float; if the rendering is much more than half an inch thick do it in two coats, scoring the first one as it dries to provide a key for the second. If the rendering is textured try to match this with the edge of the float or a brush. Pebbledash is rendering sometimes pre-mixed with small stones, but more usually applied flat and then having small stones flung against it from a shovel and pressed in with a float; examine it carefully if you want a good match. Brush down walls to get rid of dust (scrub them with a broom if they are very dirty), and apply masonry sealer if the surface is powdery. Repaired cracks and other bare areas should be given an under-coat of emulsion paint. A surface which has never been coated should be wetted a square yard at a time before painting; if it has been painted but is very absorbent thin the first coat by 10 per cent. or so. The second coat (you'll need two) should be put on full strength. Wash off all splashes as you go. Where possible keep the painter's rule: don't let an edge dry before you paint the adjoining section.

After patching damaged rendering, a coat of emulsion paint will act as an undercoat, but give the repair time to dry

Previously unpainted rendering should be wetted before first coat, powdery surfaces should be sealed with masonry sealer

Brickwork doesn't usually need attention beyond dusting down with a brush; if it has been splashed or looks dingy it can be cleaned with a weak solution of spirits of salts (buy it from your builder's merchants); a tablespoonful to a bucket of water. Brush it on, rinse and brush down with a wire brush. Take care; though the acid is weak it can still burn, so wear goggles and rubber gloves. Brickwork can be painted with emulsion (wet first, as with new rendering) or with cement or sand-texture paints (follow the maker's instructions).

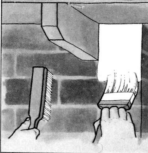

Treatment for dingy brick: brush down, brush with dilute acid, or paint with emulsion, cement paint or textured paint

The five-year protection plan

All bare wood should be coated first with a lead-based primer. Pay special attention to the end-grain of wood, to nail holes and to crevices; brush the paint well in to give strong adhesion for the putty or fillers which will follow. When the primer is thoroughly dry sand lightly with medium sandpaper, then fill nail holes and other small deep indentations with putty. For filling the face of wood where the grain or surface is irregular, and for hardwood sills which weathering often leaves rough, use a paste oil filler (from your builder's merchant) applied with a broad flat scraper. Use the scraper slightly skewed so surplus filler is forced out to one side.

After filling, undercoat. A lot depends on this; it should be even, opaque, smooth as possible – marks will show through the finishing coat. Two undercoats are better than one, especially if slightly thinned. When dry rub down lightly with wet-and-dry paper, used wet, to remove bits, then sponge

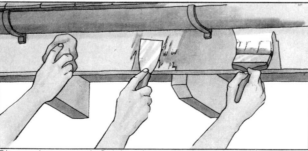

Stages to a good finish: above, washing down, face-filling, painting. Below: danger spots include cracked putty (replace) and decay in sill (scrape out, prime, then use paste oil filler)

and leather off the sludge. (If non-drip undercoat is used you'll need a much thicker coat to get a good finish.) Lay off top coat the long way of the timber, and try to make breaks between new dried and fresh paint at corners to hide join. When painting windows it's best to open them fully to paint inside edges of frames and edges of sashes first, and finally paint the face surfaces. Keep a non-fluffy rag handy to wipe paint off inside frames and glass. Always remember

you are not only making the timber look good; you are providing its only protection against the next five years of rain.

Renovating the guttering

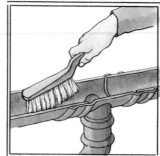 

After cleaning and rust-treatment, experts often paint inside of gutters with left-over gloss paints mixed together, strained through a stocking. Below: card behind pipe protects wall

Always check gutters are safe before resting ladders on them. Rusty gutters may collapse. A ladder stay will hold ladder clear. Plastic gutters won't stand the weight anyway, but they don't need painting. If you want them a different colour use gloss paint; no priming or undercoat is necessary. A surprising amount of debris can collect in gutters – you may have to start by trowelling it out, followed by brushing and washing down. (Don't try to flush lots of muck away with water; you'll risk blocking the downpipes.)

If joints between metal sections leak, unbolt and separate sections, chip out old putty joint and renew with metal casement putty, then bolt together again. (We go into detail about more gutter repairs later.) If previous

paint has been bituminous, use the same again – it's very good for protecting metal, and its dark colours are more practical for gutters – unless you want a light colour.

Light colours will have to be in gloss paint, and before putting gloss on top of bituminous you must seal the old surface with a shellac sealer, otherwise the old colour will bleed through.

Doors need care and attention

Doors need extra care: they are the parts of exterior decoration seen in close-up. Take off handles, letterbox and knocker; check that the joints between stiles (uprights) and rails (crosspieces) are sound. If not, repair them (see details on page 58) – it's no good puttying-up a crack which will open again. If paintwork is bad burn it off. Do mouldings first, then panels, then rails and stiles. Use shavehook for mouldings, flat scraper for flat surfaces; keep flame ahead of scraper or you'll distort and spoil the blade. Heat an area only large enough to soften and lift the paint. Use knotting varnish over knots, or the resin from them will discolour or lift the paint. In repainting do mouldings first, then panels. For these, or any large flat areas, you use a full brush to paint a vertical stripe, spreading the paint as far as it will go; then repeat a brush-width away then fill in with diagonal brush strokes; then remove surplus from brush and even out the film with cross-strokes. Finally, lay off panel upwards with gentle strokes. After panels paint top rail, then stiles and muntin (the middle upright) down to the lock-rail (the middle crosspiece) and then the lock-rail and stiles and muntin down to the bottom rail. Lay off side stiles upwards – and look out

for runs at moulding corners. For a natural wood finish front door strip off the old finish with paint stripper (protect the floor with cardboard), rinse with white spirit rubbed into pores of wood with fine steel wool, working with the grain not across. This removes any wax left on surface; no varnish will dry over wax. Stain if necessary; easiest for the amateur is a combined stain-filler, rubbed evenly across the grain, or a spirit stain, followed by a filler (to get a really smooth surface). Lightly rub the surface with abrasive paper to smooth off, put on a thinned coat of varnish, sand gently again, and recoat; you'll need three or four coats in all, letting each one dry well before sanding. Before the last, rub lightly with 400 grade wet-and-dry paper, used wet.

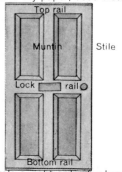

There's a right order for burning-off and repainting doors; appearance repays care given

PAINT GUIDE

The amateur housepainter is concerned with two kinds of paint: *emulsion paints* which can be thinned if necessary and washed off the brush with water, and *solvent-based* or *oil paints* – the ones you wash off brushes with white spirit or, in some, with detergent.

Both types contain *pigments,* usually white *titanium* dioxide pigment and various coloured pigments. The white used to be lead, but lead is poisonous, as well as being less white than titanium, it is used rarely now, and then only for exterior paints.

The pigments are held together, protected and stuck fast to the surface being painted by *binders,* various forms of synthetic resins, though you are unlikely to see the word synthetic on a paint advertisement. Most improvements in paint during the past 40 years have been through replacing natural products with synthetic ones, but manufacturers believe customers think 'synthetic' means imitation, cheap, ersatz, and so don't like to mention it.

In solvent-based oil paints the resin binder is dissolved in solvent, which enables you to brush on a very smooth, even coat. The solvent evaporates, which is why these paints smell more than emulsions, but the paint film normally hardens by oxidation – oxygen from the air combines chemically with the resin to make it solid. In emulsion paints there is a small amount of solvent, but the paint particles are dispersed in tiny droplets in water. As the water dries, the droplets coalesce to form a continuous film which then hardens.

Most of the long words used in paint advertising are descriptions of these resinous binders. In oil paints they are *alkyds,* the resins formed when certain natural oils – linseed oil, safflower oil, soya oil – combine chemically with phthalic anhydride and pentaerythritol. In emulsion paints the binders are based on *vinyl* acetate normally combined with ethylene, or an *acrylic* ester such as ethyl acrylate.

These materials are *monomers,* substances (usually liquids) with molecules which you can imagine as the

separated links of a chain. By the process called polymerisation the links are joined and the product is a *polymer,* another word which turns up in paint advertising. Most plastics are polymers – polyvinyl chloride, pvc; polyvinyl acetate, pva; Polythene, polymerised ethylene – but more to the painter's point, they make good paint binders. Sometimes two monomers are polymerised together to make a polymer with qualities neither would have alone and an impressive name to go on a paint tin – *co-polymer.* Acrylics are often modified with other monomers to give the correct qualities to the paint film – flexibility, hardness, good resistance to weathering.

CO-POLYMER

Polyurethane binders are hard and tough with good chemical resistance and waterproofing quality; but beware. The original paints and varnishes which gave polyurethane its good name were two-pack types – you had to mix the contents of two tins and apply it quickly before the combined contents went hard. That material, often used as yacht varnish, would retain its gloss out of doors for up to 10 years if properly applied. Single-pack polyurethanes won't reach that standard, and many sold on the word polyurethane contain very little. You won't get a 10-year gloss from a one-pack paint containing just a little polyurethane and slapped on to a poorly-prepared surface.

There are modified alkyd paints where the alkyd has been reacted with about 30 per cent *silicone* resin; these are as durable out of doors as a 100 per cent. polyurethane, but they are much more costly than the paints amateurs usually buy. *Latex* is another paint binder. Technically a latex is any emulsion which will leave behind an elastic film when it dries. So a latex paint doesn't necessarily contain natural rubber.

Apart from pigments and binders, paints contain *additives* and fillers or *extenders.* Extenders are often used, particularly in emulsion paints; usually chalks or clays. Sometimes they are overdone; cheap emulsion paints may have a very high percentage of filler which normally means a low covering power – they are cheap by the litre, but not cheap by the square yard because you have to put on more coats to get the same effect as with a smaller quantity of good emulsion.

Many additives are used to give paint particular qualities. One ensures that it stores well – the constituents don't separate in the tin. Others promote brushing characteristics, making a paint that goes on easily without leaving brushmarks and allowing knitting up so that there's no trace of a join between sections when a large surface like a wall is painted. Others, like the *silanes* – a chemical group related to silicone – help stop dirt sticking to paint. Silicone resins or oils help prevent surface defects.

Other additives make the paint *thixotropic;* the paint is almost gelatinous (hence *gel* paint) in the tin so that a large quantity can be picked up on the brush without dripping, but

POLYURETHANE

when brushed on the paint flows easily. What happens is that energy absorbed from the brushing temporarily alters the paint structure. As the energy leaks away the paint film stiffens again. Many paints not advertised as thixotropic are thixotropic – "structured" is a favoured word – to some extent; it has become very important for the amateur market, though professionals, who have learned how much a brush will hold without dripping, tend to go for paints which have other qualities (including cheapness) instead.

Silk, satin, sheen, eggshell are descriptions of how the paint will appear when dry, not of the contents; there's no silk in silk emulsion. Whatever the constituents of a paint, the surface can be varied basically by altering the proportion of pigment to resin. Lots

of pigment and little resin and you've a matt surface; roughly equal parts of resin and pigment and it will be glossy. Because of the high pigment content the matt finish will tend to cover up old colours beneath better, litre for litre than the gloss; because of the high resin content gloss will tend to be stronger, and easier to clean.

Because of the complication of paint constituents, it isn't a good idea to mix the remnants of one maker's paints with those of another maker. Resins and additives may not agree.

The chart below lists just part of the output of Britain's big three manufacturers who between them have three-quarters of the amateur market. The "outdoor use" and "kitchens and bathrooms" are the manufacturers' recommendation.

Our consultant paint experts do not disagree, but say that professionals reckon a high gloss oil (alkyd) paint is the most resistant to wear and weather; the balance between long life, appearance and convenience depends upon you.

Picking a paint for the job

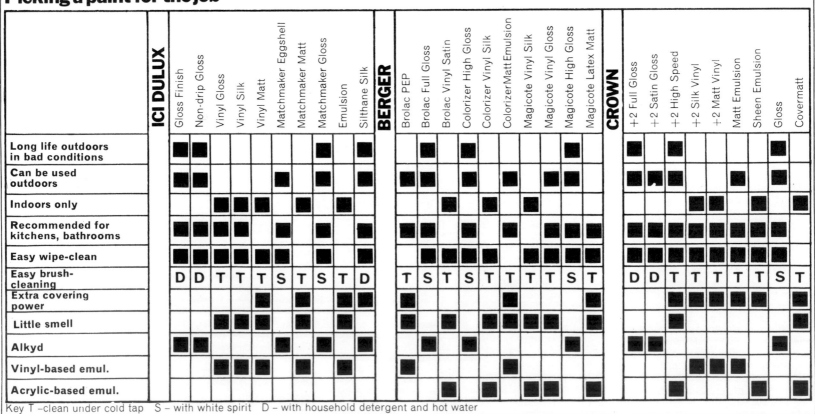

		ICI DULUX	Gloss Finish	Non-drip Gloss	Vinyl Gloss	Vinyl Silk	Vinyl Matt	Matchmaker Eggshell	Matchmaker Matt	Matchmaker Gloss	Emulsion	Silthane Silk	BERGER	Brolac PEP	Brolac Full Gloss	Brolac Vinyl Satin	Colorizer High Gloss	Colorizer Vinyl Silk	Colorizer Matt Emulsion	Magicote Vinyl Silk	Magicote Vinyl Gloss	Magicote High Gloss	Magicote Latex Matt	CROWN	+2 Full Gloss	+2 Satin Gloss	+2 High Speed	+2 Silk Vinyl	+2 Matt Vinyl	Matt Emulsion	Sheen Emulsion	Gloss	Covermatt
Long life outdoors in bad conditions			■	■						■		■		■	■		■	■				■			■	■						■	■
Can be used outdoors			■	■						■		■		■	■	■	■	■	■		■	■	■		■	■		■				■	■
Indoors only					■	■	■	■	■		■									■							■		■	■	■		
Recommended for kitchens, bathrooms			■	■	■	■		■	■	■		■		■	■	■	■	■		■	■	■		■	■	■	■	■		■		■	■
Easy wipe-clean			■	■	■	■		■	■	■		■		■	■	■	■	■	■	■	■	■		■	■	■	■	■		■		■	■
Easy brush-cleaning			D	D	T	T	T	S	T	S	T	D		T	S	T	S	T	T	T	T	T	S		D	D	T	T	T	T	T	S	T
Extra covering power						■	■		■		■							■	■				■						■	■	■		■
Little smell						■	■				■					■		■	■	■			■					■	■	■	■		■
Alkyd			■	■				■	■	■				■	■		■				■				■	■						■	
Vinyl-based emul.					■	■	■				■	■				■		■	■	■							■	■	■	■			
Acrylic-based emul.																							■								■		■

Key T – clean under cold tap   S – with white spirit   D – with household detergent and hot water

Common painting defects and why they occur

All jobs carried out in the home will only be as good as the preparation that has gone before them. Our consultant experts stress this even more so with painting (see page 19). Surfaces should be clean, dry, free from grease, dirt and rust.

Loose and flaking material must be removed, surfaces rubbed down for a better key and if necessary sealed. But if this isn't done there may be trouble. Here we list some faults, explain their causes and advise on how they are avoided

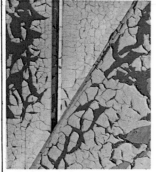

Efflorescence is a white crystalline deposit brought to the surface of brick plaster and cement indicating base material is drying out. It is unwise to apply any paint while the condition is visible. If 14 days after clearing there is no recurrence, probably safe to go ahead. Painted surfaces interrupted by efflorescence must be stripped down and left to dry until deposits stop, when surface should be safe for redecoration

Blistering highlights a fault between the top coat and its base. Where the paint film fails to adhere, usually because of trapped damp, differences in tension between films lead to blisters. Odd blisters can be removed, the edges rubbed down, and the small area repainted. Bigger areas must be stripped right down to base. Then repaint. Check damp is not getting into timber through unpainted top or the edges

Flaking or peeling occurs when paint loses adhesion with its base, as when paint is applied to a wet surface. Surface expansion or contraction will also cause flaking. Peeling often starts from a joint or split in the film. Early flaking is accelerated if paint is applied to a powdering or chalking surface. To correct: strip paint, make sure surface is dry. When it is, rub down, seal if necessary, repaint

Dripping, running or sagging is basically caused by uneven application. Fault can be accentuated by applying heavy coat to uneven surfaces or intricate mouldings. More paint added to an already wet edge which has started to set produces thick joins. This may also cause sagging. Careful, even application – brushing out – will eliminate. If sagging has occurred allow to dry thoroughly before sanding down and repainting

Crazing is splitting or crack-of a dried paint film. In more severe examples may extend through to base material. Can be avoided by using same manufacturer's under- and top-coats and making sure that each coat is hard and dry before continuing. May be possible to rectify light crazing by rubbing down. Bad crazing must be stripped, rubbed down, sealed or undercoated before top-coat

Taking the hard work out of decorating stairwells

Decorating stairwells scares some amateur decorators. Working at a height is worrying if you are not used to it, and the high walls mean long lengths of paper to be handled. Work only with a properly supported system of scaffolding. You've a long way to fall, and you can't paint or manipulate paper into position if you're unsteady. The system shown here does not take long to set up and you'll save the time because of the ease of working. Suitable short ladders, scaffold boards and step-ladders can be hired for not much more than £1·50 a day or about £3 a week; double the planks if you've a long gap to bridge. Screw a strip of wood to the stair tread to avoid the risk of ladder or steps slipping.

The same general rules apply as for rooms; work out from the source of light where possible, so that any bad joins or overlaps show up as little as possible, but if you've a big pattern, try to centre it on the wall where it will show most. This is usually the wall at the head of

the stairs. It is essential, with the long lengths of paper you'll be using, to start from a true vertical.

Use a plumb-line, and use it again each time you turn a corner. A fractional error that might not show in an 8ft.-high room will be all too plain with a 16ft. staircase wall. You won't be able to carry these long lengths of pasted paper in two big loops as you did when papering a room (see details, p. 24); they will tear, or stretch so that the pattern fails to match. Fold them into 18in. concertinas, as when papering ceilings. The bottom three feet is folded back on itself so the pasted paper won't smear all over the stairs, and a narrow folded-over strip at the top will prevent paste from marking the ceiling.

Use the double-loop for the shorter lengths at the top of the stairs. Keep a damp cloth by you to wipe off any paste that gets on the paintwork; left to dry it may damage the paint and will certainly be very much more difficult to clean off.

Paint squares side by side on stairs

When you come to the wall where the banister-rail starts, mark paper-widths from the rail into the corner, using a roll of paper. It will probably need an odd narrow strip. Cut this and hang in the corner first and then work back to the banister-rail. This way the rail will fall neatly where two lengths of paper join.

When painting staircase walls it isn't possible to follow the room system of painting in rough squares starting at the top and working down. (The squares system leaves the shortest time between painting adjacent sections, so avoiding marks where you're joining up to almost-dry paint.)

Stair walls being shorter sideways than downwards, you'll get the best results by painting the squares side by side. It's easier from your scaffold, too, than hopping up and down a ladder. A time will come when you've got to move the ladder to paint behind it. Make sure new paper or paint is dry before you rest the ladder on it. Pad top of ladder to prevent marking.

How to hide the bad join

Start beside the window; that way bad joins show up least as you move away from the light. With a big pattern start in centre of chimney breast and get non-matching joins in a corner where they show least; it's probably worth papering a long narrow ceiling across the narrow way regardless of window because long strips of paper are hard to handle. If walls are rough, or if they've been gloss-painted, cross-line them – hang paper horizontally.

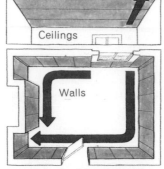

Ceilings

Walls

Pick of the pastes

For amateur paperhangers *cellulose pastes* have almost wiped out the competition. Their advantage is that if they get on to the surface of the paper they don't, as a rule, stain it; their disadvantage is that they contain more water, soak more into the paper. *Tub pastes* or *prepared pastes* are ready-made and packed in tubs; you thin them with cold water. Undiluted they stay fresh for a long while.

Flour paste is useful if you run out of paste with one wall unfinished; mix a small amount of ordinary household flour in a bucket with water. Make a thick batter; then pour in boiling water stirring all the while. Allow to cool before using. Whichever paste you use, tie a string across bucket on which to rest the brush and wipe off surplus paste. Wipe up paste splashes – they can spoil paint.

DECORATION: Wallpaper techniques

On this page we describe how to decorate rooms with light or medium-weight papers; (for tall hallways and stairs see p. 23). Heavy papers, vinyls and fabric wall-coverings are dealt with opposite. If it's your first attempt at paperhanging don't choose too light-weight a paper; they're harder to handle. Soak and strip off old paper, wash down walls, fill in cracks and give the bare surface a coat of glue size or, if you're using cellulose paste, a coat of thinned paste – it stops the surface sucking paste from your paper and makes positioning of the paper easier.

Pasting and how to match the patterns

If paper curls, roll opposite way to straighten. Cut each length with about 3in. to spare top and bottom; if it is patterned start 3in. above complete motif. Where pattern repeats horizontally – that is, matches at same level on both edges – you can cut each complete length the same way. Where it is a drop pattern, different at the two edges, you'll have to pass the next length along until you can match. You may save drop pattern paper by cutting alternate lengths from two different rolls.

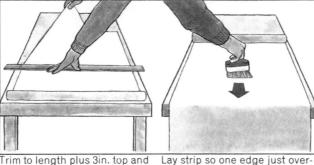

Trim to length plus 3in. top and bottom, remembering pattern; straight-edge is the easiest tool

Lay strip so one edge just overlaps edge of table; paste along the centre and outward to edge

Move paper so other edge overlaps table. Paste out, never in or paste gets on pattern side

The ceiling: beware of the angles

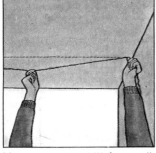

Rooms are seldom perfectly square, walls rarely perfectly straight. If you start papering from an angle like the join of wall and ceiling, chances are you'll be visibly way out before you reach the end of the room. By marking a line not quite the width of the paper away from the wall, hanging your first length to that and trimming off the overlap in the angle, you will start all square. When papering round electric fittings, for safety's sake switch off current at the mains supply box

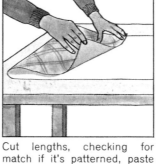

Measure paper-width from wall, mark by snapping string rubbed with chalk (a pin holds one end)

Cut lengths, checking for match if it's patterned, paste and fold over about 12in. to 18in.

Go on pasting and folding until you've a concertina of pasted paper about 12in. to 18in. wide

Leave last fold open to give you big area to begin. Brushful of paste on ceiling allows slip

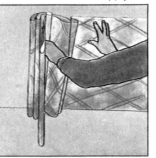

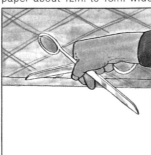

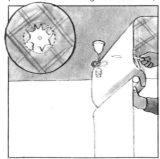

Use wooden roller, cardboard postal tube or spare roll to carry pasted strip to the ceiling

Peel open last 2ft. strip, press on ceiling, slide to chalk line or to butt on previously hung strip

Brush paper down, and move along plank letting concertina unfold. Keep on brushing down

Brush well into wall corner, rub back of scissors into corner to mark paper, peel back and cut

Paper to ceiling rose, cut star pattern, poke flex through, brush up to rose, trim round

Papering walls: use a plumb-line for a true start

When papering walls always use plumb-line to get a true vertical when you start, or after rounding a corner; few rooms have perfectly square corners and doors and windows may be fractionally out of true. Starting from window, measure paper-width from frame and hang plumb-line just inside this width, mark vertical line and hang first strip to this line. Brush edge of paper against frame and trim. Clean paste off woodwork or paint may be damaged as the paste dries.

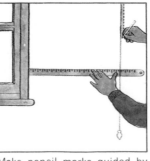

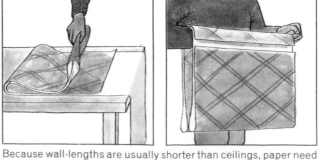

Make pencil marks guided by plumb-line or, as with ceilings, chalk string and snap a line

Because wall-lengths are usually shorter than ceilings, paper need only be folded ends-to-middle, carried over your arm. To protect ceiling from paste stains stick 4in. strip over pasted top edge

Slide into place, crease into corner with back of scissors, remove protective strip, trim

Care and patience on the obstacle course

When paper is in place brush down centre and outwards to edges to remove any air

Sometimes, in spite of care, edges don't stick: peel edge back carefully, paste and brush

Roll joins with seam roller while paper is still wet. Go gently on embossed papers, or use brush

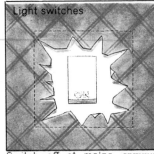

Light switches

Switch off at mains, remove flush-mounted switches, cut paper so switch hides edges

Air bubbles

If bubbles remain after paste is completely dry, cut them and paste down with fingertips

Battle of the bulges: papering into corners

Order of papering into corner

3 2 1

3 2 1

Never try to paper round corners; it hardly ever works. Turn ¼in., cut off and start again

Because room corners are rarely perfectly straight you can't paper right round them; if you do there will be wrinkles and bulges. Paste paper in usual way, measure from last strip into corner at three or four places, add ¼in. to widest measurement and cut paper to this width. Hang this strip into and just round corner, then mark with plumb-line width of remaining strip out from the corner and hang the remaining strip to that, even if it overlaps, the corner will hide overlap.

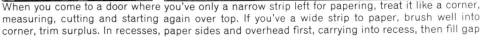

3

4 5

1 2

When you come to a door where you've only a narrow strip left for papering, treat it like a corner, measuring, cutting and starting again over top. If you've a wide strip to paper, brush well into corner, trim surplus. In recesses, paper sides and overhead first, carrying into recess, then fill gap

Hessian and fabric-type coverings

Hessians and other fabrics can be bought ready-backed for hanging, or you can use furnishing hessian at about half the price, but with twice the trouble. For unbacked fabrics, paste wall (thick tub paste) not material. Roll cut strip on a cardboard tube. Unroll to wall from top. Smooth with hands, then roll gently with foam roller. Overlap joins, leave for a while to shrink, then cut through both layers with straight edge and very sharp blade. Peel off surplus, and press the join down

Japanese grass and jute cloths

Japanese grass cloth is made of thin bark held by fine thread and backed with rice paper. Check rolls and shade them – get nearest matching colours side by side; they vary a lot. Use a fairly stiff paste, but don't soak because of the fragile backing. Hang with a soft roller. Don't roll the joins. The joins will show – they're supposed to. Jute cloths are hung the same way. Any heavy pressure risks forcing paste through paper. Japanese delicacy is called for, but is worth while

DECORATION: Decorative papers

Bold decorators who have mastered straightforward paperhanging are ready to try the more difficult wall-coverings: heavy embossed papers, flock papers, fabrics, delicate Japanese grass papers. For good results with these papers they must be hung on walls already cross-lined – covered with lining paper hung horizontally – so that the final covering has a sound base on which to get a good grip. For open fabrics and grass papers a lining of similar colour is essential. Lining paper which matches the colour of the finished heavy paper is worth while – it will help to hide any bad joins. A white lining would make them all too visible. The lining needs to be hung with a strong paste, otherwise the heavy paper may stick firmly to the lining but pull the lining away from the wall. Treat fabrics, flock papers or embossed papers gently. Rolling seams hard will spoil the surface. Avoid getting paste over edges.

Moulded, embossed and relief papers: Lincrusta, Anaglypta

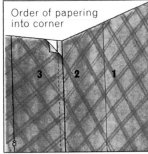

Lincrusta, unlike other relief wallpapers, has a flat, solid back. It is moulded to imitate wood panelling, ready-decorated or plain for you to finish, tiles, bricks or patterns. The material must be hung on a really well-pasted lining because it is so heavy. Lincrusta is best hung with a rubber glue – quick-drying, so be ready for speedy work. If you are using imitation panelling, remember it is important to get the pattern properly centred on main walls

Anaglypta is a heavy embossed paper, but the embossing is hollow at the back, so take care. It is hung with a paste made for this material. Paste one length at a time, leaving each to soak for about five minutes before hanging. Brush down gently or use a soft (foam) roller. Press too hard and you could flatten the embossing. If reluctant to stick, pieces can be pinned into place until dry. When dry, Anaglypta paper can be painted with an emulsion or an oil paint

Repairing wallpapers and coping with vinyls and ready-pasted papers

To repair damaged paper, tear off loose edges, then line up pattern on larger piece of paper held over hole. Next, tear an irregular patch larger than hole. Tear it carefully so that the underside of the paper doesn't show up. Paste down. An irregular outline and a tapered edge will make repair less visible than if it is cut straight. Fabrics won't tear, so lay new piece over hole, cut through new and old material together. Peel off material round hole. Patch is joined edge-to-edge

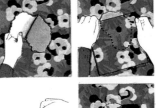

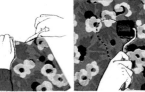

Ready-pasted papers and vinyls come with their own water containers. Cut pieces to length. Immerse lengths one at a time in water container on floor below where strip is to be hung. Allow wet paper to drip before sliding into place. For good adhesion wall may need to be coated with size first (see note on p. 24). The dealer will advise what kind of size to use. Vinyls not supplied ready-pasted must be hung with a heavy-duty fungicidal paste. Again, a dealer will advise

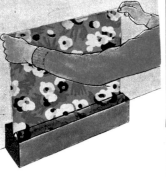

INSULATION

With inch-thick insulation in loft, 20p of heat still goes through roof; much more with uninsulated loft. With three or four inches heat losses are halved, paying for extra insulation in about three years

From every £1 spent on heating, occupants get 25p worth of warmth, perhaps less

INSULATION: eliminating the draughts

For every £1 the owner of a house spends on heating, the inhabitants get only 25p worth of warmth, often less. The rest goes to warm the great outdoors. Some heat losses are inevitable – you can't live in a vacuum flask – but self-sufficient householders can make sure the losses are halved without too much expenditure. On the left we show where the money goes and roughly how long it takes for each heat-saving to be paid for out of the heat saved. The later chapters of the book show how to make these fuel savings, but we start by discussing draughts. An average living room should be sufficiently ventilated for all its stale air to be replaced by fresh air in about 40 minutes. In a draughty house it may be replaced two or three times as often, which means that two or three roomfuls of good warm air are being wasted every hour

Cavity-wall insulation can cut loss through walls from 25p to 10p or less. Prudent householders should consider it. Can take from five to 10 years to recoup outlay

From £1 worth of heat, 10p worth leaks out through the floor. Wall-to-wall carpet and underlay can help, though recovering outlay would take a long time

With normal size windows only some 10p from every £1 of fuel gets out through the glass and another 10p worth because of draughts. Double glazing can save up to half, but some systems will take 20 years to recoup initial outlay

Cool air coming into a room causes uncomfortable draughts. Places to look (with a candle) are around windows and doors; the crack between floor and skirting board; and between floor boards. Below and overleaf we look at draught prevention

Fitting a foam strip

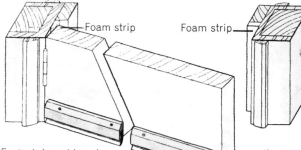

Foam strip

Foam strip

Easiest draught sealer foam strip, about 2p a foot. Re- or if repainting. Don't seal head of there rarely cause discomfort. Don't use where will get wet

is self-adhesive place when dirty doorway; draughts will get wet

Making sure doors fit

(1) Tight on hinge side with gap opposite: unscrew one hinge at a time, pack recess with cardboard. (2) Tighten loose hinges, replace worn ones – plug worn screwholes. (3) Cure gaps on hinge side by paring off wood from hinge recess. (4) For distorted doors set a door-thickness batten $\frac{1}{4}$ in. thick to frame, pencil against it on door, remove door and plane or sand to pencil mark, fit batten to edge

Using a hard plastic sealer on windows and doors

Windows and external doors best sealed with hard plastic strip, about 4p a foot. Fold strip (1), slip on metal grip supplied, and nail to side of door rebate, starting at top (2). Use a small, light hammer to avoid damage. Layer of non-hardening putty along front edge of strip on outside doors will keep rain out. At foot of door (3) trim with chisel or sharp knife, slip off grip, start other side. Run strip over lock (4); when fastened go back and cut off top and bottom beside nail (5)

Stopping draughts that flow beneath doors

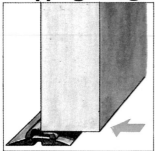

This floor-fitted excluder is rubber; others are wood or metal, with rubber or plastic inserts

Worst draughts usually whistle beneath doors, particularly if door is set to clear a carpet that doesn't reach the threshold. The choice is to bring the floor up to the door or fasten something to the door to bring it down to the floor. Raising the floor is less obtrusive when the door is shut; the excluder shows when the door is open and it can trip you up. Excluders fastening on the door are less handsome, but probably safer.

This is one of the simplest door-mounted draught excluders: a rubber strip free to move in

a wood casing. Trim rubber to fit door; with awl make holes for screws above rubber strip

housing. Press through wood to start holes in door, soap screws for easy turning

Closing the gap between floor and skirting boards

The least-expected source of draughts is gap between skirting board and floor, and where squared floor boards (instead of tongued-and-grooved boards) have been fitted. Boards shrink, gaps develop, letting cold air in from beneath house. Carpets cure these; if you've a carpet with a surround of bare boards the cheapest and easiest way to seal gaps is to cover bare boards with hardboard

Small gaps between skirting and floor can be sealed with one of the patent fillers from a tube.

A better way is to buy wood mouldings – left are just some of the patterns – and fit carefully along each skirting, using a mitre block to make sure the corners meet at the right angle. Nail to floor board with panel pins tight up against skirting. At doorways, round end of moulding carefully

Laying mineral wool [Warning: wear a mask to protect lungs]

A reminder before you begin: ceilings are fragile and ceiling-joists – the timbers to which the ceiling beneath is fixed – are awkward to walk on and painful to kneel on. Slip, and you've made an expensive hole in the ceiling. So take into the loft a couple of short planks on which to stand or kneel. A torch, a stick to poke insulation into corners, scissors, and a pair of gloves to keep insulating wool fibres out of your hands are all the tools you'll need. Metre-wide mineral wool blankets laid across the joists give better insulation because a layer of air is trapped in the cavity between blanket and ceiling, but this system makes it even harder to walk on the joists – you need to top the blanket here and there with half-inch boards screwed to the joists to form walkways – and it's almost impossible to get to the electric wiring afterwards. Narrower rolls laid between joists are cheaper, almost as effective

Get rid of layers of dust and, often, piles of shavings left by builders

Unroll mineral wool; it comes in right width to fit between joists usually 14-16in. apart

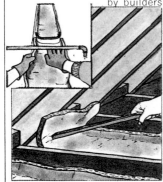

Cut insulation to pass under pipes, wires; push into corners, but don't seal eaves entirely

Don't forget to cover trap door as well; mineral wool can be tacked at edges or stuck down

Spreading loose-fill vermiculite

Loose-fill insulation is simply poured from bag between joists, smoothed over with board cut to give right depth when resting on joists. To reach into corners nail board to broomstick. Most ceiling joists are 4in. deep; filling to $\frac{1}{2}$in. of top gives good degree of insulation

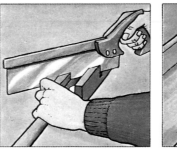

Spreader, cut to fit joists

Lining the rafters

Modern houses have a layer of waterproof felt between rafters and tiles; older houses don't and irregularities of tiles let wind drive in dust and snow – enough snow sometimes to wet the ceiling and spoil decorations. Cure is to line underside of rafters with $\frac{1}{8}$in. hardboard. Get it in 4ft. x 2ft. sheets – easiest to carry through trapdoor – and screw to rafters; nailing can disturb tiles. Start at top – the ridge board – and work sideways round roof.

Where sheets don't join over a rafter, overlap them slightly and Scotchtape the join. Next row of sheets down should overlap first by an inch. Aluminium-backed fibre insulation board can be fixed the same way – it is dearer and harder to handle, but it insulates and seals roof in one operation – useful if you want to use the roof space. Economy method: buy tar-bonded building paper – it's tough, waterproof, untearable – and drawing-pin it to rafters

For an unfelted roof, hardboard traps air between rafters, keeps out both dust and snow

With tile-hung gable ends and other odd roof shapes hardboard sheets must be cut to fit

INSULATION: sealing your roof space

Insulating the roof space of a house gives the biggest fuel saving for the smallest outlay of time and money. The material used for insulation is always the same – air; the various insulation materials are different ways of packaging it. The package needs to be fire-resistant and discouraging to mice, and for the householder the first choice is between blankets of mineral wool or a layer of vermiculite – a soft, fluffy relation of mica – spread above the top-floor ceiling. The thicker the layer the more effective. When fuel was cheap a one-inch layer was regarded as economic; now three or four inches are worth-while. If you've already an inch layer it will pay to put another two inches on top. But don't insulate under tanks – the rising heat holds off frost.

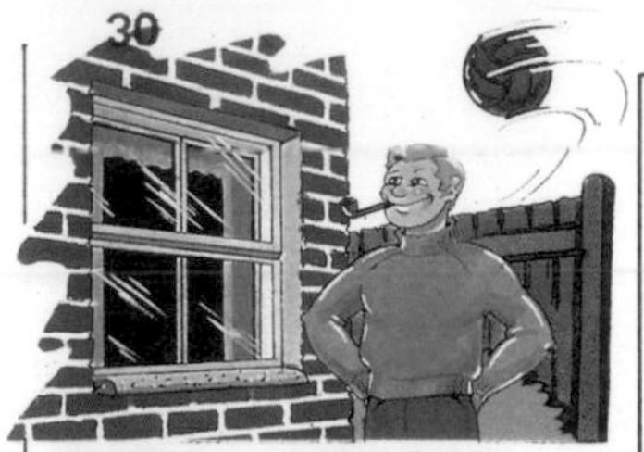

INSULATION: Methods of double glazing

The most neat and trouble-free method of double glazing is to replace the existing glass with sealed double-glass units; unfortunately this is also the most expensive, with the sealed units costing roughly £2 a square foot. The methods we suggest on the right use a second pane of glass fitted to the existing window with a frame of timber. This, when painted to match the existing frame, is inconspicuous as well as cheap. The gap between the two panes need be only half an inch to cut heat losses by half. Because you are then removing a large cold area from the room and so cutting radiation losses and draughts, the warming effect feels very much greater.

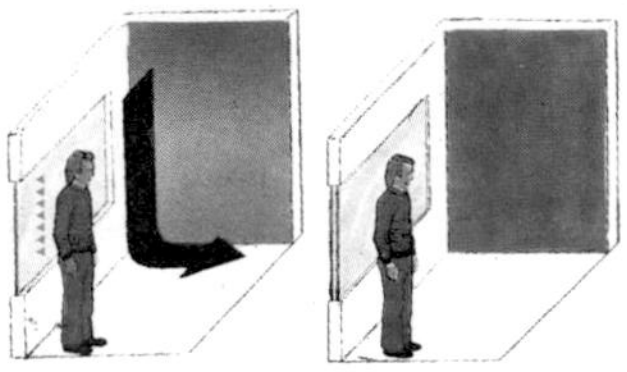

Double-glazing wood-framed windows and glazed doors is a straightforward job of screwing a new frame against the face of the existing frame or into its recess (below, left and right). With metal-framed windows (below, centre), it is necessary to fasten a new wooden frame into the window opening first. For the once or twice yearly taking down of the double glazing, the screws are taken out and that's it. You'll be handling the glass then without any frame to protect your hands, so have the glass merchant smooth the edges – or smooth them yourself by rubbing gently with an emery stone used for sharpening tools. In each case the airtight seal for the second pane is a strip of self-adhesive plastic foam draught excluder obtainable from most hardware shops.

Double-glazing on opening window: order the glass little bigger than existing area, and stick the adhesive foam round flush with the edge of the pane. The frame is 25mm. x 12mm. (1in x ½in.) timber rebated (cut to an L-shape) as shown – the timber merchant can do that; or you can make your own moulding from two ¼in. strips of wood glued and panel pinned together. Cut the moulding to fit the glass (mitred corners look best), and drill every foot or so to take a No 8 raised-head screw. Screw bottom moulding loosely to the window frame and rest glass in it while you fit the other three sides; then tighten screws to compress the foam strip. Double-glazing sliding sashes this way the new pane fits inside the bottom sash, outside the top – and you'll need heavier sash weights

Where metal windows fit direct to the wall drill and plug the wall and screw a 25mm. x 18mm. (1in. x ¾in.) fillet of wood all round. Make a wood frame with a ⅛in. groove for the glass. This frame should be about ⅛in. smaller than the opening so that it can slide into place. Drill the frame for fixing screws, have the glass cut to fit frame and glue frame to glass all round. For the opening parts of metal windows, an elegant but expensive solution is to replace single glass with sealed double-glass units. Alternatively, use the system shown here, but with a thicker (say 25mm. x 25mm.) fillet; make a frame to fit *inside* this, not against it, and hinge it to open inwards into the room. Easiest way out is to double-glaze all but one opening pane, leaving that single glazed – you'll still be making considerable heat savings.

Double-glazing fixed window in a wood frame, you'll need the glass cut about ¼in. shorter and narrower than the opening. The glazing moulding is simply screwed to the side of the frame. With fixed metal windows in a wooden outer frame the double-glazing units can be screwed to the wood, if necessary glueing a strip of wood to the mullions – the broad vertical metal bars separating the window sections – with impact adhesive. It will be strong enough; there's a solid frame top and bottom. Always fit double-glazing on a dry day to minimise risk of condensation between panes, and make sure there are no cracks to let damp and draught creep in, if you still find condensation, a few crystals of silica gel sewn into a tiny bag and left in the space between the panes will absorb moisture.

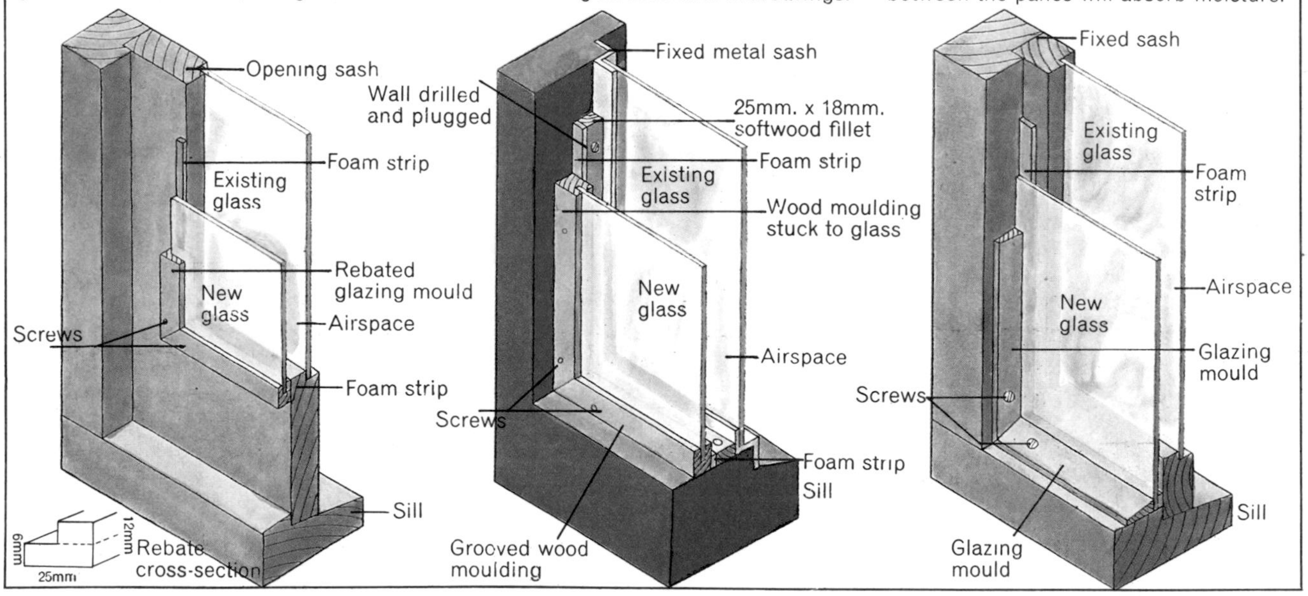
Opening sash
Existing glass
Foam strip
New glass
Rebated glazing mould
Airspace
Screws
Foam strip
Sill
6mm
12mm
25mm
Rebate cross-section
Fixed metal sash
Wall drilled and plugged
25mm. x 18mm. softwood fillet
Foam strip
Existing glass
Wood moulding stuck to glass
New glass
Airspace
Screws
Foam strip
Sill
Grooved wood moulding
Fixed sash
Existing glass
Foam strip
Airspace
New glass
Glazing mould
Screws
Sill
Glazing mould

Within these walls: a job for the experts

What double-glazing was a few years ago, cavity-wall insulation is today – a keeping-up-with-the-Joneses form of economy. Both can save a lot of fuel, both can cost a lot of money. Wall insulation gives the greater saving because on most houses there is more wall than window, but there is this difference: you can try double-glazing one room and fit more if you find it worthwhile; it isn't really practical to insulate only part of the walls of a house. And there's this even bigger difference: you can save much of the cost of double-glazing by fitting it yourself, either with ready-made kits or (as we have shown above on this page) by making your own frames. But cavity-wall insulation is no job for amateurs, though some have done it and been well satisfied. They were, say our own experts, very lucky. Much can go wrong; and if it *does* go wrong, the cure is likely to involve knocking half your walls down. So our considered advice is: if you can afford it, fine – but leave this particular job to experts.

Cavity walls were an improvement in house design not generally used until the Thirties. Until then houses usually had a solid wall, 9in. or more thick. Cavity walls are two thinner brick walls with an air space in between; air is a better insulator than solid brick, and, most important, if the outer wall gets soaked through with driving rain the water can't cross to the inner wall; it runs harmlessly down the inside of the outer wall and your rooms stay dry.

The flaw in cavity wall construction, by modern standards, is that air is free to flow up and down in the cavity, taking with it heat coming through the inner skin from the warm rooms. Fill the cavity with some kind of insulation, the air can't move and the heat loss is halved.

One kind of insulation is mineral wool fibres (like the material with which lofts are insulated) blown into the cavity under pressure. To get it in, 2½in. diameter holes are drilled in the outer leaf of the wall, hoses inserted, and the material forced in; when the cavity is full from top to bottom the drilled-out cores of brick are replaced. It takes one or two days to complete the work on a typical three-bedroom house, leaves hardly a mark, cuts fuel bills appreciably. A firm worth hiring will give a guarantee of around 20 years on the work.

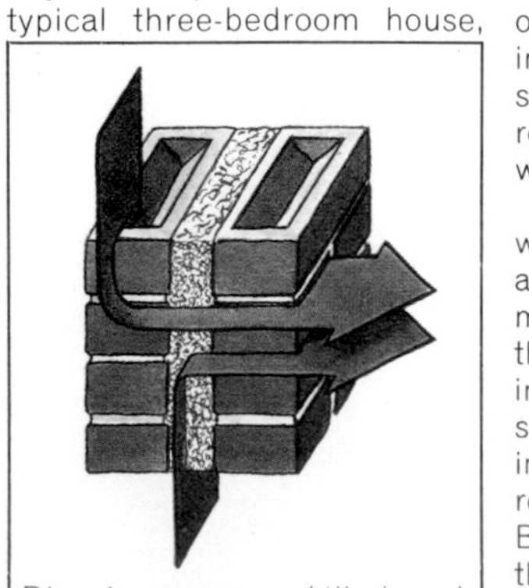

Disaster area: unskilled work can let insulation form bridge for damp through wall or rising from beneath damp course

The other kind of insulation is a form of made-on-the-spot plastic foam, pumped in through a series of ¾in. holes drilled in the outer walls about a yard apart; the foam sets inside the wall and the holes are then sealed with mortar coloured to match the bricks. The insulation value is roughly the same as with mineral wool, and reputable firms guarantee the work in the same way.

What are the snags? It won't work with some houses; a tile-hung house, for example, may not be sufficiently tight for the pressures needed in injecting the insulation. Some designs of house make it almost impossible for the insulation to reach every part of the cavity. But the real difficulty is that if the quality of the material, or the pressure with which it is pumped in is wrong, the material may not be waterproof. Rain driving against the outer wall may pass through, cross the bridge provided by the insulation, and soak into the inner skin: at once you've a damp wall to your room, and you can't get into the cavity to take out the defective material.

This doesn't happen with reputable firms employing expert workmen. It does happen with fly-by-night firms, so if you are considering wall insulation check carefully. Ask for the names of previous customers, the longer ago the better, and ask them if they are satisfied or if they've had problems. Above all, beware of the friendly operators who have "just finished a job down the road" and so can offer you a cut price. Ten to one it's a rip-off. Remember too, that guarantees are useless if the firm goes broke.

And although it is possible to hire the equipment for pumping in the insulation, and to buy the insulating material, don't be tempted to try it for yourself. There are other ways of insulating walls which we will deal with later in the book. Putting something into a cavity wall demands skill – and you can't undo mistakes.

Keeping out the cold with polystyrene

Thick (at least an inch) slabs of expanded polystyrene make excellent insulation for tanks. The material is light, cuts easily with a sharp knife (try a bread-knife) and is simply taped together round the sides of the tank. Don't cover the bottom of the tank, even if it is accessible. Another slab makes the top, which should not be airtight; slip a chip of wood beneath it to leave a small gap. Cut-outs to allow for pipes should be taped back in place

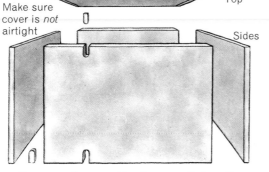

Make sure cover is *not* airtight

Top

Sides

Cylinder jacket

For hot water cylinders, ready-made padded jackets are available; they cost about £5, and the cost is recovered in fuel savings in a few months. If your cylinder is already fitted with a jacket, check the thickness. An inch of insulation used to be thought enough; with soaring fuel prices it isn't; buy a thicker jacket, or you can even wrap a second jacket over the first

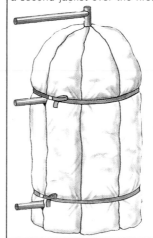

INSULATION: The water system

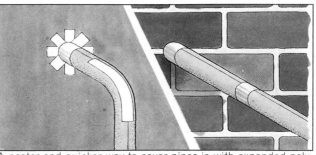

If a loft has been insulated in the way we described on page 29, it's going to be a lot colder than before because the warmth is staying down below where you need it. That leaves a problem: roof space can now become cold enough for pipes and tanks there to freeze in really cold weather, even when the rest of the house is warm. As long as no insulation is put directly under any tanks in the roof, they will get a small amount of warmth from below, but tanks and pipes must be wrapped; there are several ways to do it. Note where stopcocks are fitted: in watery emergencies quick action can save a lot of damage to the ceilings and to the decorations below.

Glass-fibre treatment for awkward-shaped tanks

[*Warning:* wear a mask to protect lungs]

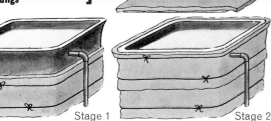

Stage 1

Stage 2

Circular tanks or tanks with pipes placed too awkwardly for sheet insulation can be insulated with mineral wool or glass-fibre blankets or bandages; it's a cheap and easy way to insulate other tanks as well. Always wear gloves when handling this material

How can you tell if your house was fitted out by an extra-careful plumber? Look at the outlet of the overflow pipe, above water level in the cold tank. In some positions a cold draught can come whistling up this pipe from the open air. Extra-prudent plumbers fit an anglepiece to this with a short down-pipe dipping just below the water surface when the tank is full, to block the draught. There may be another angle bend at the other end of the overflow pipe, or a hinged flap

Building an insulating box for the tank

Mount blocks on floor to secure box in position

Where a tank stands on a floor of planks it can be insulated by fitting round it a box of hardboard on wood framing (right), the gap between tank and box filled with vermiculite, cork chips or expanded polystyrene granules. Construction of the frame does not have to be particularly neat or strong because the hardboard panels provide extra strength and bracing, but the corners must be tight enough to prevent filling trick-

ling out. Similarly-made boxes of two or three sides can sometimes be used to insulate a hot water cylinder fitted too closely into an awkward corner to slide an insulating jacket round it. Where hot pipes run down a kitchen or bathroom wall they can be insulated in the same sort of way with battens screwed to the wall on each side of the pipe, covered with hardboard and the cavity filled with pour-in insulation like cork chips

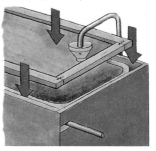

Cut two hardboard panels tank-depth and 6in. longer than the tank sides; frame them with

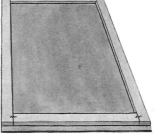

Cut two more panels tank-depth and 6in. longer than ends of tank. Frame similarly, but set ends of frame an inch from each panel so the four sides

2in. by 1in. Join the frame with screws, or hammer in corrugated fasteners. Pin the hard-

assemble with both frames and panels butting. Cut out panels to slide over pipes, reinforcing frame where needed. Assemble four sides pinning and screw-

board to the frame, with the smooth side to the outside, fastening with ¾in. panel pins

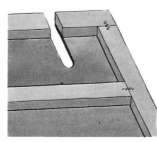

ing corner joints. Tape cut-outs back to fill holes. Make top from two panels with frame between. Fill cavity, taking care insulation doesn't get in tank

Wrapping the pipes to guard against freezing

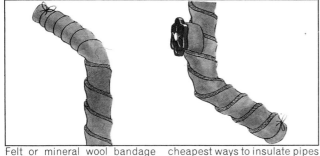

Felt or mineral wool bandage wrapped round pipes and taped or tied at intervals is one of the

cheapest ways to insulate pipes – but don't wrap round stop-cock valves set in the pipe

Where pipes run between joists and close to the ceiling, just spread the insulating blanket or granules over the top. Where they run above the joists they must be wrapped; cold pipes to keep the cold out, hot pipes to keep the heat in. Wrap right up to walls, taping if necessary; a one-inch gap is all that's needed to freeze a pipe. Pay particular attention to pipes running close to the eaves; hardest to get at, they are the ones in most danger.

A neater and quicker way to cover pipes is with expanded poly-styrene or flexible foam-plastic sections taped together. With rigid insulation you will have to bandage round all the bends

ELECTRICAL WORK

Wires and their colours: each one has a job to do

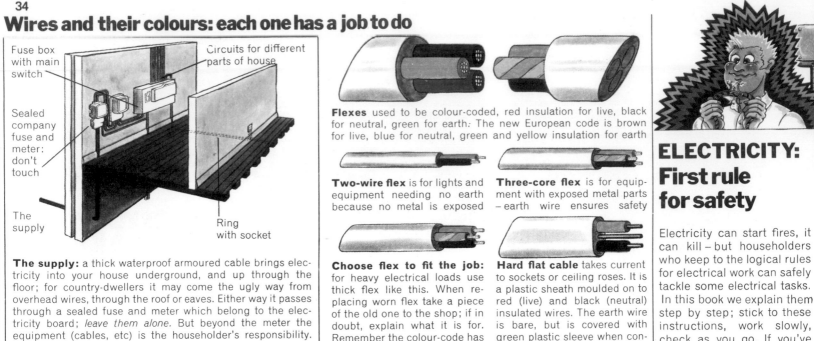

Fuse box with main switch

Sealed company fuse and meter: don't touch

The supply

Circuits for different parts of house

Ring with socket

Flexes used to be colour-coded, red insulation for live, black for neutral, green for earth. The new European code is brown for live, blue for neutral, green and yellow insulation for earth

Two-wire flex is for lights and equipment needing no earth because no metal is exposed

Three-core flex is for equipment with exposed metal parts – earth wire ensures safety

Choose flex to fit the job: for heavy electrical loads use thick flex like this. When replacing worn flex take a piece of the old one to the shop; if in doubt, explain what it is for. Remember the colour-code has been changed; when replacing flexes new brown goes in place of the old red (live), new blue in place of the old black (neutral), and the new green and yellow in place of the old green (earth). Tighten screws securely

Hard flat cable takes current to sockets or ceiling roses. It is a plastic sheath moulded on to red (live) and black (neutral) insulated wires. The earth wire is bare, but is covered with green plastic sleeve when connections are made. Cables must be big enough for load they will have to carry. Any wire carrying its full rated current may become warm; heavy current through a thin wire causes overheating (see fuses, below)

The supply: a thick waterproof armoured cable brings electricity into your house underground, and up through the floor; for country-dwellers it may come the ugly way from overhead wires, through the roof or eaves. Either way it passes through a sealed fuse and meter which belong to the electricity board; *leave them alone.* But beyond the meter the equipment (cables, etc) is the householder's responsibility. How it looks depends on the age of the wiring, but it will include one or more main switches, sometimes heavy, iron-clad ones; more recently, heavy plastic switches. Next to these – joined in more recent installations – will be the fuse boxes from which wires emerge to supply power and light on different ring circuits to different parts of the house. Before you touch fuses, always TURN OFF the main switch.

ELECTRICITY: First rule for safety

Electricity can start fires, it can kill – but householders who keep to the logical rules for electrical work can safely tackle some electrical tasks. In this book we explain them step by step; stick to these instructions, work slowly, check as you go. If you've doubts, STOP, get advice from an electrical contractor or your electricity showrooms. The first rule for safe working is: SWITCH OFF, don't take any chances.

Fuses: the necessary weak link in the supply line. Switch off before starting work

Fuses are thin wires designed as weak links in electrical circuits. In older installations there are usually two, one for the live wire, one for neutral. More recently only one fuse is fitted, to the live wire. Fuses melt when overloaded, slowly with a small overload, with a bang if, for example, two bare wires touch in a worn flex. To replace a fuse, SWITCH OFF at mains. Remove fuse carriers. Replace cartridge with another of same marked capacity. On others, remove old wire, fit correct new fuse wire. Turn on

Cartridge fuse in carrier. If it fails, fit a new one. Cartridges are marked with the capacity

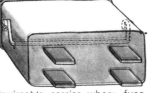

Rewireable carrier where fuse wire is protected. Wire anticlockwise round screws so it doesn't stretch when tightened

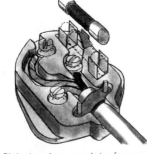

Flat-pin plugs contain fuses; if something goes wrong this melts, nothing else is affected

Bridge carrier, melted fuse is visible. Rub marks off bridge before fitting a new fusewire

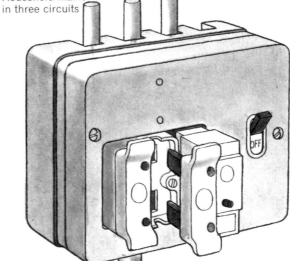

Household mains in three circuits

Power supply

Fusewire card will be marked 5amp, 10amp, 30amp. NEVER fit bigger size than that marked on fuse carrier

Fuse wire

Above, one pattern of *fuse box* – a 'consumer unit' with an integral mains switch. Others may have separate mains switch, or fuses behind a door in the box. Always SWITCH OFF before touching fuses. Right: a very few houses have *circuit breakers* instead of fuses

The fuse box is the householder's insurance against electrical fires. If a circuit is made to carry more current than it was designed for – perhaps by running a heater from a lighting point – the fuse for that circuit will overheat and melt, cutting off the current. If fuse is replaced by heavier wire, instead of the fuse melting, it is the cables, out of sight under floors and against wooden joists that overheat, a real fire risk. A fire started that way could invalidate a householder's insurance policy and upset any damage claim

Circuit-breakers are switches that turn off when overloaded by current. They can be reset

How to wire a square three-pin plug

In place of plugs with *two* or *three round pins* (below), *flat-pin plugs* have been used in new work since about 1947. These carry *cartridge fuses,* 13-amp for big loads, 3-amp for small. New plugs are sold with 13-*amp fuses* but the shop will change it for a 3-*amp fuse* if you ask

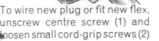

To wire new plug or fit new flex, unscrew centre screw (1) and loosen small cord-grip screws (2)

Trim brown and blue wires shorter than yellow/green. Pare off carefully. Avoid damage

Brown joins fused terminal, green/yellow the big earth pin, blue the other. Tighten screws

Replace cord grip. It should grip the outer covering, not inner wires, to take the strain

Electric lights: moving a ceiling rose

Pendant ceiling lights in your house may not be where you want them. They can be moved – if your house was built, or has been rewired, within the past 15 to 20 years or so. If your wiring is older *leave it alone*. You can check the age by whether it is in plastic-sheathed cables. *If it's not, don't touch.*

You'll need a medium and a small screwdriver, a knife, wire-cutting pliers, a bradawl. You will need tools to lift floor-boards – narrow-bladed pad-saw, bolster chisel, hammer; and a drill. You'll need a 4-terminal bakelite lighting junction box, 300mm. of green pvc sleeving, cable clips, and enough 1·5mm. 2-*core-and-earth pvc insulated and sheathed cable*.

■ SWITCH OFF MAIN AT FUSEBOX. Unscrew cover of ceiling rose you want to move. Remove wood screws that fix it. There will be two or three cables running into the rose. Label carefully the hard pvc-covered wiring which links to the red or brown flex of the lampholder, and that which links with the black or blue flex. Loosen terminal screws securing the hard

wiring (NOT the lampholder flex). Remove rose, flex and lampholder complete. DO NOT untwist any wires.
■ Measure carefully to locate old and intended new position of rose, and mark on floor above. Lift floorboards over both positions (Fig. 1, below).
■ With square-edge boards, run back of knife between boards until it is stopped by a joist; drill small holes across the board at angle sloping away from joist, insert padsaw and make sloping cut across board, lever up. With tongued-and-grooved boards padsaw through tongue of boards before cutting across. Always feel carefully with back of saw as you go; pipes or wires may be underneath. When you replace boards, nail 2in. by 1in. wood against joist for cut board.
■ Pass new cable from old to new light position, leaving six inches spare each end. If it has to cross joists (Fig. 3) drill 12mm. holes in them at least 2in. down for safety. Alternatively notch tops of joists to take cable, and protect with short length of metal channel (from electrical

shop). If room is beneath loft space clip cables to joists.
■ Push screwdriver through ceiling from below at new lighting position. If it hits joist make new hole to one side. Wire can then come through that hole but still be concealed by ceiling rose screwed to joist. If your new light position falls between joists, fix a "noggin" – a piece of timber just touching ceiling, nailed to joists each side (Fig.2). NEVER fix rose to plaster alone.
■ At new position feed cable through hole in ceiling, strip pvc sheath exposing about 3in. of the red and black insulation and earth. Remove about ½in. (12mm.) of black and red insulation, sleeve all but 12mm. of earth with green sleeve.
■ Push cables through holes in back of ceiling rose. Connect red wire to rose terminal with brown or red flex of bulbholder, black wire to terminal with black or blue flex, green-covered wire to E – earth – terminal (Fig. 6). Pull surplus through ceiling.
■ Screw rose into position on joist or noggin (Fig. 2).
■ On floor above pull old cables

back through old hole in ceiling. Break out slots in junction box to take them (Fig. 7). When you removed ceiling rose there were probably three red hard wires joined together, two black wires joined, one black wire on its own, and three bare or green-sleeved wires. If so, now join three old red wires *and no others* to one junction-box terminal, the two joined old black wires (formerly linked to the black or blue flex) and the black of your new cable to another terminal, the remaining black wire (formerly linked to the red or brown flex) AND your new red to the third terminal. The three old and one new earths go to the fourth.
■ If you had only two cables when you removed the rose the two old reds *alone* go to one terminal. The *new* red joins the old black, formerly linked to the red or brown flex of the lamp-holder. The new black joins the old black, formerly linked to the black or blue flex. All earths to the fourth terminal.
■ Screw box to noggin or side of joist (Fig. 5), replace boards. Fill old ceiling hole.

ELECTRICITY: The little extras

This section of the book describes two small electrical jobs in a house with modern wiring. If your wiring isn't modern, don't attempt them; we will be talking about large-scale rewiring later. NEVER work on exposed wiring unless the supply from the fuse box is SWITCHED OFF. It's not safe, for example, to work on a lighting circuit with only the room switch off. Electricity rules require an expert to check major alterations

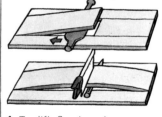

1 To lift floorboards you can drill small hole and cut with padsaw, then lever up; it may be easier to lever board in middle, force chisel across to provide gap so board can be sawn without harming others

2 When ceiling rose is removed it will have two or three cables; when refitting, only one, as here

3 Threading wires through joists; by holes at least 2in. down, or in protected notches

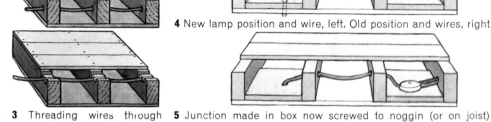

4 New lamp position and wire, left. Old position and wires, right

5 Junction made in box now screwed to noggin (or on joist)

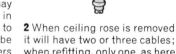

Ceiling rose   Ceiling rose   Ceiling rose

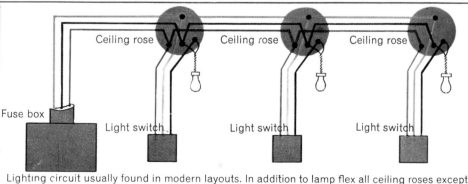

Fuse box

Light switch   Light switch   Light switch

Lighting circuit usually found in modern layouts. In addition to lamp flex all ceiling roses except last have three cables – one in, one to switch and back, one on to next rose. Last rose will have only two cables, one in, one down to the switch. Turn off at the mains before starting any work.

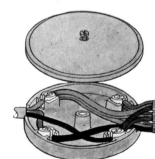

6 Ceiling rose wired up in new position. Patterns vary but wiring principle is the same

7 Wiring now joins in junction box instead of ceiling rose. Here, cable to new lamp position is on left. Entering right are cable from supply, switch and next lamp in circuit.

Power at hand: extra sockets in a room

11 Flush-mounting socket in box

12 Surface-mounting socket

13 Double socket outlet; easy to wire up as single

Overleaf we explain how to add a new power point to your wiring. First step is cutting out the wall; it is neater and safer than surface-mounting where socket may be damaged by feet or furniture. Six inches to a foot from floor is usual height. Mark round new socket box and cut out plaster with bolster, and brickwork if necessary. Cut a chase – a shallower recess in the plaster – straight down to and behind skirting for cable and its protective channelling.

For flush-mounted socket cut away plaster with this broad chisel – it's called a bolster

To get socket-box depth you may have to cut into brick. Use masonry drill, then join up holes

Fishing with hooked wire sometimes reaches cable, saves lifting many boards; worth trying

How to fit additional sockets to a ring circuit

Long trailing flexes are dangerous; it is safer to have an extra socket nearer where it is needed. If you've a house wired recently, or rewired with a ring circuit, here's how it's done. If your wiring is more than about 15 to 20 years old – that is, if it isn't in plastic-sheathed cables – or if it isn't on a ring circuit, or if the room has a solid floor, DO NOT attempt this work.

In modern house wiring, power points are distributed along a cable which runs from the fuse box, round all or part of the house, and back in a ring to the fuse box. As well as sockets on

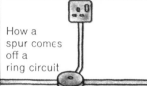

How a spur comes off a ring circuit

the ring there can be spurs – like the one we show how to fit here – of cable running from the ring to outlying sockets, NOT more than two to each spur.

To fit it you'll need the same tools as for the lighting operation overleaf, a 13-amp flush socket, a metal flush-socket box, a 20mm. rubber grommet, (see Fig. D) 300mm. of metal channel, 300mm. of green sleeving, a 30-amp 3-terminal bakelite junction box, and the wire – ask for 2·5mm². 2-core-and-earth pvc insulated and sheathed cable. You *can* use a surface mounted socket screwed to the skirting, but a flush socket sunk into the wall looks neater and is less liable to damage. You'll also need to make up a test lamp from a 25-watt bulb in an ordinary plastic bulb-holder joined by

a short length of flex to the L and N terminals of a 13-amp plug.
SWITCH OFF AT MAINS.
Remove a power point near where you want the new one. If it has only one set of wires entering, put it back and try another; you've hit an existing spur. If it has two sets of wires (Fig. A) it's probably on the ring, but it could be the first of two on a spur. To check, disconnect and part the wires, tape over bare ends of the red and black wires (Fig. B), turn on the mains switch again.
Go round all other power points plugging in your test lamp. If all light up, you've disconnected a socket on the ring. Work from that. If one doesn't light up then you are on a spur and must SWITCH OFF at the mains, reconnect, replace the socket and try another.
Having found a socket on the ring, make sure the mains SWITCH IS OFF, lift floorboard (see overleaf) and another next to your new socket position. Mark round socket-box in new position and mark out chase – a recess in the plaster – for cable straight down to skirting. Cut out plaster and brickwork if necessary with bolster, as shown overleaf; chisel behind skirting (you may have to remove it) so your cable can run down from box and under the floor, to the ring cable near existing disconnected socket. To cross joists, drill them as explained for lighting, overleaf. Leave plenty of slack (Fig. C). How it will look depends on cable-positions, but should be something like Fig. C new cable end alongside ring.
Push out hole in socket box,

fit grommet (Fig. D), screw box to wall and feed in cable allowing about 150mm. to protrude. Cut channelling to protect cable between skirting and box, and plaster over channel.
Strip outer pvc sheath to within 20mm. of box revealing red and black wires and bare earth wire. Fit green sleeve to protect earth, strip about 20mm. of red and black insulation (with knife, like sharpening pencil) double over ends of all three and fit to new socket, red to L, black to N, green to E (Fig. E). Screw socket into box. Cut slackest of ring cables running to disconnected socket (Fig. C), strip sheathing and insulation from both ends and from your new cable, sleeve earth wires again and connect up to junction box as shown in Fig. F, reds together, blacks together, greens together. Fit lid, replace floor. Untape wires at disconnected socket, reconnect. Check red to L, black to N, green to E – and refit socket into box. Turn on, check all points are working. *Now ask the electricity board to test your wiring.*

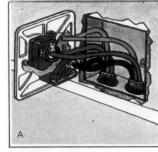

A

SWITCH OFF at the mains. Carefully remove the socket. You will probably find there are two sets of wires entering it

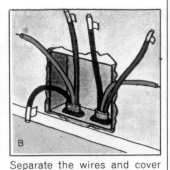

B

Separate the wires and cover the ends with insulation tape while you check with test lamp if the socket is on a ring circuit

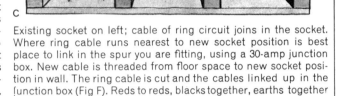

C

Existing socket on left; cable of ring circuit joins in the socket. Where ring cable runs nearest to new socket position is best place to link in the spur you are fitting, using a 30-amp junction box. New cable is threaded from floor space to new socket position in wall. The ring cable is cut and the cables linked up in the junction box (Fig F). Reds to reds, blacks together, earths together

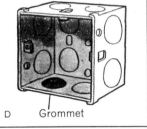

D   Grommet

Box which protects flush socket in wall. Knock out hole in best place for cable to enter. Fit grommet to hole to protect cable from edges. Drill and plug wall, screw box in place

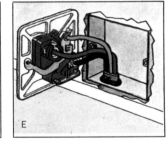

E

Thread cable through grommet and wire new socket like this: red to terminal marked L, black to N, earth wire (don't forget to fit green sleeve) to E. Fit socket to box. Careful: don't trap wires

F

Link cut ring-cable and cable to your new socket in junction box. All terminals must be tight. Poor connections could overheat. If cables reach, screw box to joist

WARNING!

It cannot be stressed too often that great care is needed when dealing with electricity.

The first rule to remember is:

SWITCH OFF AT THE MAINS

It is not sufficient to switch off at a wall switch.

At all times,

IF IN DOUBT, STOP

To get advice from an electrical contractor or from your electricity showrooms may delay work, but it is better than taking chances.

NEVER TAKE CHANCES

A power supply to workshop or garage

Fitting a light and a power point in a garage is easy; you use surface-mounted fittings, complete with plastic boxes, and run cables on the surface – no hacking out plaster. The supply can be from a spare fuseway in your consumer unit (fit a 15-amp fuse) or a spur off the ring circuit (fit a large 30-amp junction box): see instructions p. 36). If the garage is attached to the house the cable can be run through the wall (use a special large masonry drill or a cold chisel). If you are supplying a detached garage or garden shed the cable must be buried at least 18in. underground in an inch-diameter heavy galvanised steel pipe, earthed; or run overhead in the same pipe; or, the easiest way, run overhead clipped to a steel catenary (supporting) wire firmly anchored at each end to stout screwed hooks and earthed. This wire can be a stout single-strand fencing wire or a multi-strand steel cable. It must be high enough to be safely above anyone walking beneath. Inside the garage the cable runs to a fused, un-switched 13-amp spur unit with a 3-amp fuse. From the feed terminals of the spur unit (the terminals to which the supply cable is connected) run 2·5mm.² two-core and earth PVC insulated and sheathed cable to the 13-amp socket. From the other, fused, terminals, run 1mm.² 2-core and earth PVC insulated and sheathed cable to a 3-plate ceiling rose, and similar cable from the rose to a surface 5-amp, one-way, one-gang switch. At the rose, the flex for the lamp-holder is connected to two of

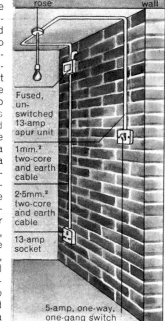

3-plate ceiling rose — House wall — Fused, un-switched 13-amp spur unit — 1mm.² two-core and earth cable — 2·5mm.² two-core and earth cable — 13-amp socket — 5-amp, one-way, one-gang switch

Wiring and fittings in garage are all surface-mounted; clip wires with plastic clips every 8in. Catenary (support) wire must be very firmly anchored; the strain on it is heavy. Leave loop in cable each end to ease strain and stop rain running into wall. Tape wire to cable before fitting buckle clips to stop clips cutting or sliding

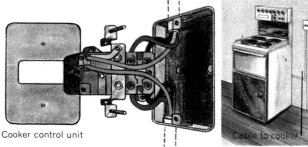

Connections for fused spur unit (left) and 13-amp socket (right)

the terminals; the two red wires of the two cables are joined and connected to the rose terminal which has no flex, the black wire of the supply cable to one of the flexed terminals, and then the black from the switch cable to the other flexed terminal.

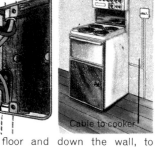

Connection for the light switch

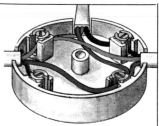

Garage wall — Ring circuit — Earthing clip — Earth from pipe — Cable to garage — Protective pipe — Junction box

Support-pipe enters wall both ends. Support-wire, weight taken by hook each end, enters house only, with cable. From either support, earth runs to junction box or consumer unit

Strong screw-in hook — Wrong: no loop — Support wire — garage end — Buckle clip — Cable — Right way loop in cable

See items on pages 35, 36, 38, 39, 40, 41 for how to run cables under floors and behind plaster and further diagrams on wiring power points, switches and lamps. Before uncovering any live circuits *turn off main switch*. Make sure you understand instructions before starting. If in doubt, seek expert advice. Major circuit changes should be tested by an expert or by your electricity board.

ELECTRICITY: More light and power

Fitting four wall lights

Few people like lights dangling from the ceiling, but most houses are still fitted with them. Here's how to replace a centre pendant with four wall lights, all controlled by the existing switch. You'll need 1mm.² 2-core and earth PVC insulated and sheathed cable, some green plastic sleeving (for the bare earth wires) a 4-terminal plastic junction box, four conduit wall terminal boxes complete with earth terminals, 4 double-pole 5-amp connectors, plastic or metal channelling, screws, wall plugs and cable clips.

Turn off main switch. Disconnect and remove the complete pendant, pull cables back from above ceiling and connect them into the junction box. In a 3-plate ceiling rose the three red wires will have been joined in one terminal, two black wires in another, one black wire on its own and finally the three earth wires, green-plastic-sleeved, into the fourth terminal (see details on page 35, on moving a light). Transfer these in their existing

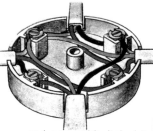

Junction box: wires moved in original sets from ceiling rose...

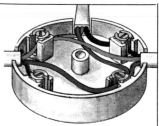

... and new cable linked to take supply to first wall-lamp

groups to the junction box. Lift boards and drill joists where necessary (at least 2in. from top of joist) for cable route.

Mark positions of four wall lights, about 6ft. from floor; cut out brick and plaster and fix conduit box so its face is just behind face of the plaster. Cut out plaster between ceiling and box wide enough to take protective channel. Run cable from junction box to nearest wall light, another cable from first box to second, second to third and third to fourth, allowing 6in. of each to protrude at each box. Fix protective channel over cables in wall and make good the plaster. Return to junction box and connect the new cable's red to the terminal with one black wire, new black to terminal with two black wires; and bare earth, green-sleeved, to terminal with other three earth wires. At each wall light remove outer sheath from both cables, connect two red wires together and fit them halfway into one pole of a connector, two blacks into other pole; green-sleeve earth wires, then connect to earth screw at back of box. (There will be only one cable at the last wall point.) Wire up wall fittings to empty side of connectors, and fix fittings to threaded holes in the boxes with the connectors tucked neatly away inside.

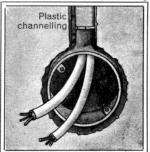

Plastic channelling

Cables run into conduit box in wall. Remember that the last box has only one cable. Note protective channelling.

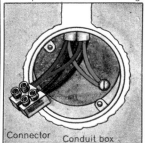

Connector — Conduit box

Two cables wired to connector; earths to terminal. Wires from wall fitting go into other end of connector and fitting fixes to screwed holes in box.

Installing a cooker control unit

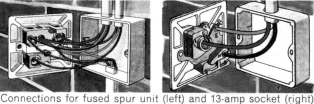

Cooker control unit — Cable to cooker

Some very small electric cookers may be fed from a 13-amp socket, but full-size models must have a cooker control unit wired on a separate circuit which supplies nothing else, using 6mm.² 2-core and earth PVC insulated and sheathed cable, and controlled by a 30-amp fuse. Very large cookers may need 10mm.² cable and a 45-amp fuse; check when you buy the cooker and check, too, with your electricity board because the house main fuse may have to be changed for such a load. Most modern consumer units take 30 or 45-amp fuses. Run cable from consumer unit under the ground floor and up the wall, or through the first

floor and down the wall, to cooker control unit which must be within 2 metres (6ft. 6in.) of cooker and accessible at all times to switch off the cooker supply for cleaning or in emergency. As most cookers have a high back the best place is about 4ft. 6in. from the floor and a foot to one side.
Cooker control units can be surface mounted or sunk into the wall – harder to fix but easier for cleaning. With a sunk-flush unit you'll need some means of removing the unit-to-cooker cable so that if you change your cooker no potentially dangerous cable will be left sticking out of the wall. So buy a short length of 25mm. conduit

and sink that in the wall from the control unit, emerging from the wall somewhere behind the cooker. That way the cable can always be disconnected at the control unit and withdrawn from the conduit. This control-to-cooker cable should be of the same 6mm.² or 10mm.² size as that feeding the control unit and long enough for the cooker to be moved for cleaning.
Connections: at the consumer unit, red wire to fuse, black wire to neutral connector, plain wire to earth terminal after fitting with green sleeve. Cooker control unit and the cooker itself will be clearly marked for which wire goes where.

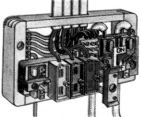

Consumer unit: cooker supply should have 30 or 45-amp fuse, best fitted in the position nearest to the main

Cord pull switch for bathroom: no other kind allowed

Water plus electricity equals danger, so bathroom lights are totally enclosed or fitted with sheathed flex and shrouded lampholders

Confusing until you see how it is done: two-way switch system enables stair light to be switched on or off from two or more places

This house has wooden (suspended) ground floor, so cables can run underneath. With solid ground floor, ground-floor power cables would be between ceiling and first floor, and run down inside walls

Key

Cooker/heater cables
Ring circuit
Lighting circuit
Two-way switch wiring
Switch cables

You can have an unlimited number of 13-amp sockets on a ring circuit; for clarity we've shown only a few. For clarity, too, we've left out the doors of our diagram house – switches almost invariably are mounted beside handle side of door

Shaver point for bathroom: contains isolating transformer for safety; no other portable appliance is allowed in a bathroom

Immersion heater: a special fused spur outlet

Modern consumer unit. This is a small one; they can have four, six or more fused circuits

Cooker point

Notice how wiring always runs straight up and down or across, never at an angle; not only easier, but safer; there's less chance of later builders hitting concealed wire unexpectedly

REWIRING: Ring in the new circuits

Earlier in this section we described one way to fit an extra 13-amp socket to a ring circuit; but supposing you've an older house without ring circuits, probably with the old round-pin 5- or 15-amp sockets and not enough of those? The chances are the wiring is at the end of its useful life. Old wiring can be dangerous and should be renewed; while you are doing it you can fit safer up-to-date 13-amp (flat-pin) sockets and more of them. And there's a safety advantage in rewiring as we describe it here; you'll be dealing with wiring not yet connected to the mains. Before planning new ring circuits check the picture (left) of a typical modern installation. Later we will describe rewiring lights, cooker and immersion heater.

New colour-coding of flex is confusing to amateurs. Once all live wires were red, neutral

wires black, earth wires green. To match European codes, British *flexes* are now brown for live, blue for neutral, green/yellow for earth; the two are shown at top. But the hard permanent wiring of a house is still, new or old, colour-coded red for live, black for neutral, green for earth (usually a green sleeve slipped over the bare earth wire) as shown above.

The rules for fitting ring circuits

Ring circuits allow the most sockets for the least installation cost, but must obey certain rules or the electricity board won't connect to them.
■ No ring circuit may serve more than 100 sq. metres of floor area. (That's about the size of a three-bedroom semi; except for very small houses it's best to have two rings anyway, one for upstairs and one for down if you've wooden ground floors; one for front and one for back of the house if ground floor is solid.)
■ The ring cable must be at least 2·5mm². (Ask your sup-

plier for 2·5mm² 2-core and earth PVC insulated and sheathed cable, and tell him what it's for.) *Both ends* of the ring must connect to supply.
■ The fuse controlling the circuit must be 30 amp.
■ The sockets must be evenly distributed round the ring. (That doesn't mean checking to the nearest inch, but avoiding a dozen sockets close together, then a long unsocketed run.)
Within these rules you can have as many sockets, single or double, as you like; the secret of the ring system's flexibility is that no house-

holder is likely to use more than a few sockets at once. Each 13-amp socket can't be asked to supply more than three kilowatts – a three-bar electric fire, say. Any load above that will blow the 13-amp fuse in the plug. The whole ring circuit will take seven kilowatts – which might be, for example, two big fires, a TV set, a fridge and one or two table-lamps. If you put more than seven kilowatts on one ring, the 30-amp fuse controlling the circuit will blow. To control your new ring circuits you'll need new fuses,

because the existing fuses will be only 5 amp or 15 amp. If the power circuit needs rewiring the chances are the lighting circuit is also due for replacement, so it is worth planning for this and taking the chance to fit a modern *consumer control unit*. A small one is shown above; they can be larger and it is best to get one which will provide for your ring circuits, all your lighting, cooker and immersion heater circuits, and to have one or two spare fuse positions available in case you want to extend the wiring later. You can buy a new consumer

unit, fit it to the wall, and wire from it to your new ring circuits and lighting circuits, but **don't try to connect it to the mains leads from the meter.** That's a job for professionals; you *must* get an electrical contractor or the electricity board to check your wiring and connect it up at the same time. Leave all your old power circuits alone; their main switches can be disconnected by the expert at the same time as he checks and switches on your new ring circuits and you can then remove the old sockets in safety.

Installing the ring circuit

Having decided where you want your sockets, place new metal flush socket box against wall, mark round it allowing ¼in. extra all round. Do this at each position, and for neatness keep them all the same height, usually about 8in. to 10in. from the floor. Don't mount them too low. Mark a chase – a channel in the plaster wide and deep enough to take the metal or plastic channelling which protects the wiring. Two cables will run into each socket so make it wide enough.

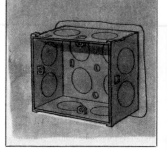

Box into which socket will fit; pre-marked circles will knock out for cables to enter

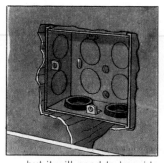

Cut into plaster and wall to depth of box; chase for cables need not be quite so deep . . .

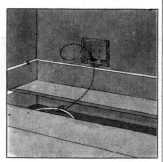

. . . but it will need to be wide – wide enough for two cables plus the protective channelling

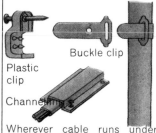

Stiffish wire with hook may enable you to fish cables from under floors if you are lucky

Plastic clip

Buckle clip

Channelling

Wherever cable runs under plaster or across notched joists directly under floorboards cover it with channelling (above) for safety; where cables are run beside the joists use plastic or buckle clips and pins (top)

Beneath wooden ground floor cables can be looped under joists, through honeycomb sleeper walls, supported here and there. When in space between first floor and ground floor ceiling, cables cross joists either in holes at least 2in. from top, or in notches covered with protective channelling (see illustration on page 35)

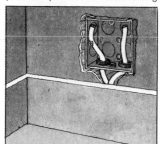

Cable runs into box through one hole, out through the other. Rubber grommets protect the cable from risk of cutting by rough metal edges of box

With each socket box screwed into the plugged cavity in the wall, cut the new ring cable and feed both ends up into the box, one cable to each grommeted hole, allowing about 6in. to protrude into the box. Fit protective channel over the exposed cable between box and floor. Make the wall good with filler or plaster, and leave it to harden. With a knife strip the outer PVC sheath from both cables exposing the red and black insulated wires and the bare earth wire. Cut green sleeving for the earth wires.

Cable is now protected with channelling; either one channel for each cable, or wide length accommodating the two cables, before plastering into the wall.

Remove insulation from ends of red and black wires for about half an inch. (A pencil-sharpening motion is best for this; don't cut ring round insulation and pull it off; you are likely to nick the wire itself.) Connect two red wires to L (for live) terminal, two black wires to N (for neutral), bare green-sheathed earth wires to E (for earth). Twin sockets are wired in just the same way; there are the same three terminals taking the paired wires – the splitting for the two sockets is part of the construction of the fitting.

Strip off outer covering, slip green sleeving over bare earth wire. Bare the ends of wires, twist ends of reds together, then two blacks, two greens

Cables are safe provided they are intact; if they're trapped or pinched the insulation may be cut or the wires themselves damaged, with the danger of overheating, sparking and fire. So check carefully before covering them with channelling or replacing floorboards. Always run cables straight across or up and down floors and walls; never diagonally or a later builder may drill or nail through them not knowing they are there. Do not skimp on wire; too much slack is safer than wire stretched taut.

Twisted together bare ends are doubled over, to provide good grip for terminal screws. Reds go to L terminal, blacks to N, green sleeved earth wires to E

In the case of a house with a solid ground floor, the upper floor would be wired as described above; the lower floor would be wired in the same way except that the cables would run down the walls from the space above the ceiling instead of up from below the floor. This means a lot of work in cutting chases the length of the wall and then replastering them, and it's not easy to repair the plaster so that no mark shows; you may find it possible to use new or existing cupboards to conceal some of the cables.

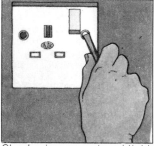

Check wires are gripped tight. Then screw socket to its box. Ease socket into box carefully, folding wires back so they are not trapped or damaged

Final operation in wiring your new ring circuit is connecting *both* ends of the ring to your new consumer unit; two red wires go to the 30-amp fuse, two black wires to the neutral terminal block two green-sleeved bare earth wires to the earth terminal. If you've decided to renew the lighting circuit (we describe how to do that on the two following pages) it's worth tackling that next before getting the new consumer unit connected to the mains.

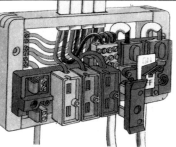

You can have both circuits tested at the same time, which will save money, and redecorate all cut-out plaster in one go, too. But don't tackle two

different rewirings at once; a mix-up could be lethal. The consumer unit shown here has a ring circuit, a lighting circuit and an immersion heater circuit already completed. Once your circuits are connected to the consumer unit, that's as far as the amateur can go. Now send for an electrical contractor or the electricity board to test your new circuits (that's a legal *must* – you put your life and your fire insurance in peril if you ignore it) and to connect the consumer unit to the meter. **Don't try to do this yourself.**

The equipment you'll need to make a clean sweep

If your house was built before 1950 and has not been rewired it is likely that, though the installation may be giving no trouble at the moment, it is coming to the end of its useful life. The lights may have been wired with lead-sheathed cables containing two rubber-insulated wires (the lead sheath acted as earth wire), or with rubber-sheathed cable, or with separate wires each rubber-insulated and wrapped in a waxed braid all enclosed in a thin-walled metal conduit. Whichever system was used, it is as well to scrap the lot and start off with a modern system using three-plate ceiling roses, flush switches mounted in metal boxes sunk into the plaster, and 1mm² 2-core and earth PVC insulated and sheathed cable. You will need 5-amp 1-way plate switches for most points, 5-amp 2-way plate switches for turning the staircase light on or off from either top or bottom, and a flush metal box for mounting each one in the wall. Individual switches are called one-gang; where two or more switches are mounted together in one box they are called two-gang, three-gang and so on. For the two-way switching on the stairs you'll need some 1mm² 3-core and earth PVC insulated and sheathed cable. For the bathroom you'll need a totally enclosed light fitting, and a 5-amp one-way cord-operated ceiling switch.

To protect cables plastered into walls you'll need plastic or metal channel, and to mark and protect the earth wires, green plastic sleeving, about 8in. for each lamp. Don't use the old flexes and lampholders again; they will almost certainly have been affected by heat. As an extra check to be sure that you get the right cables and equipment, tell the electrical dealer what it is for.

Before touching any wire make sure that the current is switched off at the mains.

REWIRING: Renewing the lighting circuit

If you plan to rewire lighting circuits get some table lamps which can be plugged into power points so that the house isn't plunged into darkness. No electrical job should ever be rushed, and rewiring lights will take more than a day. But *don't take any lamp on a flex into the bathroom*. Follow the rewiring instructions carefully; make sure you understand them. If you've any doubts, stop, check; and if necessary get the advice of an expert.

Switch off the mains and remove all the existing switches and ceiling roses upstairs. Remove the old wooden switch boxes and examine how cables have been run down walls to switches. If they have been protected by channel or conduit you may save a lot of work by connecting the new cables to the ends of the old – as shown on the right, and gently easing the old out and the new in. This needs someone in the loft where the old cable disappears down into the wall and someone else at the switch position

Old cable
Slim knot
New cable pulled through

below. Don't be too rough or the cables may part; if they catch ease them back and forth to free them. If you can't change cables this way you'll have to cut out the plaster between ceiling and switches (right). As you trace the wiring you may find there is a separate circuit for upstairs and another for downstairs, each with its own main switch or fuses. If you are certain which lamps are on which circuit you can switch on the downstairs lighting circuit while you work on the switched-off upstairs circuit. **But be careful; check and check again, and if not absolutely certain keep the main switch OFF all the time.** In installing your new cables it

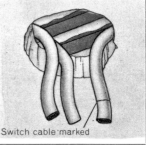
Old cable
Cutting wall over switch

is better, though not essential, to have one circuit supplying the ground floor and a separate circuit with its own supply from the consumer unit for the upper.

With modern three-plate lighting systems, a cable runs from the consumer control unit to the nearest lighting point, then on to the next, and so on until the last lamp in the circuit is reached, with another cable running from each point down to the switch on the wall (see diagrams on two earlier pages, 35 and 38). Run 1mm² 2-core and earth PVC insulated and sheathed cable from the consumer unit (*don't connect it up yet*) to the nearest lighting point. Cut it, allowing 6in. of cable to protrude through the hole in the ceiling. Run another piece of the same cable from there to the next lighting point, again allowing 6in. of cable to dangle through the ceiling at each end. Repeat this until all the ceiling-rose positions have two cable-ends except for the last which will have only one.

When all the light positions have cables in place, return to the first and, again using 2-core and earth cable, run from the hole in the ceiling to the switch position, using the old cables where possible to pull in the new ones. Allow 6in.

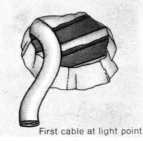
First cable at light point

at both ends. Mark switch cables at the ceiling point as you go along; you'll need later to know which is which. Repeat for all lights

Fitting ceiling rose: At each ceiling point except the last in the circuit you'll have three cables (below). Remove outer sheath from each cable for about 4in., slip green sleeve on to bare earth wire leaving ¾in. exposed, cut back red and black insulation to leave about

except the bathroom.

For safety's sake the bathroom switch must be a cord-operated switch mounted on the ceiling, so instead of running cable down the wall you bring 6in. of cable out through a hole in the ceiling where the cord-operated switch is to be. Two-way switches at top and bottom of stairs, enabling the light to be turned on and off from either position, will also need a *3-core* and earth cable run from switch to switch. The lower floor will be wired in just the same way as the upper,

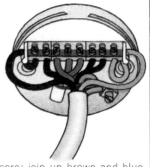
Switch cable marked

except that you will, of course, have to lift floorboards to change the old cables. **Make sure the circuit is switched off at the mains.**

three red wires to terminal without a flex connected to it; join black wire from switch cable to brown flex terminal, and two remaining black wires to blue flex terminal. Finally join bare ends of three green-sheathed wires to terminal marked E or Earth. Screw the ceiling rose to joist or noggin (see illustration on page 35) where the original rose was fitted. If you've a metal lampholder and a metal shade which needs earthing use 3-core flex instead of 2-

Even in roof space don't take shortest route between points; always run parallel with joists or at right angles to them. Keep cables away from gas, water and central heating pipes. It's worth the cost of a few extra yards of cable to be sure the wiring is safe. Clip cables to side of timbers for extra protection using plastic clips or, right, buckle clips. If you are running cables behind plaster always run them straight up and down or across, never diagonally, so that later builders don't hit them by mistake when

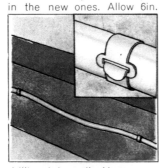

drilling into wall. Always protect cables with channelling. Don't economise on cable; one that has a little slack is safer than one which is stretched.

Grommet

Clear out holes in walls left by old wooden switch boxes and fit new metal ones so that they are just behind face of plaster. Don't forget to fit grommets

If chasing out walls for switch cables, cut chase wide enough and deep enough for cable with protective channel covered by at least ⅛in. of plaster

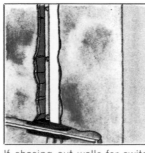

½in. exposed. Cut flexes to required length and fit one end to new lampholder and other end to new ceiling rose. Trim the outer sheath carefully so as to allow the brown and blue wires to fit into the cord grips, but not so much that these wires show when covers are fitted. Now bring complete ceiling rose to wires at ceiling point. Join all

core; join up brown and blue wires as before and the flex earth wire, green with a yellow stripe, to the earth terminal in the ceiling rose. With last lamp position in the circuit where only two cables are present, two red wires are connected to the terminal without a flex, the black wire in the switch cable to the brown flex terminal, the other black wire to the terminal with the blue flex.

With the plaster made good round the switch boxes and over any chases for switch cables. you may have had to make, the switches can be connected; with the one-way switches you are using, except for those controlling the stairs light, this is simple. Strip the outer sheath of the switch cable for about 4in., bare the ends of the black and red wires and connect one wire to each of the two terminals on the switch – it doesn't matter which goes to which. The bare earth

wire, with green sleeving, is connected to the earth terminal of the switch box (above).

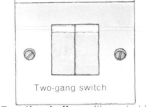

Two-gang switch

For the hall you'll probably need two switches, one for the hall light and the other for the landing light upstairs. They can be separate, but for neatness we recommend using a two-gang switch like the one shown above. With a two-gang switch both will be two-way switches though the one for the hall light will be wired as a one-way switch. Deal with this one first. You'll have two cables coming into the top of the switch box, one two-core and earth, one three-core and earth, as in the top picture, far right.

For the hall light you need the two-core and earth cable only, with its red and black wires, either one of which goes to the terminal marked Common. The other wire goes to one of the other two terminals, marked L1 and L2. Switches are usually labelled to show whether L1 or L2 should be used for one-way switching, but picking the wrong one means only that the switch will be (wrongly) up for on, down for off. If you find this when the circuit is tested simply switch off at the mains and change the wire to the other (L1 or L2) terminal. Earth the earth wire, (all but the end sleeved in green) to the metal wall box.

The second switch in the casing – don't get the two mixed up – is for the landing light and has a *three*-core and earth cable

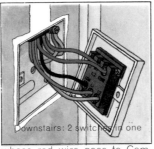

Downstairs: 2 switches in one

whose red wire goes to Common, blue to L1, yellow to L2, sleeved earth to the box. The completed double switch will look like this (above).

When all the wiring has been completed and all switches and ceiling roses are in place, it's time to have the circuits tested. **This is an electrical regulation which must be obeyed;** all major alterations must be checked by a qualified electrician, which means sending for an electrical contractor or the electricity board. It costs money, but is essential for the safety of you and your family. If you have fitted a new consumer unit, but have not

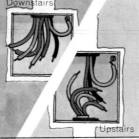

Downstairs

Upstairs

Upstairs a two-core and earth cable enters the box from above, the three-core from below. Fit a two-way switch, red of the three-core to Common,

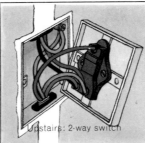

Upstairs: 2-way switch

black and blue wires to L1, red of the two-core and yellow to L2, bare earth wires to the box (above). Your hall and landing wiring is now completed.

yet had it connected to the supply from the meter, you can

join your new lighting circuits to the consumer unit; the red wire of each lighting circuit goes to one of the 5-amp fuses, the black wire to the neutral terminal block, the bare earth wire (don't forget the green sleeving) to the earth terminal, as shown on the left. If your consumer unit is already connected to the mains, get an electrician to test the circuit and connect it up for you. **On no account try to connect the consumer unit to the mains yourself.**

Rewiring bathrooms

Extra precautions must be taken in wiring bathrooms; a shock that might be merely painful to someone with dry hands would be lethal to someone who was wet, so every means is taken to ensure that wiring or apparatus can't be touched. The light switch is on the ceiling, worked by a cord. When the casing is unscrewed

you'll see that the fitting inside (left) has two terminals; connect the red wire of the switch cable to one, the black wire to the other. The earth wire goes to the earth screw (though there's nothing in these switches to be earthed). The best lights for bathrooms are totally enclosed so that condensation can't get into the wiring. They usually contain a short length of special heatproof flex to join the bulb-holder to the built-in ceiling rose; check that you've got this heatproof flex when you buy the fitting. If you must have a lamp on a flex in the bathroom – because of a high ceiling, for example – make sure the lampholder is made for use in bathrooms. It will be plastic, not metal, and have an outer sleeve to cover the part where the bulb fits. Use sheathed flex, not the cheap braided kind. **The only portable electric apparatus allowed in bathrooms is a shaver,** and this must have a special shaver point with an isolating transformer; tell your dealer it is for a bathroom.

THE KINDEST CURRENT CUTS

In the years of plenty, electricity companies never tried particularly hard to tell customers how much any piece of equipment cost to run. Now, with a sudden real need to reduce electricity used, it is important. Official exhortations to switch off lights, for example, are of little use. Below is a guide to the big spenders in electricity – and savings worth making. At about 1000 shaves for a penny an electric shaver is cheaper than heating water for a soap-and-blade shave

Drawings by Su Huntley

One unit of electricity – a kilowatt hour or kWh – is the amount used by a 1000-watt (kilo=1000) piece of equipment – like this one-bar fire – in an hour; by a 2 kilowatt heater in half an hour, or by a 100 watt bulb in 10 hours. Many gadgets are marked in watts or carry a plate marked in volts and amperes: volts multiplied by amps equal watts.

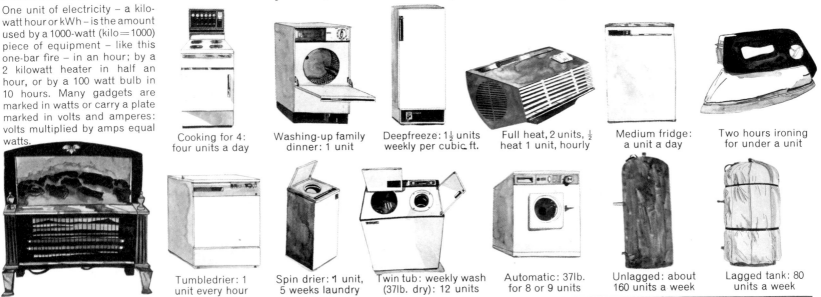

Cooking for 4: four units a day

Washing-up family dinner: 1 unit

Deepfreeze: 1½ units weekly per cubic ft.

Full heat, 2 units, ½ heat 1 unit, hourly

Medium fridge: a unit a day

Two hours ironing for under a unit

Tumbledrier: 1 unit every hour

Spin drier: 1 unit, 5 weeks laundry

Twin tub: weekly wash (37lb. dry): 12 units

Automatic: 37lb. for 8 or 9 units

Unlagged: about 160 units a week

Lagged tank: 80 units a week

A guide to what you get for one unit

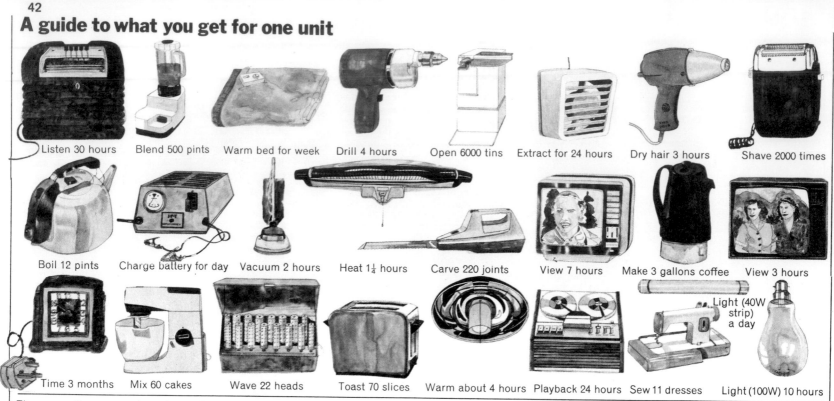

Listen 30 hours · Blend 500 pints · Warm bed for week · Drill 4 hours · Open 6000 tins · Extract for 24 hours · Dry hair 3 hours · Shave 2000 times

Boil 12 pints · Charge battery for day · Vacuum 2 hours · Heat 1¼ hours · Carve 220 joints · View 7 hours · Make 3 gallons coffee · View 3 hours

Time 3 months · Mix 60 cakes · Wave 22 heads · Toast 70 slices · Warm about 4 hours · Playback 24 hours · Sew 11 dresses · Light (40W strip) a day · Light (100W) 10 hours

There are three ways to cut electricity bills: by having a colder, darker house; by using less heat by holding on to it more tightly; and by making use of the White Meter system. The first way is uncomfortable and possibly dangerous; the other two ways are worth exploring.

Insulating lofts, walls, floors and windows and keeping draughts out saves money whichever way you heat your house.

You'll save a lot by insulating an electric hot water system: an unlagged hot tank with an immersion heater inside it wastes enough heat for about 20 baths a week, and an electrically-heated bath uses about five units, about 7p

worth, even when the tank is lagged.

Electric cookers use about four units a day to cook for four people; save by using the oven *or* the hobs but not both for the same meal; use triangular saucepans which fit three to one hob. Making toast in an electric toaster is much cheaper than turning on the large grill on the cooker.

Electric room heaters – fires, fan-heaters, storage heaters – are big users, varying from ¾ unit to 3 units an hour or more, but they should not all be banished for the sake of economy. If you need to heat a room quickly, it is cheaper to switch on an instant-heat fan heater for a few minutes than

to leave a central-heating radiator on all day.

Big savings are possible using the White Meter system, but not for everyone. The system is worth while if you have night storage heaters, or if you're a night bird, or an early riser. The meter has two sets of indicators, for night and day. The changeover times vary from district to district; usually 10.30pm to 7.30 in the morning. Any current used at night is cheaper – again, the precise rate varies from district to district. The local showroom can provide details.

There's a higher standing charge for the White Meter – another £1 or so each quarter – so you need to be able to trans-

fer a reasonable amount of your electricity demand to the night hours to make the change worth while. In most areas, if you use 20 or so units a week in the cheap time this extra cost will be covered and you can go on to make savings. Night storage heaters will certainly use more than 20 units a week, but even without them most people can save. Automatic washing machines, dish washers and clothes driers used last thing at night or first thing in the morning, will transfer some of the heaviest demand for electricity to the cheaper period; so will switching the immersion heater on at night, off in the morning.

As a check before taking on the White Meter system, try

some night and morning meter readings for a few days. With digital meters one simply records the figures and deducts one from the other to see how much has been used overnight or during the day. Dial meters are a little more tricky. Ignore the one-tenths dial, and move from right (single units) to left (10,000s units). Write down the lower number a pointer has passed, not the one it is approaching (adjacent dials revolve in opposite directions). If a pointer is directly over a figure, look at the dial to its right; if that pointer is between 9 and 0 record the previous number; if it is between 0 and 1 write down the figure the pointer covers.

PLUMBING
and
DRAINAGE

Before starting work turn off at the main

Before even renewing a washer you must be able to turn off the water. For that you need to know where and how the water flows, and that depends on where you live and the age of your house. For some water authorities insist on the 'direct' system where all cold water in the house comes from the company main; others insist on the 'tank' system where only the kitchen tap is fed from the mains and the rest of the taps and appliances are fed from a storage tank.

The direct system means that water from any cold tap is drinkable, and a smaller tank is needed in the roof; it holds 25 gallons, because its only function is to maintain a supply for the hot water system. The tank system needs a minimum 50-gallon tank and (because the water is stored) you shouldn't drink from any tap except that at the kitchen sink – though people with houses plumbed in this manner have been cleaning their teeth in the bathroom for many years without

coming to harm. An advantage of the bigger tank is that you can go on washing or flushing the lavatory should the mains supply be interrupted.

In the diagram below we show the pipework for both systems, though you'll only have one, of course, in your house; there will be only one pipe feeding cisterns, only two – hot and cold – feeding basins. With the diagram and a little looking around in kitchen, bathroom and roof space you'll be able to recognise which system you've

got and find the various stop valves which control the water supply.

In working on taps, valves or pipes always use a second spanner or a wrench to take the strain when you are unscrewing components or screwing them up; heave too hard on an unsupported fitting and you may finish with more plumbing repairs to do than when you started. Joints that stick can often be freed by gentle tapping, pouring on hot water, or with a little penetrating oil.

PLUMBING: See how it runs

Leaky taps and overflowing cisterns can be dealt with by an unskilled householder: but first, see where pipes run.

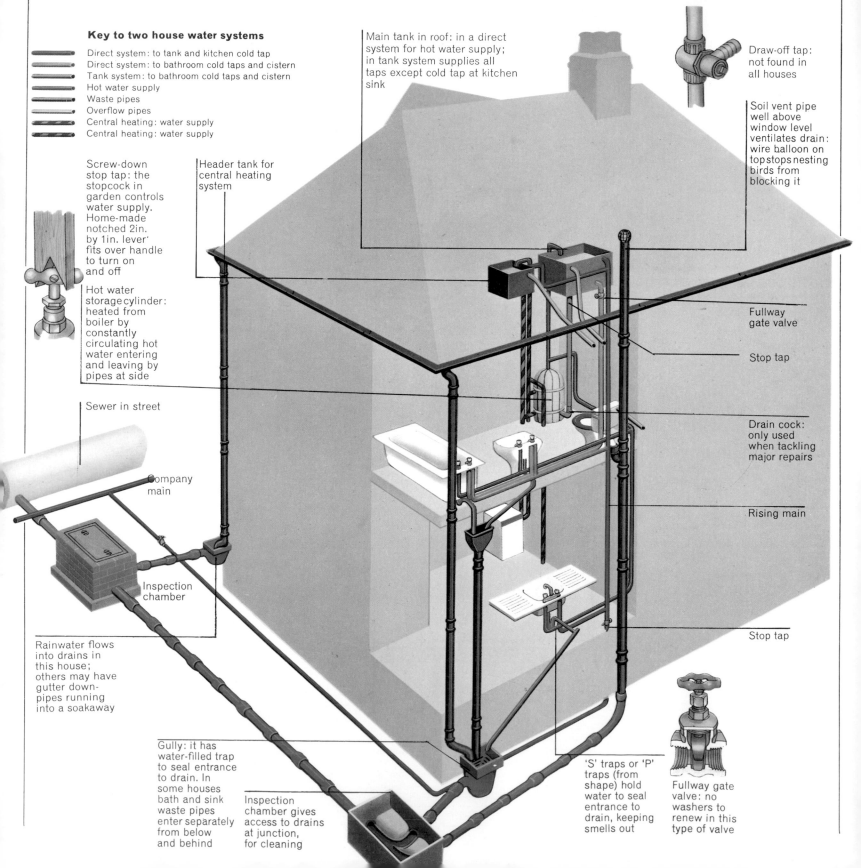

Key to two house water systems

- Direct system: to tank and kitchen cold tap
- Direct system: to bathroom cold taps and cistern
- Tank system: to bathroom cold taps and cistern
- Hot water supply
- Waste pipes
- Overflow pipes
- Central heating: water supply
- Central heating: water supply

Screw-down stop tap: the stopcock in garden controls water supply. Home-made notched 2in. by 1in. lever fits over handle to turn on and off

Hot water storage cylinder: heated from boiler by constantly circulating hot water entering and leaving by pipes at side

Sewer in street

Company main

Inspection chamber

Rainwater flows into drains in this house; others may have gutter down-pipes running into a soakaway

Header tank for central heating system

Main tank in roof: in a direct system for hot water supply; in tank system supplies all taps except cold tap at kitchen sink

Draw-off tap: not found in all houses

Soil vent pipe well above window level ventilates drain: wire balloon on top stops nesting birds from blocking it

Fullway gate valve

Stop tap

Drain cock: only used when tackling major repairs

Rising main

Stop tap

Gully: it has water-filled trap to seal entrance to drain. In some houses bath and sink waste pipes enter separately from below and behind

Inspection chamber gives access to drains at junction, for cleaning

'S' traps or 'P' traps (from shape) hold water to seal entrance to drain, keeping smells out

Fullway gate valve: no washers to renew in this type of valve

Plumbing the mysteries of the household tap: leaks round the top

Dripping taps and overflowing cisterns are simply dealt with – once you've found, with the help of the diagram overleaf, where to turn off the water if necessary. The tools you will need are: pliers, screwdriver, one, or better still two, adjustable wrenches, and a pair of thin open-ended spanners to fit tap and ballcock nuts (a good tool-merchant will advise you). Never use a wrench straight on the chrome "easyclean" cover of a tap – you're bound to scratch it. These covers can stick; if the ways of freeing them listed on the right don't work, a plumber would use a strap wrench – a leather strap fastened to a lever. The strap is

wrapped round the thickest part of the cover and heaving on the lever undoes the cover without damage. If you can't borrow one, or make one, then tape round the cover, grip wrench firmly and hope for the best.

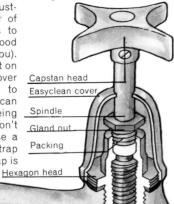

Capstan head
Easyclean cover
Spindle
Gland nut
Packing
Hexagon head
Jumper
Washer

Water leaking round the spindle of a tap means that the gland packing (see left) is at fault

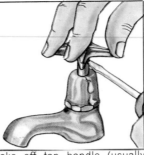

Take off tap handle (usually a small screw holds it). It may need *gentle* tapping with wood

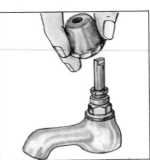

Easyclean shield unscrews; if stuck try pouring on hot water, tap it, or use penetrating oil

Try giving now-exposed gland nut (the top, not the lower nut) a quarter-turn or so clockwise to tighten it. If that fails to stop the leak remove nut completely

Beneath nut will be old packing; rake it out and replace with soft white string. Plumbers grease string with tallow; lard is an alternative, they say

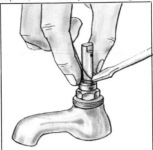

With new packing pressed in place, replace gland nut. Don't overtighten or tap will be stiff. Smear a little grease on thread of cover before replacing it

The drip-drip-drip that means a new washer

All those taps with handles on top work by screwing a non-metal washer down on to a metal seating; when washer wears tap drips. Half-inch sink and basin taps have 19mm. ($\frac{3}{4}$in.) diameter washers, $\frac{3}{4}$in. bath taps 25mm. (1in.) washers. Best kind are composition, which work with hot or cold water. Brass stem on which the washer fits is called the jumper; sometimes it is loose in tap, sometimes fixed to stem. You can buy separate washers, or jumper complete with washer

Jumper plate
Fixing nut
Washers

Have ready a new washer, or new jumper complete, turn off water supply, turn tap full on

Unscrew easyclean cover. Use thin spanner on hexagon now visible to loosen inner tap

Remove whole tap top, lift out jumper (if it is not fastened). Grip jumper with pair of pliers

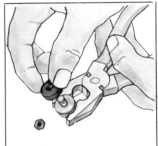

Unscrew nut, remove remains of old washer, fit new washer, replace nut and re-assemble

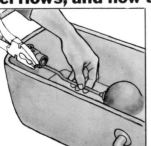

Capstan head

Taps of the Supatap type can have washers changed without turning off water. When capstan head is removed (after undoing lock nut) water stops

Antisplash fitment

Jumper and washer fit into one end of grooved antisplash fitment inside capstan head of tap which is not on top but on the water nozzle of the tap

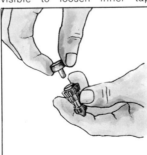

Remove jumper from antisplash fitment, replace with new one. (If you can't get a new washer, you can cut one from a piece of rubber and fit it to the jumper)

Put jumper back into antisplash fitment and return that to tap's capstan head; screw back to tap. As you screw head back, water will begin to flow again

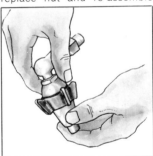

Finally refit locking nut, tightening carefully clockwise. Don't forget: always support taps when using a spanner – they won't stand much hard twisting

Why the overflow overflows, and how to stop it

Cistern control is by a ball float; when tank empties float drops, opening valve. As water comes in the float rises until it shuts off valve again. If cistern overflows check that float isn't leaking. Unscrew it from arm and shake it; you'll hear water inside. If it leaks, renew it. If float isn't leaking it may need adjustment; bending arm down will shut off water supply at lower level. If overflow persists, valve needs a new washer. Turn off water supply

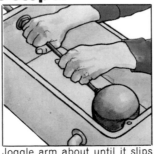

With pliers, take out split pin holding arm. You may need to remove flush handle to get at it

Joggle arm about until it slips out of slot in valve. Unscrew the knurled end cap of valve

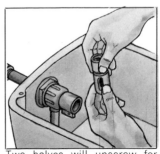

Slide out piston with screwdriver. Grip washer end in pliers, put screwdriver in recess

Two halves will unscrew for replacing washer. Clean and grease piston, then re-assemble

PLUMBING: Blockages

Blocked waste pipes and drains are among the minor domestic disasters which a self-sufficient householder can tackle easily, if sometimes messily, and by tackling them he can save the inconvenience of waiting for a plumber as well as the plumber's bill. Hour for hour, most plumbers probably charge more for clearing drains than for other work; and who could blame them?

Sinks and washbasins—the simplest methods

There are three stages in a drainage system: waste pipes (from sink, bath and basin) and soil pipes (from watercloset) lead into drains, the bigger pipes which take waste from the building into the sewer, the large drain in the street which leads eventually to the sewage works. The sewer is the drainage authority's responsibility; everything else is the responsibility of the householder. Between the sink, bath, basin or watercloset and the drain there is always a bend in the outlet pipe, called a trap because it traps a small amount of water to form a seal, stopping foul smells getting back from the drain into the house. If the bath, sink or basin outlet become blocked, the first tool to try is a plunger, a bell-shaped rubber cup fitted to a wooden handle. Buy one from an ironmonger; keep it handy. It works by forcing water down the waste-pipe and pushing the blockage away; used occasionally if the waste seems to be running slowly it can prevent a complete blockage happening.

Block overflow with cloth first, or working plunger will shoot dirty water out of overflow

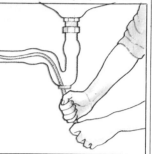

With cloth held in place, put plunger cup firmly over outlets, pump vigorously up and down

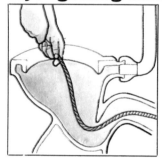

If plunger doesn't clear blockage, try poking with flexible thin cane or wire; but go gently with lead or plastic fittings

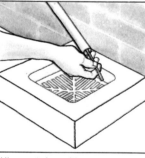

No luck? Then put bucket under trap (tray is all you'll get under bath trap) and try unscrewing brass cleaning eye or fitting

Flat bar will undo cleaning eye. Hold rest of bend, go gently, use penetrating oil if stiff; lead will not take rough treatment

Other traps may be in plastic, and whole unit unscrew. Either way, when off, use the cane or wire to clear pipe both ways

Lavatories and gulleys—getting down to basics

A makeshift plunger for a blocked watercloset can be made from a mop, with a plastic bag tied tight round it. If that doesn't work, again try a flexible cane or wire. There's no removable cleaning eye on the trap in this case. This may also work with blocked gulleys – the drains covered with a grid outside the house which often become blocked with grit or mud

Sets of rods for cleaning water closets or bigger drains can be bought or hired for the day

Where sink and basin pipes run into drain like this, cleaning rod can be inserted from below

This kind of drain, technically a gulley, often gets blocked with leaves or grit from the gutters

Lift off and clean grid. Trowelling out debris is usually enough to clear; if not use rods

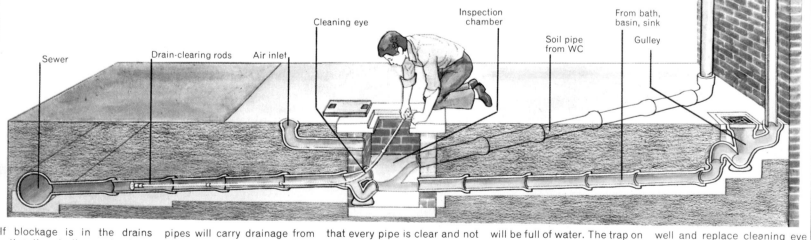

Sewer | Drain-clearing rods | Air inlet | Cleaning eye | Inspection chamber | Soil pipe from WC | From bath, basin, sink | Gulley

If blockage is in the drains rather than in the waste pipes, there's nothing for it but to get a set of drain-clearing rods (the hire rate is about £1 a day or less), take off the manhole cover in the garden, and get down to smelly reality. If the drain is blocked but the manhole is empty, then the blockage is somewhere between the manhole and the house. You'll see two or more pipes running into the inspection chamber from the house; one or more of these pipes will carry drainage from the gulleys – the water from baths, sinks, washbasins and very likely water from the gutters. Another will be the soil pipe from the watercloset. A pipe high up on the side of the chamber will be an air inlet, fitted at the top with a grid, or sometimes a hinged mica flap to keep smells from escaping. Assemble the rods and push them up each drainpipe in turn – while you've got the rods you may as well make sure that every pipe is clear and not building up for a blockage later. There are different kinds of screw-heads, brush-heads and plunger-heads available for the rods, and with one or the other you will be able to break through the obstruction. Go on scraping and brushing while water is flushed down the drain to complete the clearing.

A worse job is when the blockage is between the manhole and the sewer. In that case the chamber beneath the manhole will be full of water. The trap on the outlet side of the chamber has a cleaning eye just above it, a stopper fitting into a branch of the drain. When this stopper is removed the rods can be pushed down, with a plunger end. Pumping up and down will probably clear the blockage; if not you may have to replace the plunger with a screw end and turn the rods (clockwise only, otherwise the sections will come undone) to break up the blockage. Flush well and replace cleaning eye before replacing manhole cover – clean cover well round edges for a good seal. If you've once had the unpleasant job of fishing open the cleaning eye of a drain from inside a flooded chamber you'll understand why prudent plumbers tie the eye to a nylon cord whose other end is fixed high up near the top of the chamber.

With long drains there may be more than one manhole; the procedure is the same.

PLUMBING: Pipe dream

When lead and steel pipes went out of fashion and copper and plastic came in, it became possible for householders to tackle simple alterations and repairs to the domestic water supply. For plastic tubing there is only one technique to learn: how to join tubes. Plastic won't bend far with safety, so any bends are best made by using angle fittings. For copper tube you need to learn how to make joints and how to bend tubes. All the techniques are simple, but it's best to order an extra length of tube and an extra fitting or two and practise before you tackle the real thing.

Copper tubing and how to bend it into shape

If copper tube is bent more than a small amount it will become oval in section and eventually flatten completely. To avoid this, plumbers use bending springs or bending machines which keep the tube section round. Bending machines are not worth buying, but you can hire them for about £2 a day, £4 a week. Springs can be bought or hired; they are steel spirals about 2ft. long. The easiest kind to use fits round the outside of the tube – it's easier to slip on to the correct position and take off again after bending. Internal springs which slip inside the tube are more commonly available. With the spring in place you simply grip the two ends of the tube, set your knee against the place to be bent, and pull. With the tube bent, internal springs tend to jam inside. If the bend is at the end of a tube, so that part of the spring is sticking out, slip a screwdriver into the ring on the spring end, twist to wind up the spring a little and the spring will slip out. If the bend is in the middle of a long tube you'll have to fasten

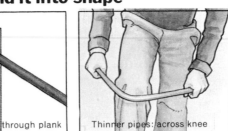

Thick pipes: bend through plank | Thinner pipes: across knee

Copper tube bends easily; thicker tubes can be bent by fitting into a hole bored in a piece of timber; press down on the ends. For smaller tubes, it is enough to hold ends of tube in each hand and bend tube over your knee. Section to be bent must be protected by bending spring or it will flatten and finally collapse

Internal pipe-bending spring

External pipe-bending spring

the spring ring to a strong wire, measure carefully and mark the wire so that you can slide it in to the right position. Bend the tube a little further than you need, then straighten it a little to release the bending spring.

Bending machines, usually on a portable stand, can be hired, make tube-bending easy. The tube is held in a groove so it can't flatten while being bent

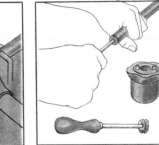

Copper or plastic pipes full of water are heavy and will sag if not supported by fittings like these for copper (top) and these for plastic (above)

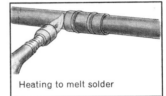

If you've a lot of joints to make these small tools are worthwhile: wire brushes for cleaning inside and outside of tubes. Make sure you get right size

Capillary fittings: the neatest joints

Capillary fittings make the neatest joints and are the only ones for fitting underground which we'd recommend an amateur to tackle. The design is such that even if you aren't good at soldering you'll be able to make a sound joint. There are two kinds of capillary fittings; those where you must add solder and those, shown here, easiest for amateur use, which have a ring of solder already fitted inside as an integral part of the fitting.

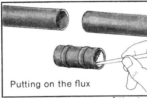

Putting on the flux

Cut the ends square of the two tubes to be joined (use a fine-toothed hacksaw or miniature hacksaw) and file off any roughness (use a round file for inside). Thoroughly clean inside of fitting and outside of tube

Scratch with a nail

with glasspaper or the special cleaning tools (above, right). Put flux on outside of tubes and inside of fitting. Push tube into fitting as far as the built-in stop. Scratch tube with nail at joints to be sure solder grips well.

Heating to melt solder

Play the flame of blow-lamp on fitting; solder will melt and creep up the narrow space between tube and fitting (by capillary attraction, hence the name) until you see a bright ring of solder all round the joint.

Adapters

If your existing plumbing is in lead, you'll have to pay a plumber to make a lead-to-copper joint, and you pick up the job from there. He's likely to charge you fairly steeply, to make up for the work he's losing, but you'll still save money in the end. If your plumbing is in steel tube, unscrew a convenient joint and fit a steel-to-copper adapter (below) or T-piece. You can buy these adapters from a builder's merchant; buy some *PTFE tape* as well, wrap the steel thread with the tape, then screw on the adapter and from there on you can work in copper tube. Similar

adapters are made for steel-to-plastic, permitted only for cold water and waste pipes.

Compression joints are the simplest for copper

Compression joints are the simplest for joining copper tube; there's no heating or soldering and the only tools needed are a hacksaw, file and spanners. Cut square the ends of tubes and file off any roughness (use a round file to smooth the inside). Slide the nut on the tube, then the compression ring. Push tube into the fitting making sure it reaches the stop ridge inside. Then push the ring into the mouth of the fitting, and tighten as far as you can with your

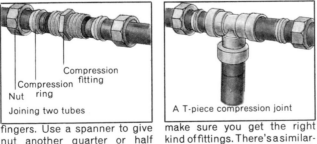

Compression fitting
Compression ring
Nut
Joining two tubes

fingers. Use a spanner to give nut another quarter or half turn. Don't overtighten or the joint may leak. This kind of joint is called *non-manipulative*;

A T-piece compression joint

make sure you get the right kind of fittings. There's a similar-looking *manipulative* joint, which needs a special tool to widen tube ends before joining – not

Tightening: go carefully

quite so easy for amateurs. If a joint leaks, tighten a little more with spanner; if that doesn't cure it, remake the joint with a new compression ring.

Plastic pipes: for waste and cold water only

Plastic pipes are for cold water and waste pipes only. They can't be bent cold; the manufacturers supply instructions for bending after heating them, but it's best, where possible, to use the various angle fittings. Water supply pipes are joined with solvent cement after cleaning the inside of the fitting and outside the end of the pipe with special cleaning fluid. Buy both when you buy the pipes and fittings. The tube ends must be cut square; use a fine-toothed

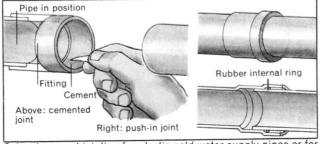

Pipe in position
Fitting
Cement
Above: cemented joint
Rubber internal ring
Right: push-in joint

Solvent-cement jointing for plastic cold water supply pipes or for plastic waste pipes. For plastic waste pipes only: pipes push into expansion fittings where rubber inserts seal the joints

saw, and chamfer the end with a file. After cleaning, paint outside of tube and inside of fitting with solvent cement, and immediately push pipe into fitting and allow to set. (Work fast or cement will dry before you've made the joint.) Wipe off the surplus cement, and wash out the brush immediately in the cleaning fluid. Bigger pipes for waste systems can be joined in the same way, or they can be joined with simple push-on fittings. These have rubber

rings inside which grip the outside of the pipes. Cut pipes square, chamfer the ends. Wipe the outside of the pipe with liquid soap. Check that the rubber inserts are seated correctly in their recess in the fitting. Push the pipe home carefully so that it doesn't displace the rubber ring. Plastic pipes should be kept an inch or so clear of hot pipes if they are running side by side; if they must be close, they should have insulation between them.

Off with the old, preparing for the new

Begin by disconnecting the waste from the old sink: this will be fastened either by a bolt running down through the centre of the waste fitting, or by a large nut beneath the sink tightened on to the threaded stem of the waste fitting. You may have to tap the waste fitting to break the seal of old hard putty which will hold it to the sink. Then slide the sink forward off its supports (take care: it's heavier than you think). If you are replacing it with a similar fireclay sink,

simply clean off beneath the tiles where the old sink fitted and slide the new one into place. Grout joint between new sink and tiles carefully – it's a dirt trap. Reconnect the waste with fresh putty. If you want a modern sink in its place, there's rather more to do. If pipes to taps over sink are sunk in wall, hack off tiles to reach them. (Keep a piece as a sample if you want to match them.) Dismantle any cupboards under sink; take away any wooden sink supports.

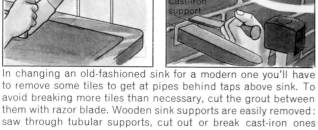

In changing an old-fashioned sink for a modern one you'll have to remove some tiles to get at pipes behind taps above sink. To avoid breaking more tiles than necessary, cut the grout between them with razor blade. Wooden sink supports are easily removed: saw through tubular supports, cut out or break cast-iron ones

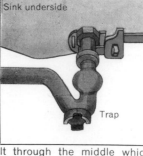
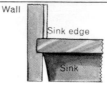

Waste fittings are held by a bolt through the middle which unscrews (left) or by a nut beneath. When undoing nut, take care to avoid damaging the trap; lead fittings are not very strong

Cut tubular sink supports (left). Cast-iron ones built into the wall (left, below), can be cut out with a cold chisel; or you may be able to break them off by a blow with a heavy hammer – cast iron is brittle. Set the new sink temporarily into its cupboard unit and stand that against the wall, marking where

sink top, bottom of tap stems and waste will come. Move it out again and cut a groove in the wall so back edge of sink fits snug behind line of tiles.

PLUMBING: Replacing the kitchen sink

Modernising an old kitchen starts at the sink, and it's not difficult. Replacing a sink with one of the same kind is straightforward; replacing an old fireclay sink with a new enamel or stainless steel unit is more complicated, but not beyond the skill of a householder. For details of bending and joining water-pipes, see details on p. 47. On p. 51 we describe a very similar job of replacing a bathroom basin; and on page 92 we explain how to make a kitchen unit.

Fitting the new taps and the waste outlet

Some sinks and taps will be supplied complete with fitting instructions; if yours hasn't such instructions this is what to do. Fit the taps in place, each one with a thin nylon washer on top of the sink (this makes the tap-to-sink joint watertight and, with enamel sinks, protects the enamel from the metal of the tap). Underneath the sink comes a thick, shaped nylon spacer washer with the flat side against the underside of the sink. On to that goes the backnut, with its flat side against the washer. If you are installing a mixer valve instead of individual taps, there will be the same thick washers underneath, but one large sealing gasket on top of the sink instead of the thin nylon washer for each tap. Tighten the backnuts. There are different kinds of waste fittings. If the sink has no overflow the waste will be a plain threaded one. Fit the nylon or rubber washer supplied, inside the sink beneath the chrome outlet and another outside (beneath) the sink above the nut which tightens the fitting. If the sink has an overflow,

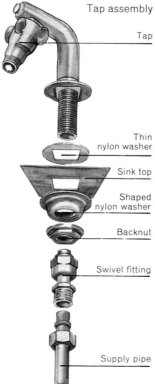

Tap assembly

Tap

Thin nylon washer

Sink top

Shaped nylon washer

Backnut

Swivel fitting

Supply pipe

it must have a *slotted waste*, similar to the plain waste, but with slots cut in the waste just below sink level to let in water from the overflow. This overflow may be built in as an integral part of the sink, but in a modern unit it is most likely to have a flexible plastic pipe which runs from the overflow fitting (like a miniature waste) to a collar which fits round the slotted part of the waste. This kind of waste unit will have three nylon or rubber washers, one below the chrome waste inlet inside the sink, one

immediately below the sink above the overflow unit, and one below the overflow unit between it and the nut which tightens the whole assembly together. (Metal-window putty is an alternative to nylon or rubber washers for sealing metal fittings, but putty should never be used with plastic fittings.) Tighten the waste assembly. Now fit the sink unit to its base: small angle brackets screw into the framework and hold the turned-up lip of the sink top down to the base.

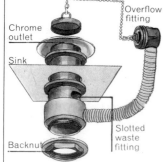

Overflow fitting

Chrome outlet

Sink

Slotted waste fitting

Backnut

Overflow assembly: make sure flexible pipe is fixed firmly at each end or overflow will leak

Turning off the water supply

The cold water supply to your sink will be direct from the main; turn it off with the stop tap in the house (sometimes below the sink) or by a stop tap outside, usually in or near the path (see illustration, p. 44). Hot water should be controlled by a valve in the pipe from the cold tank in the roof to the hot cylinder. If your house hasn't such a valve (many haven't) having turned off the cold stop tap simply turn on all hot taps until no

more hot water comes out. Switch off immersion heater and turn down boiler to stop water in the hot cylinder overheating, but there's no risk of damage because while the 25 or 50-gallon cold tank will empty, the hot water cylinder itself remains full. (If you can't bear the thought of wasting all that hot water, turn off heating the night before.) If hot water is supplied by a separate gas or electric heater, turn off the valves on the heater itself.

Adapting and extending the pipework

If the existing hot and cold supply is in copper, your problems are simple. Compression joints (with nuts) can be disconnected and new lengths of pipe run to the new taps using compression joints. If the joints are capillary (soldered), heating with a blowlamp will enable them to be pulled apart and new joints made. If the supplies are in steel pipes you'll have to locate a threaded joint in the steel pipe – there's one where the old taps join on but there

Sink top

Bracket

Sink base unit

How sink is held down to its base

may be others more convenient for your new pipe run farther back. Unscrew steel joints – you may need to heat them first – and fit a steel-to-copper adaptor using PTFE tape for the steel side, then run new piping in copper. If the supply is in lead you'll need a plumber to make a lead-to-copper joint

from which you can pick up in copper, or to connect the lead pipes to your new taps; joining lead is a skilled job. Pipes coming down to taps over the sink will have to be extended below the sink and there turned up to meet the threaded ends of the new taps. Pipes to the side of the new unit can run low down (where they will be hidden by the sink cupboard) and up to the new taps; pipes from below are easiest of all because they will only need cutting short to connect to the taps. Pipes on the surface of the wall are easiest to deal with but present problems if they must pass from above, behind the back of the sink unit to reach the taps.

Turn pipes to run parallel with the sink top, dropping down at the end of the unit to enter through end panel, or hack a channel in the wall. Ideally this channel should have a removable cover, but most houses survive without such a refinement. Drill sink base for fitting to wall, stand it in place and mark wall for drilling and plugging. Now fix the waste pipe; unless the old one is sound and in precisely the right position it's quicker to scrap it and fit a new waste pipe in plastic. Cut holes for waste and supply pipes in unit where necessary. With sink unit away from wall fit swivel couplings loosely to taps; complete running supply pipes to sink position. Now tighten swivel couplings to taps using fibre washers or jointing paste and hemp for a watertight joint. Put complete unit in place, screw it to wall and connect hot and cold supplies. Turn on water and check for leaks. When you are sure everything is sound, make good any plaster and tiles.

What's what in the smallest room

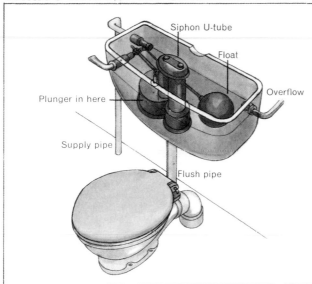

Siphon U-tube
Float
Plunger in here
Overflow
Supply pipe
Flush pipe

A lavatory cistern – Water Waste Preventer or WWP to builders' merchants – works on the siphon principle. An inverted U-tube runs from just above the bottom of the cistern, up above the water level and down again to join the flush pipe to the pan. Pulling the handle moves a plunger in the thick part of it, pumping a little water up this tube; as the water falls down the other side it pulls the rest of the water in the cistern after it. The ball-shaped float opens and closes water inlet valve according to water level in the cistern. Pipe from inlet valve to bottom of cistern helps cut out splashing and gurgling noise as water comes in to refill cistern

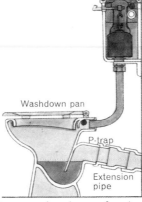

Washdown pan
P-trap
Extension pipe

There are two types of water closet; the *washdown* pattern, above, is the cheapest and most common; it is effective but often noisy. The flow of water from the cistern simply washes everything through the trap – the water seal – and down the drain. Its efficiency depends on the force of water; with the old high-level cistern this was no problem. With low cisterns there's less force to the water. Bigger pipes and better design get over this; but it isn't a good idea to change to a low cistern with a pan originally installed for a high one

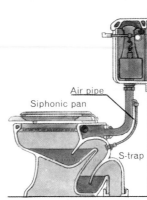

Air pipe
Siphonic pan
S-trap

Siphonic water closets (above) are more complicated, more expensive, but claimed to be more efficient; they're certainly quieter and can be installed with the cistern mounted directly on the pan – far neater. They have two traps, one visible and one in the bend of the outlet. When flushed, the flow of water sucks air through the small pipe at the back, out of the space between the two traps, pulling the contents of the first trap over to empty by syphonic action; the water washes down the pan and reforms the water seal. They can have either P or S traps

PLUMBING: The new loo guide

Replacing a damaged or out-of-date lavatory is not the most pleasant of plumbing jobs; plumbers usually charge a lot for it. In most cases it is a job the householder can carry out; and at the same time if necessary replace an old high cistern with a modern low-level one.

Stripping out the old equipment – take care – and fitting the new

Apart from the different kinds of lavatory pan (above, centre and right) there are different ways in which the drain end of the pan – the pan spigot – points to join on to the drain – the soil pipe. A P-trap is made for a drain which runs out through the wall like the one above centre, and overleaf. An S-trap is made for a drain which runs down through the floor, as shown above and below. Make sure you get the right type; and check also that the

new pan will match as nearly as possible the height of the drain it must join – matching up new pan with old soil pipe can present difficulties. If you are changing from a high cistern to a low one it may be necessary to fit the new pan farther out from the wall than the old one, to make room. You can do this using extension pipes; if that isn't possible you can buy very thin (3½in. or 4in.) cisterns – though you'll have to allow extra height and width for them,

because the cistern must contain approximately two gallons of water. In removing the old pan, take very great care; if you damage the soil pipe which it joins, the repair may be expensive and need an expert. Before starting work, flush the pan well, then turn off the water and flush again to empty cistern. Water in the pan can be mopped out. For how to turn off the water supply and how to bend and join water pipes, see the details on p. 47 for guidance.

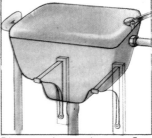

Disconnect supply, overflow and flush pipes; lift down cistern carefully – it's very heavy

New low cistern sits on concealed brackets and screws to wall. Pierce wall for new overflow

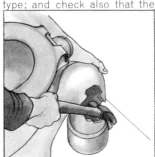

Remove screws holding old pan in place, disconnect flush pipe, lift pan from outlet pipe. If anything sticks you'll have to break the pan. Make sure pieces don't go down drain. Push wad of cloth into pipe (careful it doesn't fall right down) to keep bits out and smells in. Take great care not to damage outlet pipe connection

Chip away cement or putty seal very carefully with small cold chisel. Chip inward at the pan spigot; don't knock pipe. Even iron pipes are brittle

There are three ways of connecting a new pan to the drain. On a solid concrete floor the joint can be made with spun yarn topped off with a 1-3 cement-sand mix. On wooden floors where there will be inevitably a certain amount of movement, this joint would be too rigid and possibly cause the pan to crack, so use spun yarn topped off with putty. Or, for connections on either floor, there are patent Multikwik joints, shown overleaf; finned tubes which simply fit inside pipe and outside the pan spigot.

Put new pan in place. Check there's room for low cistern behind it. Mark on floor round pedestal and for screws. Drill – plug solid floors – for screws

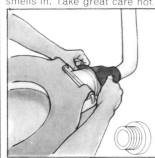

Neat and easy way to join flush pipe to pan is finned rubber fitting (inset). Less neat, is rubber wrap-around joint above. Make sure seated correctly

If a solid floor is uneven, bed the foot of the pan on a cement-sand mix. Use 3in. or 4in. brass screws to secure it. Don't over-tighten or you may crack pan

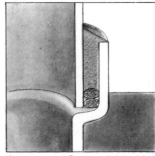

Place one or two turns of spun yarn round joint and pack well down with thin tool. Take care of the pan spigot and pipe; you don't want to crack it now

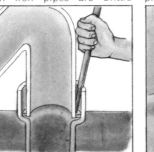

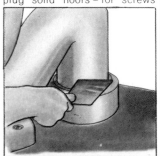

If on a wood floor, paint inside joint, use yarn, then fill with putty. Push well down to make good seal, finish edge neatly and paint. If on a solid floor, use spun yarn, then fill with cement-sand mix, trowelling edge to neat 45 degree angle. When dry, connect supply and overflow pipes to the cistern; then flush and check for leaks

Fitting a new lavatory pan

A ground-floor WC is more likely to have an S-trap – that is, the pan outlet will run straight down into the floor; though this is not always the case. A WC on an upper floor is most likely to have a P-trap, where the spigot runs out at an angle to join the waste which goes through the wall to join soil pipe on the outside of the house. The P-trap can present problems, since the centre of the pan outlet and the pipe must coincide. Most modern lavatory pans have the

Offset connector · *Extension pipe* · *Bend connector*

If pan and pipe don't match up, Multikwik connectors or extensions make adjustments possible

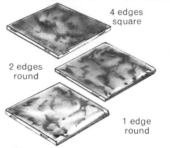

Straight connector

WC on an upper floor will most likely have P-trap, pipe running through wall to join soil pipe

outlet at a standard 7½in. from floor to pipe centre. Old ones were more variable, and if you are replacing an old pan you may find that the new one is too high or too low for a perfect match. If the pan is too low it can be raised by mounting it on a piece of wood of the necessary thickness – trace round the bottom of the pedestal and cut out the wood to fit neatly. Since the height of WC pans is set to be anatomically right for the average person, this packing

shouldn't be overdone – an inch or so at most. Further adjustments between the pipes can be obtained by using offset Multikwik connectors that provide a further ¾in. adjustment in any direction. These connectors – straight, curved or offset (far left) – are fitted first to the pan spigot and the assembled pan and connector, smeared if necessary with a little soft soap for easy fitting, are carefully manoeuvred into the outlet pipe and then slid home.

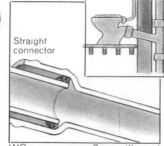

When carrying out bathroom or kitchen alterations it may be necessary to replace missing or damaged tiles. Six-inch square tiles can be obtained for repairs (take a sample with you: even white tiles are not necessarily the same white). They will probably have been fastened with sand and cement; you'll have to chip this away with a small cold chisel for the new tile to fit flush. If part of the rendering behind the tiles comes away, renew it with a 1-3 cement-sand mix or with plaster so that the new tile will be level with the others. Leave until plaster is completely dry before fixing tile with tile adhesive, then for another 24 hours before grouting the joint. If you are tiling a new area it is far easier to work in the thin 4¼in. square tiles made for easy fixing.

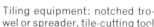

4 edges square · *2 edges round* · *1 edge round*

4¼in. square tiles have spacing lugs, come in three types

Tiling equipment: notched trowel or spreader, tile-cutting tool

TILING
All square

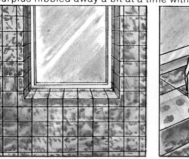

Floors may be uneven, so if you start from skirting board tile joints may show up in wavy lines. Instead mark one-tile height from lowest point, nail a batten to the wall with its top at mark. Check it is horizontal using a spirit level. When the rest of the tiles are in place remove batten and fit bottom row of tiles, trimming to fit

Tiling should start at wall or window centre with equal size cut tiles in corners. Mark tile widths on another batten, and measure to find centre point

Using plumbline, nail another batten vertically on centre line. Hold tiles in place in the angle formed with horizontal batten to check two battens are truly square. Spread adhesive according to maker's instructions over about a square yard, press tiles in place – not too hard. Mark, then score tiles to be cut for corners

Rest tile on matchstick, glaze uppermost, press down both sides and it will snap on scoremark. If you've trouble marking out these odd tiles compare with floor tiling on p. 74, the principle is the same. Awkward shapes are marked, scored on glaze, then the surplus nibbled away a bit at a time with pincers. Go carefully . . .

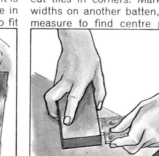

. . . to avoid waste (you are bound to spoil a few) and because broken tiles are sharp as glass. Smooth edges with carborundum (tool-sharpening) stone

In some awkward spots it may be easier to spread adhesive on back of tile rather than wall. When fitting cut tiles into corners, the cut edge goes into corner and the edge with spacing lugs goes against neighbouring tile to preserve spacing. As you go, scrape out adhesive from joints with matchstick; keep tile face clean

At window ledges and similar external corners, full tiles go to the edge, cut tiles at back – and remember to use curved edge tiles on the horizontal surface to cover the square edge of vertical tiles, not the other way round. Keep checking wall with straightedge at all angles to ensure tiles are flat and that they're all square

When tiling is complete on one side of vertical batten remove it and tackle other side. With all tiles in place mix tile-grout to stiff paste, rub it all over tiles and into joints with cloth or sponge, scrape off surplus with plastic or cardboard scraper. When dry go over joints with pointed stick, rub off tile faces with soft dry cloth

Fittings like soap dishes can be obtained already mounted on a tile; because of their weight hold them in place with sticky tape until the adhesive is dry

Fitting a new bathroom basin: fragile, handle with care

Bathroom basins are fitted in much the same way as sinks – but vitreous china is much more fragile. You'll save time and trouble by making sure that the new basin's tap and waste positions are the same as for the old one; if not, adjust supply and waste pipes very carefully so they put no strain on the basin. Basin taps are not a precise fit in the tap holes and will move unless you do as good plumbers do and wrap a small piece of sheet lead round the

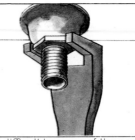

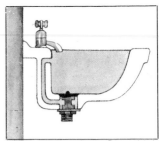

tap stem to make a snug joint. Spread metal-window putty beneath the tap to make a waterproof join; beneath the

basin a thick shaped plastic washer seals the joint and protects from the pressure of the back-nut. Fitting taps to basins

is difficult because of the curve of the basin; there's no room for an ordinary spanner. Buy a basin wrench (above). Basins

have an integral overflow which drains into a slotted waste. Cover top of basin brackets with putty for even support

The saving shower

Now you've learnt how to bend and join waterpipes, how to replace sinks, basins and WCs, and how to tile walls. Replacing a bath? It's just like a sink or a basin, only bigger. So now here are details of three more jobs for transforming an old bathroom: an easy way to cover old tiles and to fit a decorative illuminated ceiling for a bathroom or kitchen; and a moneysaving way of installing that bathroom moneysaver, a shower. It costs about 8p to 10p to heat the water for one bath. A shower uses around one-fifth as much. So a family of four which switches from daily baths to showers six days a week, enjoying a good wallow only on the seventh, can save about £100 a year – enough to cover the cost of installing a shower in the first year. A separate shower can go anywhere there's a spare square yard of space; bathroom, bedroom, or, with a doored-off dressing area, at the end of a corridor.

Complete shower cubicles are the most simple to install; but their prices start at about £100. With some straightforward woodwork, tiling and simple plumbing an amateur can produce a shower stall for much less. Before starting, check with your local council and water board if there are local regulations about plumbing installations. The best shower fittings are thermostatically controlled to keep the shower temperature steady, but they are expensive; ordinary mixers, though liable under some conditions to run hotter or colder as other taps in the house are turned on, are cheaper; in either case ask for fittings which are water board approved. If you haven't a convenient hot water supply, ask at your electricity showroom about electric shower heaters which work off a cold supply only – they cost from about £25, but they must be professionally installed which will add to this. Shower trays are made in fireclay (everlasting but heavy) or

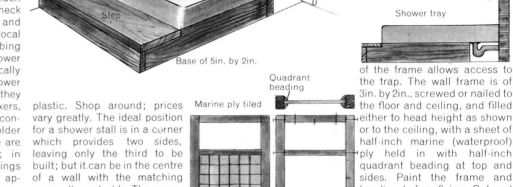

Waste: alternative positions

Tray

Access to trap

Step

Base of 5in. by 2in.

Shower tray

Trap

plastic. Shop around; prices vary greatly. The ideal position for a shower stall is in a corner which provides two sides, leaving only the third to be built; but it can be in the centre of a wall with the matching new walls each side. The essential is that there should be a way out for the waste pipe through the wall into a drain.

Make a base for the shower tray in 125mm. by 50mm. (5in. by 2in.) timber the width of the tray and about 6in. longer. The 5in. height leaves room for the waste pipe and trap under the

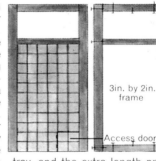

Quadrant beading

Marine ply tiled

3in. by 2in. frame

Access door

tray, and the extra length provides for a step up to the tray. The gap which is left at one side

of the frame allows access to the trap. The wall frame is of 3in. by 2in., screwed or nailed to the floor and ceiling, and filled either to head height as shown or to the ceiling, with a sheet of half-inch marine (waterproof) ply held in with half-inch quadrant beading at top and sides. Paint the frame and beading before fixing. Cut and hinge a flap in the ply for access to the trap; then fix tiles both sides of ply with tile adhesive, grout and polish. Cut hot and cold pipes at a convenient point, insert T-pieces and run supplies to shower fitting; if you are retiling they can be sunk into the wall for neatness.

New tiles on old–and a bright ceiling

In renewing an old bathroom with discoloured or cracked tiles you can hack off all the old tiles and start again. If you do it, wear thick gloves to avoid cuts from splintered tiles; make good any damage to the walls to leave an even surface for re-tiling. It is easier to fix new tiles on top of the old. Wash down walls and dry them; fix any old tiles that are loose, and see the surface is reasonably even. Then spread tile adhesive and re-tile. If the old tiles reach only

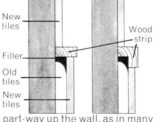

New tiles

Wood strip

Filler

Old tiles

New tiles

part-way up the wall, as in many old bathrooms, plug the wall and fix a wood strip – polyurethane-varnished hardwood looks very good; fill the gap where the old

tiles curve in, and tile up to the bottom of the strip. You can go on tiling above it.

Bathrooms in older houses were often tall and narrow. The aquarium look (and sound) this gave them can be overcome by fitting a false ceiling lower down; once a sizeable task, it has been made easy by manufacturers of illuminated ceiling kits. Aluminium strips are fixed to the walls all round at the new ceiling height, rather like a picture rail. From these, more

strips cross the room at right angles, dividing the area into squares into which light flexible translucent plastic panels fit. The strip is easily cut with a hacksaw, and the plastic can be cut with scissors for the smaller panels necessary to fit different size or shape rooms. In the space above the false ceiling, the light bulb should be replaced by fluorescent lamps. Ask at electrical shops for fluorescent fittings which plug into an ordinary lampholder.

Plumbing in a washing machine

Most washing machines will work with their inlet hoses temporarily attached to the hot and cold (sometimes only the cold) taps and with the emptying hose hooked over the edge of the sink, but they are much better permanently plumbed in. Temporary tap fixings are liable to leak, and their use means that the sink taps are out of action until the washing cycle is complete. When fixing the machine permanently, the hoses are still used, both so

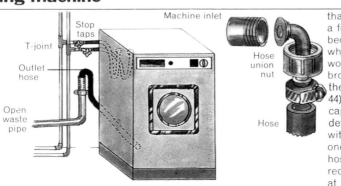

Machine inlet

Stop taps

T-joint

Outlet hose

Hose union nut

Open waste pipe

Hose

that the machine can be shifted a foot or two for cleaning, and because fixing a machine which vibrates to rigid pipes would sooner or later mean a broken pipe or joint. Turn off the water (see instructions p. 44) and fit T-pieces, either capillary or compression (see details, p. 47), to supply pipes, with stop taps close to each one. Connect the blue machine hose to the cold supply and the red to the hot. Fasten the hoses at both ends using hose clips.

For the outlet run a waste pipe of at least 1¼in. in diameter through the wall to a suitable drain. At the machine end, use angle connectors to turn the pipe upright, with the open end well up towards the top of the machine. The hooked end of the outlet hose fits into the open pipe – it must be open, or there is a risk of the water in the machine siphoning out all the time instead of being removed only when the emptying pump is working.

The parts of your guttering, and what can go wrong

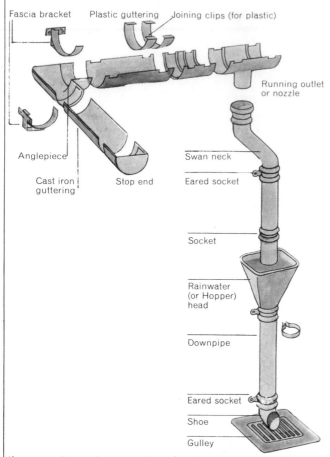

Fascia bracket Plastic guttering Joining clips (for plastic)

Running outlet or nozzle

Anglepiece

Cast iron guttering Stop end

Swan neck

Eared socket

Socket

Rainwater (or Hopper) head

Downpipe

Eared socket

Shoe

Gulley

If you need to replace a section of guttering, take a small piece of the old gutter, or a sketch with dimensions, to the builder's merchant to help him match it. If you are replacing one length of gutter downpipe, stick to whatever was the original material. If you are renewing a large run of gutter you may sometimes be able to mix new plastic with old cast-iron, and plastic is probably the best material for the amateur to handle: lighter, less brittle, easier to saw and needing no painting. Above are some of the names of the standard gutter sections and fittings; there are dozens more so that any house can be fitted with very little sawing and joining including interior and exterior right angles and obtuse angles for the corners of a window bay.

The decorative 'ogee' gutters (below) are normally fixed to fascia boards by mushroom screws through holes in the gutter, but they can also be fixed on brackets. Half-round gutters are laid on brackets previously screwed to the fascia board, brackets fastened to the brickwork, or brackets screwed to the top or side of rafters. All gutters should have a fall toward the downpipe of not less than 1 inch in 10 feet. Guttering is made in standard length

Rust can eat away sections of gutter out of sight, reducing capacity so heavy rain causes overflow. Replace section, or board and wall will be damaged

Grit and moss from roof, leaves from trees, reduce capacity of gutters, cause overflow. Clean out with trowel or wooden scraper cut roughly to shape of gutter. When clean, flush

sections; cast iron, steel or alloy gutter sections are joined with bolts and the joints sealed with putty or red lead. Asbestos cement gutters are joined the same way or with a proprietary mastic compound instead of putty. Plastic gutters are joined by special clips, with rubber joints, or by jointing cement, or both. Gutters and downpipes come in different widths according to the type of building and size of roof; if replacing parts, stick to the original size.

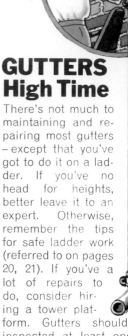

Gutters should have steady fall to downpipe, at least 1in. in 10ft. If section has dropped, renew brackets or screws; renew joints if they are leaking

out; pools left behind indicate section has begun to sag. If water stays around outlet to downpipe, downpipe is blocked. Clean with flexible rod; you may have to dismantle sections

GUTTERS High Time

There's not much to maintaining and repairing most gutters – except that you've got to do it on a ladder. If you've no head for heights, better leave it to an expert. Otherwise, remember the tips for safe ladder work (referred to on pages 20, 21). If you've a lot of repairs to do, consider hiring a tower platform. Gutters should be inspected at least once a year and any repairs carried out quickly. Most of us forget about them until they begin leaking or overflowing, by which time a cheap and simple job may have become a long expensive one. And remember: water spilling down a wall from faulty guttering means a risk to decorations and house timbers and even, in frosty weather, to the bricks themselves.

Renewing a section of gutter or rainwater pipe

Cast-iron rainwater pipes are fixed by means of lugs – ears – cast on to the thicker collar section of the pipe; these are held by pipe nails driven into wooden plugs about ½in. in diameter driven into holes drilled into the joints between bricks. All pipes fixed this way should have spacers, lengths of iron or lead pipe about ¾in. long, to hold the rainwater pipe clear of the wall so that the back of the pipe can be painted. Another way of fastening cast-iron pipes is by split clips (called 'hold-a-backs') whose spiked ends are driven into plugs in the wall, the clip then being screwed together to hold the pipe; this automatically holds the pipe clear of the wall. Plastic downpipes are fastened by means of plastic brackets screwed to the plugged wall, to which plastic clips are bolted. Where rainwater pipes are blocked take down sections of pipe and clear with a flexible rod; you may have to break one length to get at the others. Downpipes can drain into waterbutts, gulleys or into soakaways: see next page.

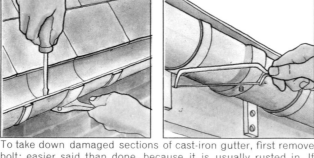

To take down damaged sections of cast-iron gutter, first remove bolt; easier said than done, because it is usually rusted in. If penetrating oil won't free it, then saw the bolt off with hacksaw

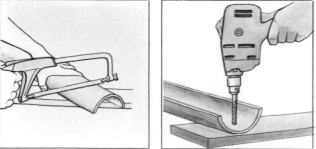

If you are replacing a standard length of gutter the new piece will have a hole for the bolt. If you have to cut a length to fit, start by sawing through bottom and gradually turn the gutter as you go, then drill hole. Cast iron is brittle; support on piece of wood. Paint new sections well, before fixing hides the back

Now lift off the damaged section. Be careful – cast iron gutter is heavy and awkward to handle on a ladder. Scrape old putty or red lead jointing from socket end of sound pipe, and wipe clean

Clean off and paint any rust patches, too, and paint joint where the new putty is to go in: paint helps putty to stick. Use metal-window putty for jointing; work it in your fingers until it is soft, press new gutter section until surplus squeezes out and joint is flush. Locate and line up holes with nail, bolt together

Zinc gutters - if you know how to solder

Valley gutters (right) and parapet box gutters (behind flat roof parapets) are usually made from zinc sheet, on the spot. They can be renewed by an amateur provided he has some skill in soldering. (See details below where you are given some useful soldering tips.) Measure old gutter to be replaced; remove a couple of slates or tiles to see how far up the roof the metal goes on either side, and draw a sketch of it with all dimensions (check these carefully). Buy sheet zinc from a builder's merchant (it comes in rolls 8ft. by 3ft.; ask for 12 or 14 gauge) and mark it from sketch; allow $\frac{1}{2}$in. overlap for corners. Cut out with tin snips. Shape the zinc with a block of wood on one side, a mallet on the other (experts use a sort of flat mallet called a dresser). Clean off all corners and solder them, using tinman's solder and Baker's Fluid as a flux. Starting at lower end of gutter take off sufficient tiles, remove section of old gutter, check that boarding is sound and sweep it clean. Then lay a soft felt (from builder's

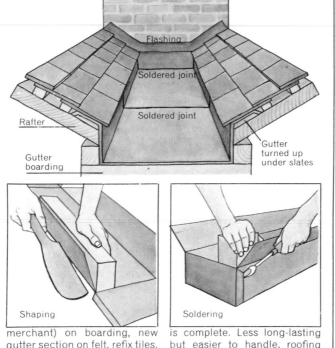

merchant) on boarding, new gutter section on felt, refix tiles. Next new section is laid with 3in. overlap and the joint soldered, and so on until gutter is complete. Less long-lasting but easier to handle, roofing felt can be used to line box-gutters. Fold corners, stick with mastic, lay edges under tiles

Soakaways - first dig a pit

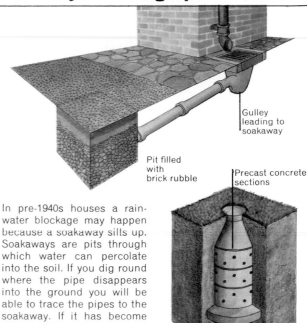

In pre-1940s houses a rainwater blockage may happen because a soakaway sills up. Soakaways are pits through which water can percolate into the soil. If you dig round where the pipe disappears into the ground you will be able to trace the pipes to the soakaway. If it has become silted up dig another pit about 6ft. deep, 5ft. across, not less than 10ft. from the house and re-run pipes. Then use perforated concrete rings (from builder's merchant) with cover (right) or fill pit with brick rubble to 1ft. from top, cover with two layers of building paper, level with earth

Tips on how to tackle soft soldering

Soft soldering, the kind which any amateur can tackle with a little practice, is essential for some building jobs - like making a box gutter (as in item above). Zinc, lead, copper and some other metals can be joined with a low-melting point alloy of lead and tin called solder, provided the metals to be joined and the bit - the business end of the soldering iron - are chemically clean. This means rubbing them bright with a file or emery paper and coating them with flux, a substance which helps solder to flow and keeps air from the clean metal. For most building jobs an iron heated with a bottled-gas blowlamp is better than an electric soldering iron. An alternative to the seam soldering shown right is 'sweating' two longer areas together; coat faces to be joined with solder, clamp them, then heat outside of joint until solder fuses.

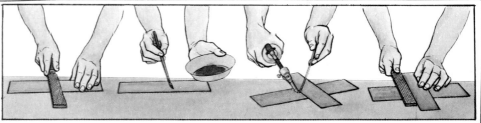

Rub surfaces to be joined clean, then coat with flux (your supplier will advise best for the metal - builders commonly use Baker's Fluid for zinc). Clean and flux the soldering-iron bit in the same way; heat iron and coat the bit with some solder

Hold surfaces to be joined together (clamp if you can) and melt solder into joint, rubbing it with tip of iron. If solder won't run easily, soldering iron or metal being soldered is probably too cool. When solder is hard, clean up with file

DOORS

Hanging a new door

Panelled or solid flush doors can be hinged either side; 'cored' flush doors are reinforced at the hinge positions only on one edge, and at the lock position on the other, and so can be hung only one way round. Makers usually mark these reinforced places; if you have to plane these edges pencil round edge on to door face so you'll know where hinges and lock must go. With door against frame (a wedge underneath raises it for clearance) mark where door is too large, plane until there's ⅛in. clearance all round. Then mark door edge to correspond with the existing hinge marks on frame. Put open hinge same size as old ones on door edge, mark with pencil, then carefully chisel a recess so hinge fits flush into edge. Fit each hinge with one screw only, in centre holes, first to door, then to frame. Check closing. When fit O.K., put in remaining screws

Hinges or butts can break away from a door or frame causing enlarged screwholes. Often caused by rust build-up on hinge – oiling will prevent

Badly hung door will be draughty, cause the closing stile to wear. Door must be rehung

1 Mark round new door against frame, plane to size; pencil existing hinge marks from frame to door. Check cored door is right way round

2 Using the same size hinge as previously fitted to the frame, open, position on the edge of the door, and mark with a pencil and cut recess

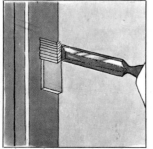

3 If new frame has been fitted, or a repair made at hinge position, chisel out the space for the hinge to allow it to fit flush with edge of the door

4 Offer door to frame and fix top and bottom hinges with single screw. Carefully close door, note fit; when correct screw home remaining screws

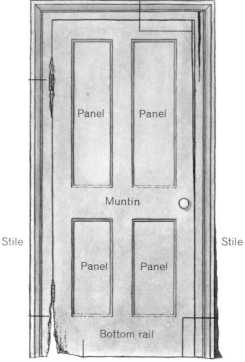

Rotting or splitting of the hanging or closing stiles needs treatment (see overleaf); neglect means buying new door

Bottom rail can rot or split through advanced age, ill fit, or poor protection by paintwork. On external doors, a badly fitted, rotted or damaged weatherboard can allow rain penetration into bottom rail and possibly into house

Poorly fitting frame can wear, or cause the whole frame to become loose through the effect of constant banging

Door diagram labels: Panel, Panel, Muntin, Stile, Stile, Panel, Panel, Bottom rail

DOORS: The key to efficiency

Correctly fitting doors mean fewer draughts, less heat loss. This page and the following ones show how to adjust ill-fitting doors and how to repair split or rotted doors and frames. A spot of oil on hinges, a few minutes work with plane or sandpaper can save money and hours of work. If a door is beyond repair a new one can be bought from a timber merchant who will show you the various designs available. Doors are available in a standard range of sizes (still in feet and inches rather than millimetres), the most common being 2ft. 4in. or 2ft. 6in. by 6ft. 6in. for internal doors and 2ft. 8in. by 6ft. 8in. for external doors. Left, we hang a new door

Making a door secure with a mortise or a cylinder lock

After a new door has been hung the next task is to secure it in position. The alternatives are a mortise lock, cylinder lock, rimlock or a ball or roller catch. All can be obtained from your local ironmonger's shop. By far the safest is the mortise lock, which fits into the door and is best employed on external doors. The rimlock and cylinder lock are effective to a lesser degree. The ball or roller is best left for internal use. You'll need: pencil, brace, bit, chisel, mallet, bradawl, screwdriver

5 Offer lock to face of door and pencil round. Drill into edge of door slightly smaller than mark

6 Chisel hole to allow lock to slip in. Mark face plate on the edge of door. Cut for a flush fit

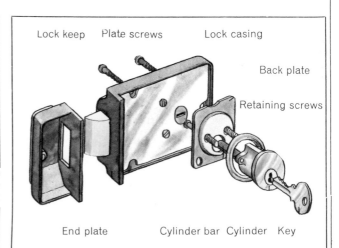

Lock diagram labels: Lock keep, Plate screws, Lock casing, Back plate, Retaining screws, End plate, Cylinder bar, Cylinder, Key

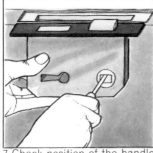

7 Check position of the handle and keyhole on the face of the door. Mark handle and, keyhole positions accurately and drill

8 Position lock in door. Check handle and key operate. Screw lock and face plate into edge of the door. Fit the handle

Labels: Latch, Bolt

9 Mark position of latch and bolt on frame, chisel out. Mark striking plate, chisel into frame for flush fit. Screw home

Label: Striking plate

A cylinder lock can be used in conjunction with a mortise or rimlock when it should be fitted at shoulder height. You'll need: cylinder lock, brace, 30mm. (1¼in.) wood bit, chisel, mallet, screwdriver, pencil. Measure from centre of cylinder position to outside of lock casing and mark distance on the door. (This distance will be given by makers, or the fitting instructions may include a pattern.) With 30mm. wood bit and brace, drill through door frame on your mark. Fit cylinder into hole from the outside. Hold cylinder in place and fit back plate to inside of door. Screw in cylinder retaining screws. Fix lock casing on back plate and see cylinder bar engages in casing. Screw home end plate screws. Shut door and mark lock keep on frame. Open door, chisel frame for flush fit. Screw home

Quick and easy door maintenance tips

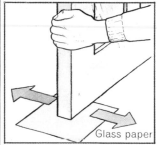

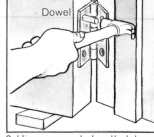

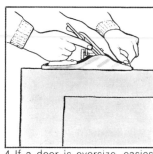

1 A door slighty oversize can be reduced a little by pulling backwards and forwards over a sheet of glass paper

2 Hinge screwholes that have become oversize, through misuse, can be filled with a piece of dowel and then used again

3 If too much wood is removed when cutting a hinge recess, packing with cardboard or thin timber will give correct fit

4 If a door is oversize, easiest way to reduce to the correct $\frac{1}{8}$in. all round clearance is to take it down and plane off excess

DOORS: Attention to the details

A little attention to doors and frames will help to prevent the faults that we describe here. Hinges will last longer, work smoothly, ward off rust if they're lightly oiled. Correctly fitted hinges have less chance of pulling out of a frame or door and splitting the timber. Properly primed and painted timber will resist rotting and attack by damp. You'll need the following: hand and tenon saw, brace and bit, rule, plane, wood chisel, mallet, cold chisel, hammer, pencil, screwdriver, adjustable square, trowel, sand, cement, and water.

Renewing a damaged hinge fixing

Most household hinges carry a lot of weight and survive much rough treatment for their size. A little oil on the moving parts will make them last longer, work smoothly, reduce strain on the retaining screws and reduce the possibility of repairs. Rust and paint build-up will put undue strain on the retaining screws and possibly cause them to pull out of the stile, perhaps splitting the timber. If this happens the timber must be replaced. Remove screws from hinge on frame and take the

door down (Fig 5). Saw at right angles to face of door, and chisel out the damaged section of stile. Cut a new piece to fit. Drill and countersink screwholes for fixing, making sure that they do not foul position of the hinge retaining screws. Glue new piece of timber and stile, fit and screw into position. Rehang door (as shown on p. 56), prime and paint new timber. It is not a good idea, and probably uneconomical, to try to repair a cored flush-faced door fixing using this method.

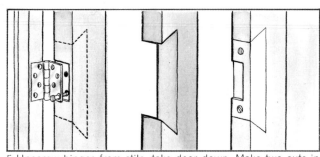

5 Unscrew hinges from stile, take door down. Make two cuts in stile, as above, and chisel out damaged timber. Cut new piece of timber to fit accurately. Drill and countersink screwholes for refixing, making sure they do not foul hinge-screw positions

Repairing a split or rotten frame

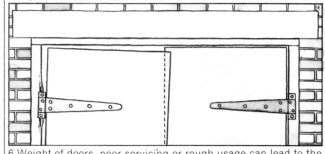

6 Weight of doors, poor servicing or rough usage can lead to the hinge screws pulling out and frame splitting, making opening or closing of the doors difficult. Doors will have to be removed and the damaged part of the frame cut out and replaced

Poor care of exterior or heavy-duty hinges such as T-hinges – cross garnets – or cup hinges, can lead to the frame splitting. The weight of the door and rough usage makes this a common fault on garage doors. Damaged timber must be cut out and replaced with new timber. This is glued and screwed home. Make sure that these screws are not so placed that the hinge fixing screws foul them. Cutting these sections to fit neatly isn't easy; buy enough timber to allow errors

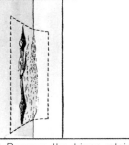

7 Remove the hinge-retaining screws and door to allow access to split frame. Mark wedge-shape that is to be replaced

8 Chisel out damaged section. Cut a new piece of timber to fit, apply glue and screw to frame. Avoid fouling hinge screws

Rotten or damaged frame base

A common defect found on exterior timber frames is a rotten base where the frame is in contact with the floor, and gets wet. Painting or creosote are easy preventive measures; the only cure is surgery. Break up concrete at foot of frame, cut out and replace rotten timber. Tip: cut the awkward joint on the new timber first, leaving something to spare at the other end to be trimmed off only when you've got a correctly fitting joint. Few amateurs will get a perfect fit first time round.

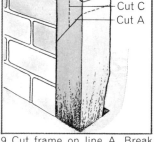

9 Cut frame on line A. Break concrete, using hammer and cold chisel. Remove rotten section. Make hole about 4in. deep, fairly wide. Cut lines B and C

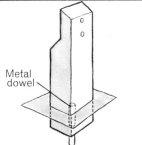

10 Cut timber and allow 50mm. (2in.) to insert in ground. Give two coats primer or preservative. Insert metal dowel 50mm. by 12mm. in base or use big screw

11 Check that new section is a good fit and that it seats squarely in ground. Drill and countersink screwholes, apply waterproof glue to joint. Screw home

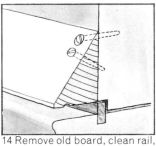

12 Mix sufficient sand and cement (one part cement, three parts sand) with water to form fairly soft mix. Push into hole. Make sure no air pockets form

Dealing with a loose frame

A badly fitted frame continually banged can become loose in the wall. Remove the door and architrave at loose side of frame. Debris between frame and wall must be removed. (Material will indicate type of wall.) Place length of timber X across doorway and force frame upright, closing gap Y. Drill frame. Drill brick wall 2½in. deep, using masonry drill, plug holes, screw frame home. If breeze-block wall, drill frame only and drive in cut nails. Replaster.

Replacing a defective weather board

Rotten or defective weather boards fitted to external doors can, in time, cause the bottom rail to rot or swell. They're normally of two types: tongued (Fig 13) or planted (Fig 14). Each will have a groove on the underside to stop water from getting into the house. A defective tongued board should be removed, the groove in the door cleaned, new board fitted. See that it doesn't foul the frame. A planted board should be glued and screwed home

13 A tongued board should be removed and the door groove cleaned. Shape new board, drill, countersink, glue, screw home

14 Remove old board, clean rail, shape new board, drill, countersink, glue and screw home. Check that board clears frame

Repairing a damaged panelled door

Rotten or damaged timber in a panelled door must be cut out and new timber fitted in its place. Remove the screws from the hinge on the frame and take the door down. If stile (upright) is damaged, cut through it at an angle (Fig. 2) taking care not to damage the panel. Carefully tap the defective part of the stile away from the panel (Fig. 3) and it should leave the bottom rail tenons exposed (Fig. 4). Cut a new piece of stile using the old as a pattern, then use drill, mallet and chisel to cut the mortise (Figs 5 & 6). Offer the new stile into position. When correct fit, drill for screws and dowels (Fig. 7). Countersink the screwholes. Use a waterproof glue on the joints and dowels, and cut the dowels flush with the face of the door. Screw up making sure that the screw heads are below the edge of the door. Prime the new timber, fit hinge, rehang door – an ⅛in. all round is a good fit – and paint to match existing top coat.

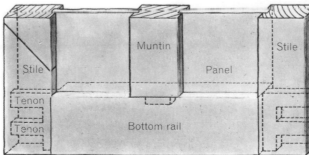

1 Part of the left-hand stile here needs replacing. Unscrew hinge from frame and take the door down. The damaged section of the stile must be removed. Cut the timber on line indicated

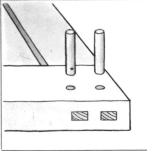

2 Cut through the stile, avoiding damage to adjacent panel. Make sure cut is vertical to face

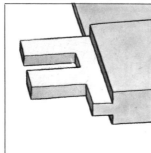

3 Tap the defective piece of the stile away from the panel with a hammer. If this is done with care the old piece of stile should come away without trouble

4 This will leave the bottom rail tenons exposed. You've now to cut the mortise for this tenon in the new piece of stile. Practise first on scrap wood

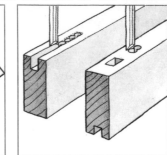

5 Accurately mark up the position of the mortise on the new timber using the old piece of stile as a pattern. Drill out to just under size. Go carefully

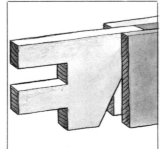

6 Final trimming of the mortise should be done with a sharp chisel and mallet. Work slowly. Too much wood removed could leave you with a weak joint

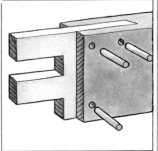

7 Offer the new piece of stile into position. When correct size, drill through door for dowels. Assemble with waterproof wood glue. Trim dowels for flush fit

8 If the stile has rotted at foot of door, the damaged tenon of the bottom rail will have to be replaced by a false tenon. Take off the damaged stile as above

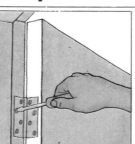

9, 10 Having exposed the damaged joint, cut off the damaged tenon. Mark position of false tenon and make two parallel cuts into edge of bottom rail. With a chisel carefully chip out between saw cuts to make an angled groove in the rail. It is into this groove that the newly-cut false tenon will be fitted, and then to stile

11 Using the old stile and tenon as patterns, mark up new timber from which false tenon can be cut. Seat it securely in groove. Don't remove too much wood

12 Fit false tenon in groove and drill holes for dowels. Fix joint and dowels with waterproof wood glue. Drive dowels home. Now fit to stile as shown above

Fitting a sliding door to save space

Fitting sliding doors in place of traditional hinged doors is comparatively simple and very useful if you need to save space in corridors or small rooms. You can re-use the old door, but this involves patching the holes where hinges, handles and locks were fitted; it is probably easier to buy a new lightweight door and start from scratch. Several manufacturers make sliding door gear; ask at builders' merchants to see what is available at various prices. Try to see sliding doors installed and check how easily they run.

Unscrew hinges and take door down. Recess may be cut in (rebated) or built up (planted strip)

With chisel lever out planted strip; or fill rebate with a strip of wood planed to the right size

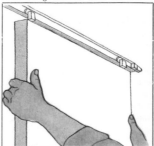

Using chisel and wooden wedge, lever off architrave moulding above and at sides

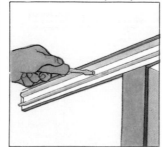

Make good plaster disturbed, then fix cover strip to both sides of frame about 100mm. (4in.) wide and thickness of the skirting, to replace architrave

Fit timber strip about 75mm. (3in.) wide, twice width of door and thickness of skirting, to head of door frame; then fix sliding door track to this strip

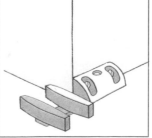

Screw hangers to top of door. Rail and hangers are covered with pelmet; some rails are specially shaped as a built-in pelmet so hangers don't show

Fix guides to floor. Various systems have different types of guide, some less obtrusive than others. Details of fitting are supplied with the equipment

Most manufacturers can supply draught-proofing strips to go with the door; it's worth having. Fit draught-proofing before hanging door on to rail

QED

An easy way to smarten panel doors

Battered panel doors can be made smart using a new over-all flush panel of 3mm. ($\frac{1}{8}$in.) hardboard or 6mm. ($\frac{1}{4}$in.) ply. Hardboard is cheaper; condition it so it won't stretch or buckle when fitted by brushing back with cold water, stand on edge for 24 hours. Cut to less than full door size – if whole door is covered you'll need to shift handles and door-frame stops, and edges will soon wear. Panel edges can be exposed or covered with moulding.

This is the easy way to plane edges of hardboard; rest sheet on floor, slip batten under edge

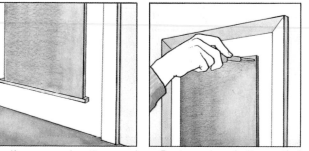

Pencil new panel outline on door. Rest panel on batten nailed to bottom rail while fastening. Glue (PVC adhesive or even old thick paint) and panel-pin (use pin-push, not hammer) in place

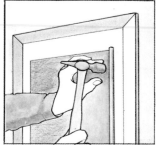

To cover edges of panel you can use moulding. Cut corners with care, using a mitre block

WINDOWS

The workings of a double-hung window

A box-framed or double-hung window, right, has an upper and lower sash. Each is counterbalanced by a pair of weights which move up and down box sections when the sashes are opened or closed.

If one of the supporting sash cords breaks it should be replaced, as should all the others at the same time. Use new, waxed damp-proof cord of correct size – take an old piece to the shop – available from most ironmongers, as are the clout nails for fixing to sash.

Access to the cords and weights is by removing the stop beads (Fig 1), sashes (Fig 2), and the pocket covers (Fig 4) in the box sections. It may be necessary to renew the beading.

You'll need the following tools and materials for the job: claw hammer, pincers, putty knife, hacking knife, pencil, rule, screwdriver, saw, plane, bradawl. Sash cord, 18mm. (¾in.) clout nails, putty, 25mm. sprigs, glass, 'mouse' (a long string tail weighted with a small bent nail or a small piece of chain), 40mm. oval brads to fix bead

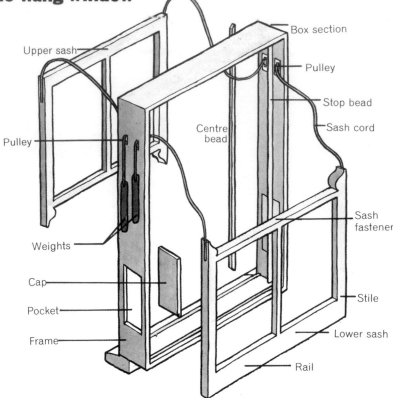

Box section
Upper sash
Pulley
Pulley
Stop bead
Centre bead
Sash cord
Weights
Sash fastener
Cap
Pocket
Stile
Frame
Lower sash
Rail

WINDOWS: The way to a safer view

Window frames, sashes and sash cords are common areas of neglect. Sticking sashes, swollen or rotten frames all go unnoticed behind drawn curtains in the winter. Some faults, like broken sash cords, are dangerous. Renovation and repair is best carried out in the autumn after dampness has had all summer to dry out. Open and survey all windows and list work to be done. If sashes are rotten or split it is more economical to go to a local joiner for new ones.

How to replace that broken sash cord

1 Carefully remove stop bead fitted at both sides of window by levering in join with chisel

2 Take out bottom front sash. Cut the sash cord if not already broken. Lower weight in box

3 Remove centre bead between sashes with wood chisel. Cut cords and lift out top sash

4 Remove the wooden caps from the frame, then carefully lift weights out

5 Use pincers to pull out clout nails which secure cords to sides of sash. Discard old cords

6 Tie cord to tail of mouse, feed mouse over pulley. Make sure string doesn't slip off pulley. Reach in pocket for mouse

7 Feed cord over pulley, pull mouse tail until cord emerges. Untie mouse from cord; see cord doesn't run back over pulley

8 So far simple: but now comes the part where amateurs slip up. Rest can be done singlehanded, but an extra hand is useful. Pass cord through hole in weight, knot end. Put weight back in box (check it is in right section. Top sash weights go on outside, bottom sash weights on room side). Place upper sash into frame, holding about 4in. above sill. Pull cord until weight is at top, hard against pulley. Pull edge of sash just clear of frame so you've room to nail the cord back into its groove

9 See cord isn't nailed too high up in groove, or sash won't close. Replace sash, raise to top. Repeat operation on other side

10 Replace pocket cover and bead, put sash on sill. Leave 2in. slack when nailing cords back. Replace sash and stop bead

Renewing a defective casement sash and reglazing

Overleaf we describe some repairs to sashes; but if a sash is rotted or badly split it's best to get a new one made at a joinery (ask timber merchant for address). Take out old sash, measure size of opening (not of old sash which may be loose or out of true). Take off fittings. It's difficult to remove old glass without breaking, but worth trying as shown on right. Cover opening with hardboard. Take old sash to joinery so they can match type and section

11 To save old glass chip away putty, pull out sprigs. You may be able to force old frame apart by tapping parallel to glass

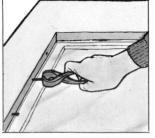

12 Check the size of the new sash against the opening. If too big mark size of opening

13 Plane to size if a fixed sash, 3mm. (⅛in.) undersize if an opening sash, for correct clearance. Mark hinge positions

14 May be easier, more convenient, to glaze new sash (as shown opposite) before fitting it into its final position

Two ways of fixing window-joints that have become loose

Ill fitting, stuck or loose-framed sashes are not only inconvenient but dangerous. Repairs to sashes that are seriously at fault should be regarded as temporary and new timberwork used as soon as possible – your local joiner will be the most economical supplier. Timber in a window can shrink or swell. Carry out repairs after a fine spell – best in the autumn – when wood is dry. Loose joints and tenons make a window difficult to open or close. Two methods overcome this. Fix window in situ using soft wood wedges (Fig 1 and Fig 2). Fix joints using angle plate and screws (Fig 3). Alternative is to remove sash and take glass out. Cramp frame (Fig 4). Drill through stiles into rails (Fig 5), insert glued dowels and drive home (Fig 6). Pin through stile and dowel, and rail and dowel. Rehang or replace sash. You'll need the following tools and materials: hammer, saw, screwdriver, bradawl, hired sash cramp, drill. Putty, glue, dowel, 25mm. panel pins, four 75mm. ✕ 75mm. angle plates, 25mm. (1in.) screws

1 Carefully cut two wedges, 75mm. (3in.) long by 13mm. (½in.) wide from piece of softwood

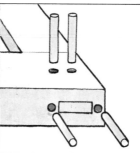

2 Close window and carefully drive home wedge in between window and frame to close gaps

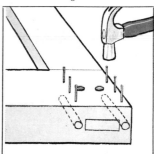

3 Mark screw holes of 75mm. (3in.) angle bracket with brad-awl. Fix using 25mm. screws

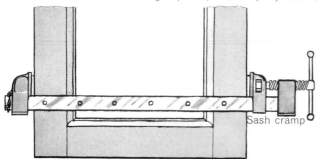

Sash cramp

4 An alternative method of fixing a loose-jointed window is to remove sash and clear putty from glass. Take glass out and cramp carefully. Hire cramp from local hire shop for economy, then drill and glue dowels through top and bottom stiles and rails

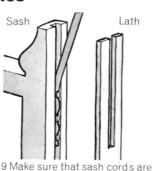

5 With the window as tightly cramped as possible, carefully drill into top or bottom rail through stile. Cut dowels

6 Take dowels and dip them in good wood glue. Position the dowels in correct hole in stile and rail. Drive home carefully

7 Fix dowels with 25mm. (1in.) panel pins through the stile and dowel, and the bottom rail and dowel. Reglaze, replace sash

Dealing with rattling or draughty sashes

8 Check for correct closure. See that sashes slide easily clear of the centre and stop beading

Casement and double-hung sashes can rattle or become draughty if badly worn. The methods above can help casement sashes. Double-hung sashes should be checked for correct closure (Fig 8). If askew, refit sash cords (Fig. 9 and also details, p. 62). If sashes stick try sanding paint edges. Check that centre bead is fitted correctly; if not, refix with 40mm. (1½in.) oval brads. Stop bead (as shown opposite) may need refixing if there are draughts. Check sash fastener

Sash   Lath

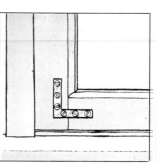

9 Make sure that sash cords are fitted correctly (details on p. 62). Lath can be fitted to worn sash

Servicing metal-framed windows

Metal casement windows need periodic servicing to preserve them. Oil the hinges and fasteners and see that they work easily. Any signs of rust should be removed at once. Remove the putty and the glass and thoroughly clean the rebates. Carefully scrape the frame down to bare metal and apply rust inhibitor (follow manufacturer's instructions). The frames should be repainted using a metal primer. Metal clips hold the glass in the frame; you need only use two or three to each side of the frame. Use metal casement putty when reglazing. Failure to do this work will see the rust spreading and eventually the glass breaking. Never force a metal sash to shut. There is probably rust or too much paint preventing closure. To force it only distorts the frame, and puts stress on the glass. Replacing broken glass in lead-framed "leaded lights" is best left to an expert. Amateurs may be lucky – but they may only increase the damage

Reglazing a broken wooden- or metal-framed window

Mending broken windows is easy; worst problems are upstairs windows, especially if you don't like ladder-work. If the broken pane is in an upstairs opening sash, it may be easier to take out the sash to work on it in comfort. Always keep glass upright, protect bottom edge with folded newspaper. Apart from new glass which glass merchant will cut for you, you'll need wood putty and a few glazing sprigs or small panel pins for wood frames, metal-glazing putty and clips for metal frames; a knife, a chisel and possibly a hammer to help chisel out the old putty. Roll and knead putty well in your fingers before using it, so it is soft. Leave putty to harden for a few days before painting it.

Remove old putty and remains of glass with chisel. When glass is out remove the bed putty

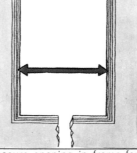

Measure opening in frame for new glass; deduct 3mm. (⅛in.) from all sides to get right size

When rebate (section where glass goes) is clean give it one coat primer or any wood paint

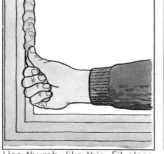

Check new glass is right size – protect your hands – remove, and press putty firmly into rebate

Use thumb, like this. Fit glass. Press edges evenly, not middle. In metal frame, fit glazing clips

In wood frame slide chisel over pane to tap in sprigs. They should just not touch the glass

Apply putty to outside, smooth off to triangular section (look at other panes) with knife

Cut off squeezed-out putty on inside, level with frame. Leave to harden before painting

A change of style: fitting louvre windows

If you are replacing a window and don't want the same style again, one of the possibilities is fitting louvre windows (right). They are available framed in aluminium (needs no painting and can't rust) and fit in well with some modern house designs. The makers supply fixing instructions; the essential is to have a wooden frame with a flat surface of at least 2in. all round; you may be able to use the old frame, or you can strip it out and fit a new subframe.

WINDOWS: Look before you decide

Wooden window frames come in standard sizes, and if one of these fits the window opening all that needs to be done is to rip out the old wooden window, prime the new frame (if it isn't supplied ready-primed) and fit the new frame with wall plugs and screws after making sure it is upright and square to the wall. The jutting-out ends of a new frame, called horns, are provided for building into the wall when windows are fitted to a new house while the walls are still going up. You can cut these off if fitting the window as a replacement, or hack out part of the wall to fit them in, making good the brickwork afterwards and replastering if necessary. It's a method of perfection, but not necessary.

Existing frames

Existing frames can sometimes be used in fitting standard wooden or metal-framed windows or the new louvre windows. The way to treat sliding-sash frames is shown far right; to fit a new window into a hinged-casement frame (right), unscrew the hinges and fill in the rebate with a piece of timber of the right size. The new window can then be screwed into place within the old frame. If the old frame is not suitable it can be removed – wooden frames are usually screwed or nailed to the brickwork – and a new sub-frame screwed to the opening. It should be of timber about 3in. by 1in. or larger.

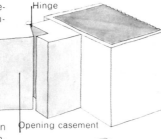

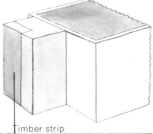

To remove metal windows

To remove metal windows fitted direct to brickwork, take out glass or open hinged lights to locate bolt heads in frame. Unscrew bolts. If they are too rusted, chip away behind frame, insert hacksaw blade and cut bolts. With window out, chisel out metal lugs which held bolts – take care to limit damage to brickwork. Position new frame with lugs loosely bolted on. Wedge frame in place square and upright, push lugs into holes and cement (1 cement, 3 sand) in place. After 48 hours remove wedges, tighten bolts.

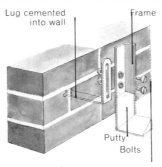

How metal window is fitted without a wooden sub-frame; lug is cemented into bricks

Sliding sash windows

Sliding sash windows are probably the most commonly replaced, since they are most common in older houses. A slice cut horizontally through the frame of such a window would look like this (right, top); at each side of the window there is a recess within the wall, a tall wooden box containing the sash counterweights. If you are replacing a sliding sash window with a new metal or wooden hinged casement window, this hole must be dealt with. Remove beadings which hold sashes in place (see item on page 62), remove sashes, then fill the gap left behind with a strip of timber (right, centre). The new window can be screwed to this. A more drastic treatment is to strip out all the old timber of the counterweight box and brick up the hole, finishing smooth with new plaster. When the plaster is dry drill and plug the brick and screw a new timber strip to it (right, bottom) and screw the new wooden or metal window on to that. Oak frames should be painted with linseed oil first, softwood frames primed.

Where a metal window is fixed in a wooden sub-frame (a better method), screws, instead of bolts, hold metal frame in place. Locate screwheads in same way, unscrew and remove window. Position new window, checking again that it is square and upright, and screw to sub-frame using sheradised or plated screws to prevent rusting. Glaze window, using metal clips supplied and metal glazing putty. Then apply mastic compound to all the joints between the frame and wood or brickwork to keep out the damp.

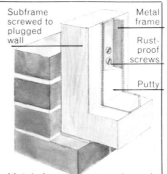

Metal frame screws to sub-frame screwed to wall. Putty or hinged window hides screws

Iron rusts and wood rots, so older houses whose walls and roofs are sound often need windows replaced. Wooden windows can be repaired if they haven't gone too far: see instructions p. 62; once metal windows have begun to fail, usually from rust getting under the galvanising, there isn't much to be done except replacement, a straightforward job. If you decide to fit a different style of window there's no technical problem though there could be an architectural one. Metal-framed or louvre windows in an early Victorian house can look as out of place as a bowler hat on a ballet dancer, and, apart from making the passers-by wince, will probably lower rather than raise the value of your house. So spend a long time looking at your house before you decide.

Occasionally, even in modern houses, the windows will have been made to measure, in which case you'll have to go into conference with a supplier about replacements. But most windows are made in standard sizes and if you take a dimensioned sketch to a builder's merchant he will be able to supply you from stock or by ordering. The tools you will need to replace most windows are: hammer, cold chisel, hacksaw, pliers, spirit level, plumb line, hawk, putty knife, screwdriver, and a medium or small trowel.

WALLS, ROOFS, CEILINGS and FLOORS

WALLS: Dealing with damp

Rising damp is a problem with many older houses; the damp-proof course wasn't adopted until late in the 19th century, and cavity walls were a 20th-century device. The problem has become worse as big open fires are abandoned – these kept up sufficient draught to evaporate moisture from inside rooms and sweep it up the chimney. Without them, damp may cause damage. Here are some ways of keeping it out (right) or at least (below) keeping damp-stains off the plaster and wallpaper.

Waterproofing walls: the damp-proof course

Bricks suck up water like blotting-paper; make them waterproof and damp will stay down at ground level. Builders' merchants sell waterproofing solutions that, painted on liberally inside the damp wall and out, will, with luck, soak through, join up in the middle and form a waterproof barrier. Painted on the outside these solutions certainly help keep out driving rain, and once dry they are invisible. A more expensive but thorough treatment is to drip silicone waterproofing solution into the wall through tubes drilled into the bricks (above). You can buy the solution and hire equipment, but it's best for a specialist firm to do it

Sometimes used with the damp-proof solution method: porous clay pipes set into the wall where a damp-proof course would be if you had one. They slope down slightly from inside to outside (where small grilles keep out the rain and inquisitive mice) and are set in a porous mortar. The idea is that moisture seeps into the pipes through the porous walls, then trickles harmlessly down the slope to the outside of the wall. No job for the amateur; your builder may be able to do it, or will more likely refer you to a specialist firm. The job should last for at least 20 years. A good firm will offer you a 20-year guarantee on their work

Electro-osmosis goes back to first principles to cure damp: what makes damp climb up a wall? The answer is that there's a minute difference between the electrical charge of the wall and that of the earth beneath it; take away the difference and there's nothing left to power the climb of the water. Electro-osmotic damp treatment consists of driving small copper rods into the wall roughly where a damp-proof course would be, joining them with a copper strip, and joining the strip to an earth rod, a metal spike sunk well into the ground. Amateurs have done it, but it's worth getting a professional job and a guarantee, usually 20 years

Cutting right through the wall to insert a new damp-proof course sounds drastic, and it isn't a job for the ordinary householder to tackle. A special saw is used to cut through the mortar or bricks, a short length at a time, a damp course is inserted and the mortar restored, before moving on to cut the next section. The complete work is usually guaranteed for 20 years or more. All these systems are fundamental cures; they stop damp getting into the wall. None are cheap. If it isn't possible to use them, for financial or technical reasons, you'll have to leave the wall damp and concentrate on protecting the inside of the rooms, below

Keeping damp stains off interior decorations

The answer of most builders to the problem of damp spoiling interior decorations and plaster is a material called Newtonite lath, a waterproof fibre sheet which lets air pass between wall and plaster, and makes a key for replastering or mounting plasterboard sheets; you can get it from any builder's merchant in rolls. But remember, interior treatment keeps damp from the interior surface of the room – it does not make the main wall dry.

Hack off plaster from damp wall, and a foot or so along any wall which joins the damp wall

Since wall will go on being damp, it's worth painting it with a fungicide to sterilise bricks

Block up
with lath while
fixing

The lathing is fixed, corrugations vertical, metal strips toward you, about 1in. off floor

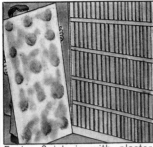

Saw it like this, supported close to saw. Vertical joins are overlapped, horizontal joins butted with a 4in. strip of bituminised felt behind the join to prevent plaster getting through join to wall and making a bridge for moisture to cross from the outer wall. Nail about every 10in. near top and bottom edges and in centre

If lathing has to be cut to let pipe pass through, make blob of waterproof mastic round it, again to prevent any bridge being formed for dampness

Professionals may finish off with plaster; hard for amateurs, though rough work may match existing plaster on old cottages. Don't go beyond lathing

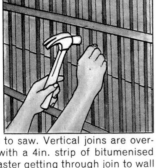

Easier finish is with plasterboard nailed in place or stuck on using blobs of adhesive, plastering joins only. Don't go beyond lathing to damp wall

By leaving small gap below skirting and at top of wall (hidden by cornice) air can pass up corrugations to help remove moisture from the damp wall

Damp patches: some alternative barriers

Where the amount of damp coming into a room is slight, it can be kept from spoiling the decorations by applying any waterproof barrier between the plaster and the paper. Ask your builder's merchant what he has in stock and what he would recommend; the materials range from paint-on waterproofing liquids, through pitch-coated lining papers to metal foils and foil-surfaced plasterboards. Pitch-coated papers are applied with a special waterproof adhesive; so are metal foils – the adhesive used with these dries quickly and you'll need to smooth the foil out at once, working gently with a soft cloth to get rid of any air bubbles, before it has dried. Overlap joins by about an inch. If you tear the foil, stick a strip of foil at least an inch wide over the tear. The foil surface can then be lined and painted, or wallpapered. Nail or stick foil-backed plasterboard in place, foil side toward the wall: this will act as a barrier against the damp soaking through and help to protect inside surfaces against the formation of condensation.

Condensation

Damp on the inside of an exterior wall is sometimes blamed on water penetrating from outside or rising from the ground when the real cause is condensation. Cooking, washing, using portable paraffin heaters – it all produces water vapour which condenses on cold walls. Totally blocking up fireplaces and draught sealing windows and doors, makes it worse, because with no draughts there's nowhere for the water vapour to go. Anything which keeps surfaces in the room warm will help; double-glazing prevents condensation inside windows, and lining cold walls with expanded polystyrene stops the damp from settling there. Buy it from wallpaper shops, and put it up much like wallpaper – instructions come with the material – except that adjacent strips are overlapped slightly. Then mark a vertical line and, using a sharp knife and a straight-edge, cut through the two overlapped sheets. Peel off

Trimming
polystyrene

the surplus and press the two edges down. You can emulsion-paint it, or paper it; don't use gloss paints.

Osborne Marks

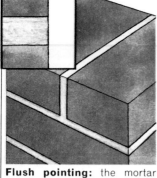

Flush pointing: the mortar finishes level with the bricks. The edge is made roughly level with the trowel and then, when mortar has begun to dry, rubbed over with a piece of wood. Work carefully; don't rub excess wet mortar into bricks, it will stain

Weather-struck and cut pointing: gives best water-defying finish; the slope helps water to run off. Formed by trowel held at an angle; then 'frenchman' (see below) is run along lower edge, on straight-edge, to leave slight overhang

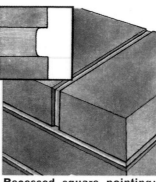

Tooled or rubbed pointing: mortar is pressed in and slightly hollowed by any suitably rounded tool – a piece of narrow pipe, an old bucket handle, or a piece of garden hose, rubbed along the mortar, giving curved finish to joint

Recessed square pointing: mortar is rubbed with a steel tool – a piece of hardwood can be as good – of the right thickness. This pointing looks very handsome with rough-textured bricks, but isn't ideal for walls going to get lots of rain

WALLS: Keeping the rain out

If the mortar joint between bricks has begun to crumble it should be repaired, not only for the sake of appearance, but to keep rain out of the wall. Rain alone is bad for a house, but the real danger is rain followed by frost, for if water has soaked into bricks and then freezes the surface of the brick can crack away, leaving a much more battered-looking wall and a much bigger repair bill. It's cheaper and simpler to mend the mortar joint – called 'repointing' by builders.

Repointing the mortar joints between bricks

Unless you've only a small area of repointing to do, and that near the ground, hire a tower platform (for cost see page 20) to work from. Repointing isn't difficult, but it will need all your attention and both hands, and that isn't possible if you are working from a ladder. It's worth practising on a small piece of wall where your first, probably messy, attempts won't show. If you are repointing an entire wall you can pick any style of repointing; if you are doing only part of a wall it will look better matched to the existing sound parts. Work from top to bottom of the wall, raking out the old pointing, and take the opportunity to clean down dirty brickwork at the same time (there are brick cleaners you can buy from a builder's merchant). If there's an odd defective brick you can cut it out with a cold chisel and club hammer and replace it with a

matching sound brick. (If there's more than one or two together, best leave the job to a builder.) Apart from the tower platform, you'll need a pointing trowel (like a bricklaying trowel but half the size) and you may find a dotting trowel (a very small one) useful too. Make yourself a 'frenchman' – file the end of an old knife to a point, then heat the blade in a flame and bend it at right angles. A straight-edge can be made from a piece of 2in. by 1in. with one edge planed to a feather-edge and a thin piece of ply or hardboard fixed at each end to hold it just clear of the wall. A hawk, to carry a small amount of mortar while you are working, can be made out of a 9in. square piece of hardboard or ply screwed to a 6in. length of broom handle. Professionals mix their mortar on a spot-board, a 2ft. square board raised clear of the ground.

The easiest way to get mortar is to buy dry readymix: it is cheaper to mix your own (one part cement, two sand) and by using coloured cements you can produce coloured pointing, but all the ingredients need to be passed through a fine ($\frac{1}{8}$in.) sieve to make sure there are no coarse particles. Whichever

material you use, add clean water slowly until you have a stiff mortar mix. If you make the mix too wet it won't stay put between the bricks and in running down it will stain them. It should be just wet enough to be worked; if you pick it up on a trowel and tip it sideways the mortar should stay put.

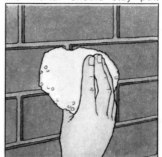

Rake out old mortar to half or three-quarters of an inch. Any hooked bit of iron will do; the tang of an old file, an old screwdriver with the end bent over

If you can't shift hard bits of mortar use a cold chisel (very carefully or you'll damage the bricks). Then brush out well and moisten – don't saturate

Much of the knack of repointing lies in picking up the correct quantity of mortar for each joint; you don't want a scooped-up lump but a little sausage

Scoop and turn and cut and roll the mortar with the pointing trowel until you've a piece the right size and shape – a wedge-shaped piece to fit joint

The mortar should be on the back of the trowel at one edge, so that you can push it into the hole. Do upright joints – 'perpends' to a builder – first

Cover square yard at a time. Always work from same side; this is especially important with *weather-struck* pointing where perpends are at an angle

Cut off surplus mortar with trowel at right angles to wall. It helps to keep the trowel clean. This is where amateur repointing tends to become messy

Now gently, with tip of trowel, press in the top and bottom of each perpend where they meet the horizontal joints between the bricks, the 'bed' joints

Tackle bed joints in the same way as perpends except that trowel position is more awkward. The obvious way (above) is *wrong*; keep hand on left

When bed joints are filled, if you want weatherproof pointing use trowel to produce the slope. Go carefully to avoid smearing mortar all over the bricks

Set up straight-edge on wall and complete the neat bottom edge with 'frenchman'. This is where the slight overhang in weather-struck pointing is made

If you want a tooled finish to the pointing do it before the mortar has hardened. This tool is a piece of old bucket-handle; a piece of garden hose is good

Gently brush down the area; the head of an old soft broom will do. Wash off any mortar stains as you go along, rubbing with a piece of brick if necessary

WALLS:
Two rooms into one

Solid though they look, walls don't have to be forever; you can knock two small rooms into one big one. It is hard work, messy, noisy, though not beyond an amateur. But before you reach for the de-molition hammer, check with the Town Hall – that's the law – and, if the house is leasehold or mortgaged, with the lessor or building society. You may need their approval – and get it in writing, too.

Which walls are safe to knock down? Not the outer walls which carry most of the load of roof and upper floors; they're a job for experts. Not the party wall between semis or terrace houses they mustn't be touched at all. Internal partition walls which hold up nothing but merely divide the internal space can be demolished with no more additional work than making good the plaster.

But there are some internal walls which carry part of the weight of roof or upper floors; these can be knocked down but only after you have, in effect, built a bridge to carry the load. You can get an idea of which is which by looking in the loft. If roof timbers rest on a wall (as in the drawing above) then that's load-bearing. Walls under or near water-tanks are prob-ably load-bearing. And where joists are divided and join just above a wall, that's load-bear-ing too. How you knock down such a wall safely is shown below.

Luckily for the amateur, any major building job like knocking down a wall – any wall – must be approved first by the District Surveyor (in inner London), the Building Inspector, or (in Scot-land) the Building Control Officer. Ask at your local council offices who and where he is, and write to him enclosing drawings of what you propose to do. These need not be per-fect, architect-style, but must be clear and give measurements. Give him plenty of time to answer; if necessary make an appointment to discuss it with him. He will check, visit, and tell you if your plans do break building laws or threaten the safety of your house. It's an offence to go ahead without his approval – you pay rates for him to protect you.

One inspector found a restau-rant which had been enlarged by knocking down internal load-bearing walls until all that kept the upper floors from falling on the diners were the nails in the floorboards ... So pick up your pen before your hammer.

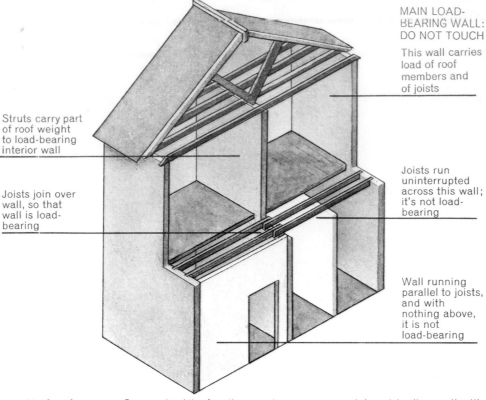

MAIN LOAD-BEARING WALL: DO NOT TOUCH
This wall carries load of roof members and of joists

Struts carry part of roof weight to load-bearing interior wall

Joists join over wall, so that wall is load-bearing

Joists run uninterrupted across this wall; it's not load-bearing

Wall running parallel to joists, and with nothing above, it is not load-bearing

Brick wall 4½in. thick plus plaster. Most likely to be load-bearing, but not necessarily so

Block wall – cheaper to build than brick, common in recent houses. Could be load-bearing

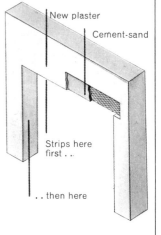

Timber frame covered in lath and plaster or, recently, plaster-board. Probably not load-bearing

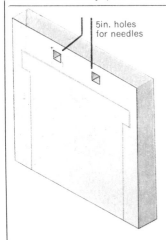

5in. holes for needles

Adjustable props
Needles

Scaffold board

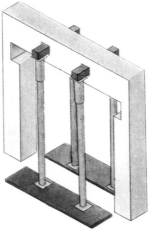

Beam

New plaster
Cement-sand

Strips here first ...

.. then here

You will need: club hammer, ordinary hammer, bolster, cold chisel, saw, steel float, hawk, trowel, spirit level, car jack, baulk of timber 6ft. long. Hire four adjustable steel props (about 70p each a week) and a couple of scaffold boards. Materials: sand, cement, plaster, pieces of slate, two short lengths 4in. by 4in. timber, some 3in. by ½in. long enough to frame hole, and a pre-cast concrete beam (from builder's merchant in standard sizes), or a 3in. or 4in. rolled steel joist ('RSJ') with expanded metal lathing to wrap it in. Pencil area to be removed

Leave at least 12in. each side to carry the beam resting on shoulders at least 6in. wide, and about 18in. of wall below the ceiling. About 6in. above where the top of your new beam will be, cut two 5in. square holes through the wall with hammer, bolster and cold chisel. Lay scaffold boards on floor either side of wall, put the 4in. by 4in. timbers ('needles' to experts) through holes and tighten steel props well between scaffold boards and needles. If wall carries joists of floor above, place length of 4in. by 2in. on ceiling and wedge firmly in place from top of needles

Now cut plaster with bolster along pencil line, exposing bricks or blocks of wall. Starting low down in centre begin care-fully breaking down wall with hammer, bolster and chisel.

Use bolster to trim bricks as near as possible to line of opening. Clear away debris. If using an RSJ wrap it (left). Lift beam to rest on shoul-ders cut in wall. Spread a mix of one part cement, three of sand, half an inch thick all over the top of the beam

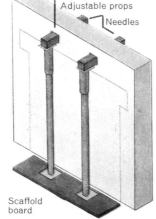

Jack beam up until cement-sand mix squeezes out. Make sure beam is horizontal. Wedge up ends by driving pieces of slate under them. Fill any cracks and joints above and below beam with 1-3 mix. Allow at least 12 hours to set. Now re-move jack, adjustable props and needles. Fill needle holes with brick and cement-sand mix. To get straight edge for making good plaster edges of the wall, run 3in. by ½in. strips below beam and against the cut of wall, wedge in position. Set strips back ¼in. from level of existing plaster. (See page 18 for illustration).

Fill in level with strips on face of wall and vertical edge of beam with 1-3 cement-sand mix. Score surface before it dries. After 12 hours, reposition wood strips level with old plaster and apply a coat of plaster – Sirapite or something similar is easiest – and smooth with steel float. When this is dry, remove strips and carefully nail to face of new plaster so they now form straight edge for similarly making good the cut edge of the wall and the underside of the beam. Make good floor, and cut old skirting board to refix round edges of the small re-maining sections of wall

Barry Jackson

Dividing a room with a timber-framed partition

WALLS: Extra room

The simplest way to divide one room in two is with a partition of plasterboard over a framework of timber.

The first step in building a wall is the same as with other major building jobs – write to the council. The local building inspector must approve your plans, check that they are constructionally safe and that the divided room meets building regulations for fire safety, light and air. The details below are for a wall with a door at one end; it could be modified to form an alcove for a baby's cot or a dining area.

The advantage of timber fram-ing covered with plasterboard is that it can easily be modified, or later removed completely without much work or mess. The door can go anywhere in the length of the wall; a window can be set over it; the wall can contain a serving hatch. Start by locating the joists in the ceiling above by probing with a bradawl; when you find a joist, probe some more to locate the centre. If the new wall is to run in the same direction as the joists, then it must be directly beneath one of them; if it is to run across the joists you'll have to locate all of the joists (they're usually 16in. to 18in. apart), but the new wall can be anywhere along them. Mark where the top of the wall is to go. The frame is made of 3in. by 2in. (75mm. by 50mm.) timber, the 3in. making the thickness of the wall, joined with 2½in. or 3in. wire nails or with screws. Cut the ceiling plate – the frame top – the length from wall to wall and saw and chisel out notches to take the studs – the uprights. The ends are notched to take the uprights which fit against the walls; another notch takes the upright forming the other side of the door frame. The rest of the uprights go into notches 2ft. apart, except for one which will probably be closer. The essential is that the edges of each sheet of plasterboard (usually 4ft. wide) must be nailed to a stud, with as little cutting of boards as possible.

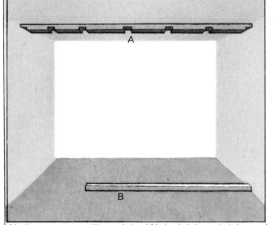

Nail or screw ceiling plate (A) to joist or joists and mark floor directly underneath (use plumb-line) for position of sole plate (B), the bottom of the frame. Cut sole plate – remember it doesn't cross doorway – and nail or screw to floor. If floor is solid, drill and plug it and screw sole plate down. Cut uprights for ends (C, D below), and inner side of door frame (E).

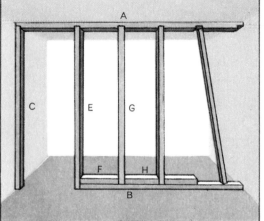

Drill and plug walls to fix outsides of wall frame; fix them also to sole and ceiling plates with nails or screws driven on the skew. Fix inner door frame (E) to end of sole plate. Cut a piece of 3in. by 2in. to same length as that between notches above and nail it (F) hard against upright (E). Fit next upright (G) into its notch, and nail or screw top and bottom

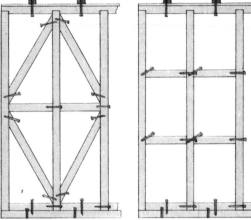

Fix another between-notches length of 3in. by 2in. (H) hard up against (G), and so on across wall. Notch doorway uprights and fit head for doorway, and fit lengths of 3in. by 2in. between other uprights, either diagonally or (easier) horizontally, and nail or screw as shown above. Now's the time, if you plan to fit wall lights or power points to the wall, to position cables

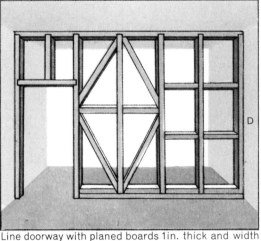

Line doorway with planed boards 1in. thick and width of upright (3in.) plus twice the thickness of the plasterboard. Hang the door and fix the door stops. Begin fitting the sheets of plasterboard, lighter side outwards. To cut plasterboard, score with sharp pointed knife, bend to break plaster, then cut other side. Smooth. Leave ¼in. gap between sheets

Nail sheets to uprights, starting at door lining, with galvanised plasterboard nails. The sheets should fit hard against ceiling; floor level is less important since it will be covered with skirting. Fix architrave round door. Fill gaps between boards with Thistle or a similar plaster, well pressed in to the gap. When dry, cover the joints with paper scrim, pasted down

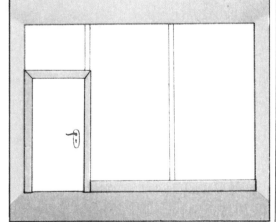

Finally, cut and fit skirting board (see details on p. 82), nailing it to the sole plate. Use filler on any nail holes. Try to get skirting to match rest of room; if room has a cornice, match that, too. If the plasterboard is lined with lining paper before emulsion-painting or wallpapering, its surface will look as good as solid wall professionally plastered

Start with a simple stretch of garden wall

Experts can lay bricks quickly and well; amateurs can usually do one or the other, but not both. If you are content to work slowly, and if necessary to knock down a piece of wall and start again (if you do it before the mortar is dry you can brush off the bricks, and all you've

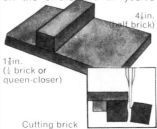

4½in. (half brick)

1⅜in. (½ brick or queen-closer)

Cutting brick

wasted is a few shovelsful of mortar), there's no reason why a householder shouldn't be his own bricklayer. Once you've begun to master the technique a whole range of jobs becomes possible, from making dwarf walls for the base of a greenhouse or garden shed to building a garage or a house extension. Start with a garden wall – if the results are a little irregular you can always claim that

the rustic look was intended. Most tools needed can be hired: brick trowel, pointing trowel, bricklayer's spirit level (a yard long with two bubbles so it can be used horizontally and vertically), club hammer, bolster chisel, bricklayer's line, a rule. Spotboards (2ft. square, raised on bricks) and a hawk can be made; so can a gauge rod (about 3ft. of 2in. by 1in. timber, straight-edged and marked with sawcuts every 3in.) and a bat-and-closer gauge for cutting bricks to the right size (left). To cut a brick, chip a groove in it with hammer and bolster and tap unwanted side sharply. When a bricklayer does it the brick falls neatly in half; amateurs can use a lot of bricks before they master the knack (though a brick which hasn't broken cleanly can still be used provided the face side is the right length). An easy way round this is to use a brick saw, a handsaw with hardened teeth set into the blade, and simply saw the bricks to size. Make yourself a large set-square from a triangle of 2in. by 1in. timber

with the sides in the proportion of 3,4,5; the angle opposite the longest side will be a right-angle. Wear working or gardening gloves; bricks and mortar are hard on the hands.

Approx 2ft. square

Spot board

For a garden wall, mark out and dig a foundation twice the width of the wall; take out topsoil until you reach a firm base. About 8in. is usually enough. Drive in pegs and level them, using a line or a straight-edged board and spirit level, so peg heads are about 3in. below ground level. Now fill trench with concrete (1 part cement, 6 of all-in ballast) to the top of the pegs and leave it to harden. There are hundreds of different types of bricks, of different strengths, colours, finishes and prices; and the mortar in which they are set depends on the brick and the job it has to do. We go into bricks and mortars on the opposite page, and also

into brick 'bonding'. Bonds are the patterns in which bricks are laid – English bond, stretcher bond, Flemish bond. Their purpose, apart from appearance, is to ensure that, for the sake of strength, no vertical joint comes directly above another. With foundations laid, stretch a line to mark where the face of the wall is to be, put a pile of bricks near each end; if it is dry weather moisten them—brick should feel damp, dust-free—mix mortar and away you go.

WALLS: Bricklaying

Everyone is willing to try papering a room, painting a door. Few householders try bricklaying – a useful skill, not quite as hard as it looks.

Scooping a trowelful of mortar out of the pile will waste mortar, make a mess, because it falls off; turn, roll and cut out a big mortar sausage from the pile with the trowel, then slide trowel under it so it lifts in one clean lump. Drop mortar onto foundation, spread it roughly along the line of the wall, about ½in. thick

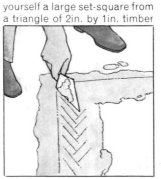    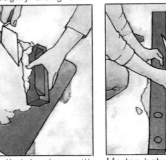

Queen-closers

With line and set-square as guide, use edge of trowel to mark precise line of wall on mortar. Remember you can use spirit level vertically to plumb down from string to foundation level so that line on mortar is precisely under the string. Make sure mortar bed is level. Mortar should be fairly stiff; if it flows, it is too wet

Lay first brick precisely at corner, and tap gently into place with trowel handle. If brick has a frog – a depression which helps the mortar to grip – it should go on top. 'Butter' end or side of the next brick (that is, spread mortar on it with trowel) about ½in. thick, to make vertical joint with last brick. Set and tap brick in place

Mortar between bricks should fill joint, squeeze out a little. Use spirit level as a straight-edge to check that bricks are in line; tap back any out of place

 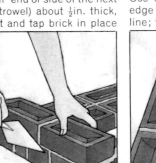 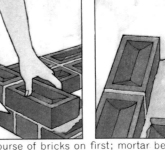

Use spirit level to check that line of bricks is level, too. This checking must go on all the time; otherwise slight errors will grow until whole wall is out

Tidy up joints as you go, pushing mortar into gaps or scooping away the excess. The joints can be left slightly raked out for pointing later, or you can complete the pointing (as shown on p. 67) before mortar has dried, using a pointing trowel. Try to ensure that all vertical joints are the same thickness, about ⅜in.

Lay second course of bricks on first; mortar between should be about ⅜in. thick when brick is in place. For details of bonds, including 'half bats' and 'queen-closers' (above right) see page opposite. Spread mortar on this second row, then lay a damp-proof course of lead-cored bituminous felt, then more mortar on top

   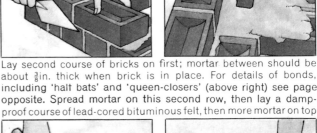 

Start to build up ends of wall, laying next course of bricks four bricks long, then three, and so on. Use gauge rod to ensure that bricks are precisely every 3in., spirit level held vertical to ensure that wall is upright. Fix line pegs into mortar joint at end of wall, use the line – keep it about ⅛in. clear of wall – as guide to fill gap

Keep checking that wall isn't bulging; level held at an angle will serve as straight-edge. When wall is at finishing height it will need a waterproof top ...

... so spread mortar again, then lay course of bricks on edge. If using bricks with frog, end bricks must have frog facing inwards. Once end bricks are in place put spare brick on top, wind line round and stretch it to other end for guide for last bricks. Finish joints between bricks, brush wall down to remove any stray mortar spots

Leslie Chapman

Pictures courtesy of The London Brick Company

WALLS: Brick jigsaw

The strength and beauty of a brick wall depends on the bond – the pattern in which bricks are laid so that no vertical joint comes directly above another – and on the choice of bricks and mortars. For a garden wall try a brick the same as those of your house, or in sharp contrast: 'near enough' matching looks worse than either. Ask your builder's merchant what suitable types he has in stock; ordering small quantities of bricks specially is expensive. Consult him, too, about mortar: one part masonry cement to four of soft sand is suitable for most work, but certain bricks may need a slightly different mix. Below are three kinds of wall bonding; try laying some bricks dry – without mortar – to get the hang of it.

The difference that coloured mortars make, here with London Brick's Milton Buff (left), Golden Buff and (right) Heather. Use coloured cement for mortar-mix, or mix in cement pigments

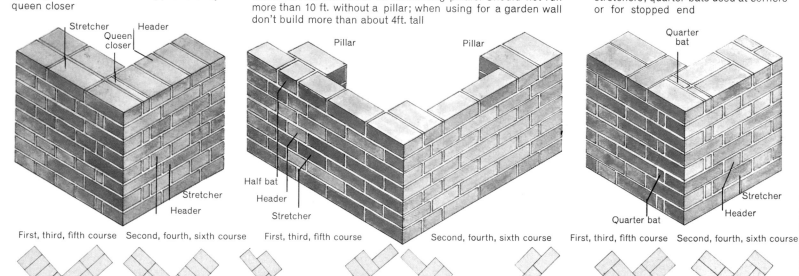

English bond: 9in. thick

Alternate layers of headers and stretchers; spacing at corners or at stopped end by queen closer

First, third, fifth course   Second, fourth, sixth course

Easy to remember: one course is all headers, next all stretchers, and so on up the wall; corners adjusted with queen closers

Stretcher bond: 4½in. thick

All courses are stretchers, staggered so vertical joints don't coincide. Half-bats used for reinforcing pillars. Should not run more than 10 ft. without a pillar; when using for a garden wall don't build more than about 4ft. tall

First, third, fifth course   Second, fourth, sixth course

Cheapest: except for corners and pillars, all bricks are stretchers

Flemish bond: 9in. thick

Each course alternate headers and stretchers; quarter-bats used at corners or for stopped end

First, third, fifth course   Second, fourth, sixth course

Every course is the same, header-stretcher-header-stretcher, adjusted with quarter-bats so that joints don't overlap

---

When a slate slips–how to hook it back

Slates and tiles are nailed or hooked on to battens running along the roof, spaced apart according to the size of slate or tile covering them. The battens are nailed to the rafters. In old houses you'll be able to see the battens and the underside of slates or tiles from inside the attic; sometimes it is possible to manoeuvre a slipped tile or slate back into place from within. In modern houses this won't be possible because of the layer of waterproof felt between the rafters and the battens which helps keep wind and driven rain or snow out. Slates are nailed in place, either at the top or about half-way down each side, and in older houses they tend to slip because the nails rust through. (Use rust proof nails for repairs.) The tool you will need for replacing slates, and possibly when replacing tiles, is a *slate ripper*; you can buy it from a good tool merchant or you may be able to hire one for a few shillings a day.

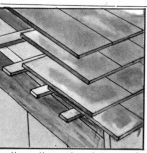

Section through slate roof: joins between slates always fall in middle of slate below

Slate ripper: thin blade slides under a damaged slate, hooked end locates the slate nails

ROOFS Replacing Slates

Major roof repairs are best left to professionals, but an amateur who doesn't mind heights can tackle replacing the odd slipped tile or cracked slate provided it can be reached without difficulty. Use long-enough ladders or a working platform and if necessary a roof ladder; if in doubt, send for an expert. Heights can be dangerous.

A sharp jerk on slate ripper will break nail without disturbing surrounding slates. Freed broken slate can then be slid gently out from its position

Nail inch-wide strip of lead or copper sheet through join between two slates beneath and into batten (nails in these slates show where batten is)

Slide new slate into place so that its bottom edge lines up with the rest of the row. Go gently or you may have another broken slate to replace . . .

Bend up the end of the copper or lead strip round the bottom of the new slate so that it is hooked in place. Lead, though dearer, matches slate colour

How to replace those broken tiles

Plain tiles are easier to deal with than slates because most are not nailed but held in place by hooking the nibs – the little knobs on the underside – over the tiling battens. Every third or fourth row is supposed to be nailed as a protection against high winds lifting the tiles, but even this is not always done. A damaged tile that isn't nailed can be removed by levering up the tiles above it – a trowel is a good tool for this – and lifting the damaged tile so that its nibs clear the batten. The new tile

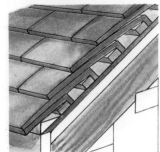

Tiled roof: extra-wide tiles at the ends of alternate rows ensure that the joins are staggered

can be pushed up until the nibs hook over the batten, and the tiles above lowered again. If the damaged tile is one of the nailed ones, lift those above it and try to waggle the damaged tile until its nails break or pull out; or use a slate ripper. There's no need to nail the new tile in its place; the nibs will hold it well enough. Tiles without nibs – like pantiles and some patent tiles – must all be nailed, though an odd replacement can if necessary be held like a replacement slate with a hook of

lead or copper strip. Don't try any roof repairs without a working platform or a ladder long enough to reach well above the gutter level (to leave you the upper rungs to hold on to). If

the work is up on the roof out of reach from a ladder, don't crawl on the roof – you are likely to break some tiles and your neck as well. Hire a roof ladder or crawling board; these have wheels at one end for rolling the ladder up the slope of the roof. When it is in place the ladder is turned over so that a large metal hook grips the roof over the ridge. Hire rates are about £2 to £3 a week. If you aren't happy working at heights don't take chances; leave the job to a builder.

Filling in holes: the way to a smooth finish

Big areas of plastering are a job for an expert; small holes in ceilings can be repaired by any householder willing to get a crick in the neck. Your builder's merchant will advise which type of plaster is best for various jobs. Lots of hair cracks in ceilings are best covered by lining the ceiling (see item on page 24) and emulsion-painting. Cut out bigger cracks so crack is wider at the back than at the surface to make a key; brush out loose plaster, damp cut and surrounding plaster by flicking water from brush, then fill with a proprietary cellulose filler. For a very big crack apply filler or plaster in layers, allowing each to harden before adding the next. Make a stiff mix and press in hard with a flat scraper; mix a little emulsion paint with the last layer if you aren't planning to paper the ceiling. Deal with cracks between walls and ceiling the same way, removing surplus plaster with a one-inch paint brush. In new houses small circles of plaster sometimes break away over the heads of nails fastening the plasterboard, as the house dries out. Tap these nails gently home (use a punch to prevent hammer damaging plaster) and fill hole with proprietary filler; let

it harden a little above ceiling surface; then sand down. Bigger holes in plasterboard, like those left when moving light fittings, should have the skim coat of plaster cut away for half an inch or so all round. Stick a piece of plasterer's scrim over the hole with dabs of plaster. When this has begun to harden, add thin layers of plaster, polishing the last one with a damp metal float or trowel. Such holes in lath and plaster need no scrim if the laths are unbroken; if they are, soak a piece of scrim or paper in plaster, stuff it into the hole, plaster up when dry. Much bigger holes – like the ones made by putting a foot through the bedroom ceiling while working in the attic – mend with plasterboard. Cut out damage to halfway across a joist and cut a new piece of board to fill space leaving about ⅛in. gap. Plasterboard can be cut with a fine saw or scored deeply, bent over a batten until it cracks, then cut the other side. Nail into place with galvanised clouts. Cover strips of scrim with wet plaster and push into the joins, flattening the edges on to the board. Then plaster the whole of the new board except the joins. When it's hard go over it again with another thin coat so the whole repair is smooth, finishing off with a steel float. Damaged cornices can usually be replaced with standard sections in plaster or plastic from a builder's merchant; in older houses they may not be standard. It's worth trying the expert way to repair them, using a zinc sheet cut to the profile of the undamaged parts (right).

Holes in lath and plaster ceiling where laths are damaged is filled with plaster-soaked paper or scrim as key; when it is beginning to harden, fill hole gently with plaster, smooth off

Useful in fitting plasterboard if you've no helpers; strut from floor to ceiling wedges new section in place until nailed. It's called a Dead Man's Hand

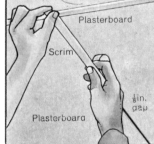

Joins between plasterboards are filled with scrim strip soaked in plaster, pressed into gap and flattened out each side. A skim coat of plaster covers it

Craftsman's ride: zinc sheet is cut to shape of cornice, fixed to wooden frame ('horse') which rides along batten nailed temporarily to wall. Plaster is laid on with trowel to damaged area, horse slid along batten scraping off excess. Repeat until damaged area is completely filled out to match the rest

CEILINGS Laths or plasterboard

Ceilings will be made in one of two ways; lath and plaster, or plasterboard. Ceilings in older houses will be lath and plaster unless they've been replaced in more recent years. The laths, thin strips of wood, are nailed across the joists; plaster mixed with hair is spread over them and grips the laths; a thin layer of smooth plaster is added to give a good surface. Lath and plaster makes a very good ceiling, but is prohibitively expensive today. A modern equivalent is using sheets of expanded metal in place of the laths, the holes in the metal providing a key for plaster. Plasterboard has a core of gypsum plaster between two layers of paper; there are insulating plasterboards with a layer of aluminium foil one side. The boards are nailed to the ceiling joists and the gaps between adjacent boards filled with plaster and scrim – open-weave thin cloth – with an all-over skim coat of plaster to make a smooth finish.

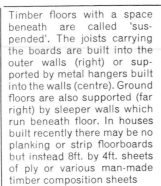

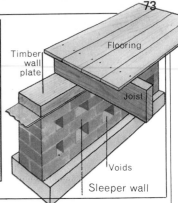

Timber floors with a space beneath are called 'suspended'. The joists carrying the boards are built into the outer walls (right) or supported by metal hangers built into the walls (centre). Ground floors are also supported (far right) by sleeper walls which run beneath floor. In houses built recently there may be no planking or strip floorboards but instead 8ft. by 4ft. sheets of ply or various man-made timber composition sheets

Joist fitted into brickwork

Joist hung in metal hanger

Timber wall plate / Flooring / Joist / Voids / Sleeper wall

FLOORS: Feet firmly off the ground

Considering the load they carry every day it's not surprising that floors show signs of wear.

In recently-built houses, ground floors – and sometimes even upper floors – are of concrete. With a solid ground floor, concrete is laid on the ground, up to the level of the damp proof course. A waterproof membrane, in effect a damp proof course over the whole area, is laid on top, then a thin layer of cement and sand – a screed – is spread on top of that and trowelled smooth. Wood blocks,

thermoplastic tiles, rubber tiles, cork tiles, or quarry (clay) tiles can then be laid on top. The essential point is the waterproof membrane – it can be sheet polythene or coats of bitumen. Some country cottages with solid floors – bricks or flags – were built long before damp-courses were thought of, and their ground floors can never be covered because of the damp which rises through them. If for

any reason the solid ground floor of a modern house has to be cut into – as it may be for running central heating pipes – the damp proof membrane must be repaired afterwards so that it remains waterproof. Where concrete is used for upper floors, the building is spanned by reinforced concrete (concrete containing strengthening steel rods), and covered with a cement and sand screed

Floorboards may be squared-edged (below, left) or tongued and grooved (below, right) which can shrink without cracks opening up to let draughts through. 'T&G' boards can be 'secret nailed' – nails in one

board covered by next. Below: parquetry flooring (top) and wood blocks in basketweave (centre) and herringbone pattern. Parquetry can be bought

Ground floor
Plaster
Skirting
Wood blocks or tiles
Damp proof membrane
Concrete
Outer cavity wall
Damp proof course
Foundations
Cement-sand screed
Hardcore over ground

Upper floor
Plaster
Skirting
Blocks or tiles
Screed
Reinforced concrete
Screed

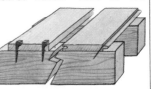

already fitted to ply, which is stuck to the floorboards

Replacing worn floorboards

To replace section of floorboard, lever up, support raised section with wedges, then by piece of wood slipped beneath resting on adjacent boards. Saw through above joist; if cut elsewhere board ends will have nothing to rest on. Cut tongue of tongued-and-grooved boards before lifting, and plane off tongue of replacement board to fit, or use square-edge board. Before sawing tongue feel with back of saw to make sure no wires or pipes are in the way.

Broad chisel or bolster levers board up, wedges hold it. Always cut over centre of a joist

If replacement board is too thick cut notches out of board over joists – not in the joists

Before lifting tongued-and-grooved board, drill holes, insert hacksaw and cut tongue

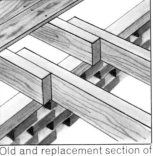

FLOORS: Repair work

Damaged floorboards or joists can be simply replaced; if damage is by rot or woodworm treat cause first – see details on pages 80 and 81.

Rotten or broken joists: how to repair with new timber

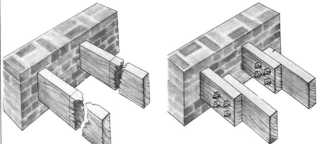

Left, joists rotted or broken (it usually happens close to wall, especially in corners). Right, damage cut away, with the new sections inserted in new hole in wall and bolted to the old joists

Ends of joists fit into holes cut in the outer walls of the house; within the house they are supported in places on sleeper walls. A joist which has rotted or broken at the ends, where they usually fail, is replaced with a new section. Cut new joist at least 12in. longer than damaged section; treat with wood preservative; place alongside the old joist and mark on the wall where the new end touches. Saw off the damaged end of the old joist and remove from wall; cut out bricks to enlarge the hole where marked. Insert new section into hole, checking with spirit level to ensure it is horizontal. Mark new and existing joist, drill, and bolt timbers with four $\frac{3}{8}$in. coach bolts. Make good brickwork and fill old joist-hole with a 1-3 cement-sand mix. Leave for 48 hours before relaying floorboards. Where there is a convenient sleeper wall the damaged joist can be cut off close to sleeper wall and the new section cut long enough to join over the sleeper wall (right).

Old and replacement section of joist joined above sleeper wall – this gives joint extra support

QED

A professional finish with plastic floor tiles

Laying plastic floor tiles is easy, but to get a professional finish spend time preparing the old floor surface. Solid floors should have small dents filled with cellulose filler; if the whole surface is rough, buy a bag of ready-mixed screed and spread a thin (⅛in.) layer all over. Give ample time to dry. Wood floors, unless entirely free of bumps and cracks, are best covered with sheets of hardboard nailed every 4in. to 6in.; best of all, if you can afford it, is resin-bonded ply. Spend time, too, on setting out – snap a chalk line from the middle of two walls, then lay tiles 'dry' up to each end and across, adjusting the lines so that odd part-tiles needed to complete the floor will be equal size each side. If you've an irregular-shaped room this will take lots of juggling. Perfectionists would be shocked, but if furniture, long curtains or even deep shadows hide the foot of one wall you *can* put the part-tiles there and have the whole tiles on the opposite side of the room.

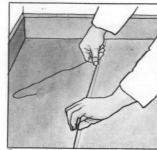
Snap chalked string to mark middle of floor; if you've no helper nail one end of the string

Set out tiles dry to get odd-cut tile sizes evenly all round; you may have to move line slightly

Spread adhesive with notched spreader about a square yard at a time. Start where lines cross

Start sticking tiles down precisely in angle formed by crossed lines, edge first. Work from this tile along and across. Butt edges; don't slide tiles

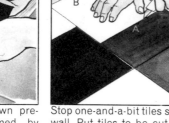
Stop one-and-a-bit tiles short of wall. Put tiles to be cut (A) in full-tile position, without adhesive; lay a spare tile (B) flush with wall so it overlaps; mark A

Score top of tile along mark with sharp knife, bend back until it breaks. Now stick down last full tile. Press tiles down firmly; a hard roller can help

Set cut tile in position; you may need to trim a sliver off. In cutting tiles it is always safer to mark and cut them fractionally too wide, then trim them

Cut tile is now set in place. So far it's simple. What do you do when you come to a doorway? Tiles should go half-way under so that the door covers edge

For awkward shapes of door frame you can use the same system of a spare tile laid over the one to be cut, to mark two edges in two or three places ...

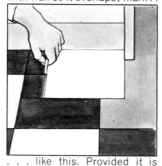
... like this. Provided it is always lined up precisely with the already laid tiles to one side or the other, the spare tile will give the right measurements

But an easier way is to buy a special gauge made for the job, like a comb with sliding teeth. Pressed against the door frame it takes up the shape precisely

... and the shape can be marked from it on to the tile. Whichever way tile is marked, score and cut it, check on floor. Now lay last row of whole tiles

Finally stick down the cut tile. Don't forget to butt each tile tightly against those previously laid – and wipe off any adhesive from top of tiles as you go

PATHS
and
DRIVES

PATHS AND DRIVES: The moneysaver

Laying your own paths and drives is a moneysaver because the materials are comparatively cheap and the labour element is large; it doesn't require great skill, though it is hard work. A cubic yard of wet concrete — enough for a path about 50ft. long — weighs about two tons; if you are mixing it by hand you'll have picked those two tons up a shovelful at a time something like a dozen times before you've finished. For large areas consider hiring a mixer or buying ready-mixed concrete. If you're starting on a new site, leave the area alone and see which way people make their

Shuttering — also called form-work — holds concrete in place until it hardens. Boards 6in. wide are nailed to stout pegs driven into the ground. You may be able to hire such boards, or scaffold boards—but brush with *mould oil* before using and they'll come away clean when the concrete hardens. Divide large areas into bays with cross-pieces. For curved drives use strips of waterproof hard-board — and lots more pegs. Smooth concrete dries quickly after rain, but you can allow an inch crossfall from one side

own paths — it may be easier to lay a path there than to persuade them to walk somewhere else. Remember that in working on the outside of your house you may want to use ladders, and it's better to stand a ladder on the path than in the middle of a flowerbed. Don't make drives too narrow; they must be wide enough to take the widest car and allow you to get out of the car on to the drive and not the garden. Measure your plot carefully, transfer it to squared paper — it will help you work out what quantities of material you'll want. Decide where to have the materials dumped. You'll have to excavate for foundations: have you somewhere to put the earth?
Whatever the top surface is going to be, you'll want a bottom layer of hardcore — broken brick, stone or other building rubble. If you are replacing badly cracked concrete don't lay new concrete on top; break into small pieces for hardcore. The final surface can be gravel or hoggin, asphalt, setts, bricks, paving slabs or cobbles — see descriptions on page 77. Or it

can be of concrete, which you'll need for a middle layer for many of these surfaces anyhow. Concrete isn't the prettiest material, but it is cheap, easy to lay and very hardwearing.
Start by marking out your path or drive with pegs and strong string, allowing an extra 3in. each side for the pegs and formwork — boards which will hold the concrete while it is setting. Dig out to 9in. for drives, 5in. for paths; if you hit soft patches of soil at this depth you'll have to go deeper until you reach a firm layer, filling holes with hardcore.
If your drive is to be level, level the bottom of your excavation checking with a straight-edged plank and a builder's spirit level; if it is sloping, check that the gradient is even by using the level on top of a board tapered to the slope you want. Construct the formwork as Fig 1, and when you've re-checked that the top of the boards is precisely where the top of your drive should be, fill the bottom with 4in. to 5in. of hardcore (3in. for paths). Ram the hard-core down well, using a large baulk of timber or a (hired)

rammer. Mix concrete (as in rules on p. 78), six parts all-in ballast to one of cement, and barrow it to the farthest part of drive. Rake and shovel it into place, prodding to dispel air and get into corners. Leave surface slightly above formwork. Another board long enough to bridge the formwork is used on edge to tamp the concrete down and then, sliding it to and fro across the formwork and gradually moving along, to level off. Finished this way the concrete will harden with a good non-slip surface. You can make it smoother by rubbing a wooden float over the surface after it has begun to set; but if you make it too smooth the surface

may crack. To work over soft concrete without leaving foot-marks, bridge formwork with planks set on bricks either side. For a coloured concrete drive, lay ordinary concrete as above to within an inch of the top of the formwork. Then — the same day, before it has hardened — add a final inch of a mix of four parts coarse sand to one part coloured cement.
Keep new concrete damp by spreading damp sacks or poly-thene sheets over it for 24 hours; when you remove them sprinkle new concrete with water. If there's a risk of frost, keep the surface covered with dry sacks for at least three days; try to avoid mixing in frosty weather.

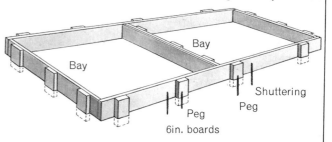

1 Formwork, also called shuttering; planks nailed to pegs hold concrete until it hardens. Also provides fixed point for levelling

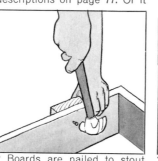

2 Boards are nailed to stout pegs driven well into the ground. If nailing loosens pegs, use two hammers banging simultaneously, one each side

3 Check with spirit level along and across formwork before and after nailing; top of boards will be level of finished drive. Pegs mustn't be above boards

4 When all levels are satisfactory, shovel in hardcore and ram down well; 5in. depth for drives, 3in. for paths. Final strength depends on this foundation

5 Rake and shovel concrete on top, prodding well into corners. It should be just a little above top of formwork. Readymix truck chute may pour it on spot

6 Tamp down with a stout plank on edge. Zig-zag plank along formwork to level concrete. Handles on plank save stooping. it's a two-man job

7 Divide large areas to be concreted into small bays, taking out the cross-planks when ready to lay the next bay. Perfectionists can put a strip of fibre-board impregnated with bitumen against crossplanks, left in place when crossplank is removed, to absorb the expansion of concrete on hot days. It's not vital

8 A good surface for paths can be made by sprinkling gently with water after concrete has begun to harden, then sweep gently to expose stones in mix

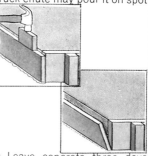

9 Leave concrete three days before removing formwork. Tap pegs down then out before lifting boards. Lifting directly up risks damaging concrete edge

Formwork against a wall; top is well below damp course — at least six inches; otherwise wall will become damp. A strip of bitumen-ised fibre-board can be pinned to wall before laying concrete, left in place to absorb expansion on hot days; it's not vital

A path or drive beside a wall must obey one rule; the top of the path must be at least 6in. (the depth of two bricks) below the damp-proof course. Since the wall is in the way the path can't be tamped crosswise; you can lay a narrow (6-in.) strip parallel to the wall and then fill in the remainder with concrete before first strip has hardened, to get a good join; keep checking surface with spirit level. Finish in the ways described above; or you can divide the area into bays and fill alternately, tamping across bay

Drainage of flat or sloping drives: (illustrations on the right) do not present any problems; where there's a steep slope toward the garage (middle right) it's wise to take precautions to avoid heavy rain flooding in. By extra digging out, the drive can be made to run down below the door level, and the last foot or two slope up into the garage. The slopes, of course do not need to be so steep as in the illustrations. Where the two slopes join, a gutter shape should be pressed into the drying concrete (top right) sloping slightly to one side towards a drainage gully. Builders favour rubbing a milk bottle along to shape this gutter. Milkmen don't, so it is best to use a non-return bottle.

Types of path, the materials and how to use them

For long drives the cheapest materials are gravel – small stones – or hoggin, a natural mixture of gravel and clay. They are less economic in the long run, however, because they need renewing at intervals, and regular weed protection.

Another problem is that these materials spread and encroach on lawn or flowerbeds. The only permanent remedy for this is to edge the drive with kerbstones set in about 6in. of concrete (one part cement to eight parts all-in ballast) with the concrete drawn halfway up the kerbstone. The foundation, of 4in. of hardcore, should be well rammed in and levelled, and 4in. to 6in. of gravel or hoggin laid on top and rolled – use a garden roller, or hire a powered roller at about £5 a day, £10 a week (plus delivery; ask about this). A slight curve from centre to edges will help shed rain; applying a bituminous solution (sprinkled on by watering can) will help stabilise the surface and keep out weeds.

Other drive surfaces are all laid on concrete; prepare the drive

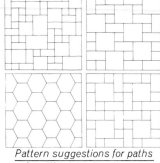

Pattern suggestions for paths

as described in detail, page 76 but finishing an inch or so below the final level. See most of the possible surfaces at a good-sized nursery or garden centre (though for cheap crazy paving it's worth asking your local Town Hall if they've any broken paving slabs for sale. You buy them by the ton, which covers 8-10 sq. yds).

Concrete paving slabs, made with crushed stone in several colours, sizes and shapes, are for drives best laid on inch of mortar made from one part cement to four of sharp sand, and levelled by tapping gently with a club hammer on a piece

To cut, chip groove, tap waste

of wood (no wood means cracked slab). Keep checking with a spirit level. Joints are filled with a stiff mix (1 cement, 4 sand, very little water), then finished by rubbing a piece of pipe along joint. Sweep slabs to remove surplus mortar. *Crazy paving* is laid in the same way. Start at the edges with the biggest straight-edged pieces, then fill in with smaller stones. *Bricks* for paving must be hard and dense, for soft bricks absorb moisture and then break up in frosty weather. There are special bricks made for paving, only 2in. thick. Ordinary bricks can be used flat or on edge; if you're using bricks with a frog – the hollow on the top – that must be underneath. *Quarry tiles* are an inch thick and from 6in. to 12in. square. Like bricks they are laid on an inch

bed of 1-4 mortar and the joints filled as for slabs. Alternatively, a dry mix can be brushed over. *Stone slabs* and inch-thick *slate slabs* are handsome but expensive, though this varies according to where you live; they're bedded in mortar too. *Setts,* usually granite, range in size from 4in. cubes to 4in. by 10in. blocks; they're laid tightly together on a semi-dry very stiff 1-4 mortar and dry mortar is brushed into the joints, surplus swept off and water sprinkled. Plain concrete drives can be given a surface of cold asphalt; thoroughly clean old concrete first, then pour asphalt direct from the bag, spread evenly and roll with a garden roller. Two thin layers are better than one thick, but the final thickness is only about $\frac{1}{4}$in., so one bag will go a long way. Paths need less thick foundations. If you don't mind occasionally lifting slabs to re-level them, they can be laid on well-compacted sand without mortar or even on a levelled bed of soil with small creeping plants and flowers planted in the cracks.

PATHS AND DRIVES: The final surface

Concrete paths and drives undoubtedly give the strongest surface for the least money; but they're not the prettiest material to have around the garden.

Laying brick and slab paths on a sound foundation

When slabs, bricks and other finishes are used for drives the underlying structure should be concrete laid on a bed of hardcore; this concrete should be levelled as carefully as if it were to be the final surface since the slabs on their thin mortar bed cannot make up for faults farther down. For paths the foundations need not be so strong; instead of mortar all over they can be laid on five blobs of mortar, or even on compacted sand or earth.

Section through strong path or drive; levelled earth, hardcore, concrete, mortar bed, slab

For paths – not drives – slabs can be laid on five blobs of mortar – at corners and centre

In each case the slab is gently tapped into place with a club hammer on a block of wood

Check each slab is level and same height as neighbouring slabs. Add mortar if necessary

Bricks, quarry tiles or stone setts can be laid in patterns – work out format on squared paper, check by setting a few out on site without mortar first

Having established pattern, sides should be laid first, checking the width carefully, and then the patterned centre filled. Check with spirit level

When bed mortar has set the surface joints should be filled with a stiff, almost dry mortar, pressing in with a trowel. Alternatively with bricks, and *always* with setts, put a completely dry mortar mix on the surface, as shown here, sweep it into the cracks, tamp down, then brush all the surplus off carefully

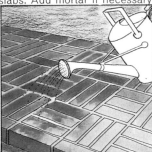

Water the surface gently using a rose on a watering can. Bricks that do get stained with mortar, can be cleaned by rubbing with a piece of brick

Curing cracked or sunken drives

If sections of a concrete drive have cracked and sunk or tilted it means the foundation isn't strong enough for the loads carried. No patching on top can cure the trouble and sooner or later the old surface must be broken into small pieces to make a new foundation and a new surface laid. But if the surface has cracked without sinking, cracks can be repaired. The repairs will always show, but they will keep the weeds and the weather out

Cut out weak edges of crack with bolster, opening out at the bottom to provide grip for repair

Clean crack thoroughly and paint with special PVA adhesive (ask your builder's merchant)

When adhesive is tacky, trowel 1-cement 3-sand mix into crack, pressing well down. dispel air

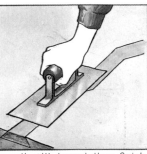

Smooth with trowel, then finish surface with float so no ridge or hollow is left around the repair

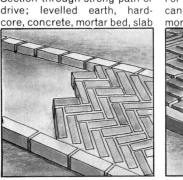

Repairing chipped or damaged edges to paths and drives

To repair damaged edges to concrete paths and drives, chip away any weak edges round the broken patch, break up the patch itself into small pieces and ram them well down, adding further hardcore if necessary to make a really firm foundation (you may need to rake out some earth to make room). Paint edges with PVA adhesive – made for this job; ask your builder's merchant – and when adhesive is tacky, fill hole with a mixture of one part cement to four parts of coarse sand.

With pegs and board, mark new edge position. *Don't* prop board up with bricks – it will shift

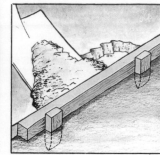

Check board is level with existing surface before nailing to pegs. Paint edge with PVA, fill

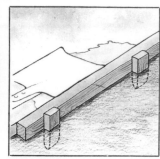

Tamp down well. Make sure there are no unfilled gaps. Smooth roughly to right level

Finish with trowel. Leave board in place for week. When removing, tap down, then out

Understanding the simple rules for concreting

For paths, drives, foundations, and floors for outbuildings, concrete is the material; mixing and laying it demands only limited skill. Here are the rules for simple concrete mixing.

Portland cement is suitable for almost anything you are likely to do. It comes in 50 kilo (1cwt.) paper sacks which are heavy and awkward to handle; try to get a spare pair of hands to help. The bags should ideally be stored in a dry shed. They must, in any case, be stored off the damp ground, either in raised timbers or at least with a waterproof sheet beneath them and with a waterproof covering.

Cement is mixed with *aggregates*, sharp sand and stones; for paths and drives the easiest material is *all-in-ballast*, a combination of stones and sand. Ideally aggregates should be stored on boards or a sheet of metal; if they are dumped on to bare earth you won't be able to use the bottom earth-contaminated layer. You can buy ballast by the $\frac{1}{4}$ yard, $\frac{1}{2}$ yard, or yard (which means cubic yards) or by eight-yard truckloads.

Cement and sand, or cement and aggregate, can also be bought by the bag, ready mixed, dry; you just add water. It is expensive this way, but convenient for small jobs. The final material for mixing concrete is water. Concrete hardens by the incorporation of water into the chemical structure, so it must be clean water.

For paths and drives, the best mix is one part of cement by volume (use a box or a bucket) to five or six of all-in ballast. In calculating how much concrete you'll make, ignore the volume of the cement and the water; that is,

a mix containing a yard of all-in ballast will make a yard of concrete, or slightly less (the moisture in the ballast bulks it up). Think of the concrete mix as a cube, a yard each way, and imagine taking slices off it; if you are laying 3in. thickness of concrete you'll get 12 slices a yard square from your cubic yard.

Don't mix concrete with a garden spade; it doubles the work. Shovels can be hired for a few pence a week – so can navvy barrows for placing concrete. Measure ballast on to boarding or metal sheet or an existing piece of concrete; anything except the bare ground. Measure the cement on top. Mix with the shovel (Fig. A, right) until the colour is even all through. Then make a hole in the middle (B) and add water, a little at a time, shovelling dry material on top. (Splosh water on too quickly and it will wash cement away, weakening the mix.) Turn the mix three times.

Most amateurs mix concrete too wet; it should be just plastic enough to be forced into corners when you lay it, but sufficiently firm so that when you push the shovel up and down across it, the marks stay sharp (C). For larger quantities it's worth hiring a mixer. An electric one small enough to fold into a car boot can be hired for about £2 a day, £3·50 a week. Start the mixer turning, add a little water, then the ballast, then the cement, then the rest of the water and leave it mixing – about two minutes is usually enough – until colour and consistency are even. And don't forget after the last batch to clean the mixer out.

For larger quantities still, consider buying ready-mixed concrete; dearer than mix-your-own but a lot easier.

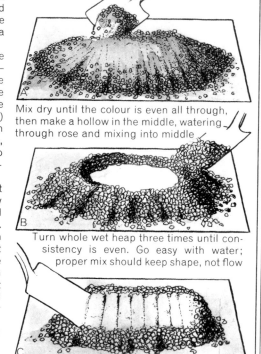

Mix dry until the colour is even all through, then make a hollow in the middle, watering through rose and mixing into middle

Turn whole wet heap three times until consistency is even. Go easy with water; proper mix should keep shape, not flow

OLD HOUSES
and
THEIR PROBLEMS

THE BATTLE AGAINST DECAY-WARDING OFF THE GREATEST DANGERS

Damp-the ever-present enemy

The worst enemy of a house is water: rain falling from above or driving sideways into the walls on windy days, and water rising from the damp ground beneath. Most modern building rules are simply standardisations of methods proved over the years for keeping water out: the damp proof course, the double skin of a cavity wall.

Some older houses will always be damp because they were built without these waterproofing device, but often a well-built modern house can become damp through neglect of small precautions that any householder can take without the help of a builder. If a house remains damp for long the materials – even the bricks –

can be permanently damaged. Biggest danger of all is of rot developing in the timbers; wet rot, which is bad, or dry rot which is very bad indeed and can in extreme circumstances quite quickly turn a des. res., all mod. con., into something fit only for demolition. Below and on the right are some of the enemies of your house.

Photographs courtesy of Dr D. Dickinson; Rentokil Limited; Wykamol Limited; Fearnley Limited; Building Research Station D.O.E.; Timber Research Advisory Service

Defective downpipe; instead of flowing down drain water from gutter escapes, soaks into wall

Moss and grit from roof washes into gutter which overflows and soaks the wall and woodwork

Split windowsill – only a small fault, but it lets water soak into a large area of wall beneath

Bill Easter

With no damp course to stop it, moisture creeps up wall. This calls for specialist treatment

Thick line in bricks shows damp course – but careless gardening has made earth bridge over it

Air bricks allow drying draught below floor. If plants cover opening, damp can cause dryrot

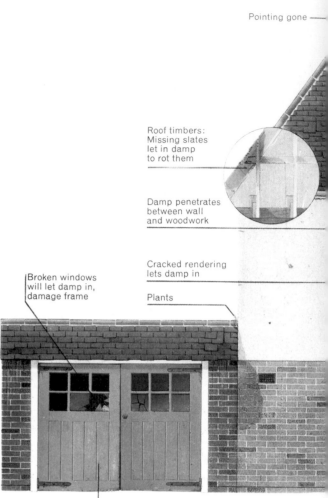

Pointing gone

Roof timbers: Missing slates let in damp to rot them

Damp penetrates between wall and woodwork

Cracked rendering lets damp in

Plants

Broken windows will let damp in, damage frame

Faulty paint admits damp, starts more paint peeling, wood decaying

How dry rot lays its seige

Dry rot: far left, cuboidal cracking left by dry rot; above, fungus in full growth; below, quick-growing threads invade a cupboard

The spores – microscopic seeds – of dry rot drift everywhere, but they can't germinate on wood with less than 20 per cent. moisture. A properly designed and maintained house won't let timber get dangerously damp, but overflowing gutters, burst pipes and other faults – even earth heaped over the damp course – can let in enough moisture to the timbers for the spores to begin growing. First thing to be seen after that will be a spreading mass of mycelium – tiny threads that sometimes look like a mass of cotton wool or felt. These threads can be white, grey, sometimes brown. Eventually fruiting

bodies form, like giant toadstool caps, which in turn will liberate more spores. Even without spores the mycelium will go on spreading, not only through wood but over, and

even through, plaster, brick walls, even stone and concrete, until they reach more wood. That's why dry rot can climb rapidly from cellar to attic – or through the party wall from the semi next door. The menace of dry rot is that it doesn't stop when it reaches the limits of the damp wood. The threads carry their own water-supply, so that perfectly sound dry wood can soon be as badly affected as the site of the original outbreak.

All this growth may go on out of sight beneath floorboards, or even behind a coat of paint. Eventually – unless the musty damp smell has made the householder start taking up floorboards – the damage will become visible inside the house as floorboards or skirtings begin to distort and eventually crack into a square pattern. The damaged wood will look dry, usually brown, and will crumble away; there may be masses of red dust – the spores. Damp

patches or fungi may appear on plaster.
Treatment must be very thorough and is best left to experts. They will cut out affected timber and sound timber for 18in. beyond, hack off plaster for two feet all round, burn off brickwork, soak everything in sterilising fluid, replace wood with treated timber – and most important of all, find and put right the cause of the damp which started it all. It's very expensive; prevention is cheaper.

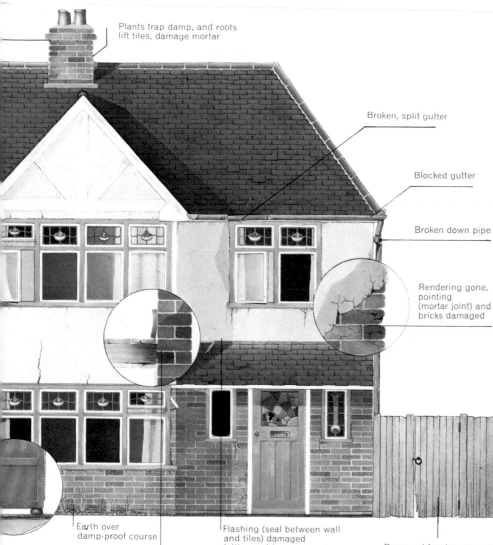

Plants trap damp, and roots lift tiles, damage mortar

Broken, split gutter

Blocked gutter

Broken down pipe

Rendering gone, pointing (mortar joint) and bricks damaged

Earth over damp-proof course

Flashing (seal between wall and tiles) damaged letting wet in

Damp joists, skirting board and floorboards rotting

Damaged fencing: sooner it is repaired and creosoted the cheaper the job will be

David Penney

Woodworm: they can eat your house away

Cutting off wet rot from its supplies

Wet rot can grow behind paint (above); cut out (top) and replace. Above: brown threads of wet rot

Wet rot is less serious than dry rot because the fungus responsible won't spread beyond the damp wood; it won't cross brick or plaster as a rule; it needs much greater moisture content in the wood to grow; and when the moisture is taken away the fungus stops growing. It should still be treated seriously because, even if the wet rot is stopped, the drying wood can be damp enough for dry rot to get a hold. It often occurs in window frames or sills, where the treatment is to scrape out small areas well back into clean wood, to cut out completely bigger areas of rot, to treat an area all round the damage with wood preservative, and to soak in preservative any timber used for repairs before fitting it. The threads in a well-developed example of wet rot are brown and the affected timber may be stained black, but it is not always easy to tell which you've got. Check surrounding timber, and brick and plaster nearby, for signs of the mycelium threads; if you find them away from the original patch you may have dry rot. If in doubt, seek expert advice. When repairs have been completed, find where the damp is coming from; around windows it may be defective paintwork or loose putty. Small cracks between brickwork and timber frames are best sealed with a non-hardening flexible sealer which allows for slight movement.

Counter-attack against woodworm

After damp, the second enemy of a house is woodworm, the grubs of various beetles which lay their eggs on timber. The grubs hatch, burrow into the wood and chew away for years before emerging as new beetles. You'll recognise woodworm attack by the holes, and sometimes by small heaps of what looks like sawdust. The Common Furniture Beetle does about three-quarters of all woodworm damage, attacking softwood or hardwood – and its name is a reminder that you can bring infection into a house by buying old furniture. The Death Watch Beetle affects mainly old houses; it lives on hardwood which has at some time suffered fungal attack. Much more dangerous in the Home Counties is the House Longhorn Beetle; its $\frac{1}{2}$ in. oval holes destroy wood fast. Smallest woodworm – you might call it the lesser of two weevils – is the Wood Boring Weevil. It favours damp wood.

Above and right: damage caused by commonest woodworm, the Common Furniture Beetle; and, below, the perpetrator – about $\frac{1}{8}$-in. long, and capable of producing up to eighty wood-eating grubs.

Woodworm infestation is not to be taken lightly; it can weaken houses seriously. At the same time, don't be panicked into signing on for expensive eradication treatment without getting at least a second estimate – and considering whether you can tackle the job yourself. The treatment is the same whichever beetle is feeding off your house; you impregnate the woodwork with a poison. The difficulty is that painted on the outside the oil-based poison may not reach grubs inside thick timbers, though sprays and injectors help, while over-generous treatment can stain ceilings and walls. Using fluid woodworm-poison is a messy job; you'll need to clear everything out of an infested attic, for example, including any insulation laid between the ceiling joists, so that you can get at as much timber as possible. The fluid can affect the insulation of some electric wiring, so you must protect wires, and perhaps take them off the timbers so that the fluid gets well into the wood. You'll need to wear a mask and gloves; the fluid could poison you as well as the woodworm. Above all keep flames, cigarettes, even electric lights, from the area (use a hand-torch). Oil vapour is explosive, and roofs *have* been blown off before now. Safer for amateurs to use are 'mayonnaise' woodworm killers.

These are pastes which, spread on top of the timbers with a brush or knife, penetrate slowly through. Up to now they have been available only to people in the trade (you may be able to get them from a builder's merchant) but one firm now plans to market its 'Woodtreat' retail. There are also slow-acting vapour insect killers which, left in the loft, will prevent beetle invasion and will eventually kill off beetles from a small infestation.

Death Watch Beetle; menace to hardwood in old buildings; great churchgoer. About $\frac{1}{4}$-in.

House Long-horn Beetle; found mainly around London. Nearly 1in. long, causes severe damage

For further information and advice on rot and woodworm treatment write to British Wood Preserving Association, 62 Oxford Street, London W1N 9WD

Removing or renewing a picture or plate rail and skirting boards

Removing a picture rail, either to renew a damaged section or to leave an un-cluttered stretch of wall, is comparatively easy; problems are filling in holes left behind and in removing many layers of paint and perhaps paper left around the rail. They must be removed or a ridge will show, even through heavy paper. If burning off paint, cover floor to protect it against burning. Wet holes before filling; rub down gently until flush.

1 Place chisel between wall and rail approximately in centre of length. Gently prise rail away

2 Slip piece of wood between rail and wall and make saw cut through rail to remove in pieces

3 Old paint can be removed by glasspapering, a blowtorch is easier. Make good damage

It's not advisable to fix picture rails to plasterboard. Concrete walls will need to be drilled (use Rawltool or percussion drill) and plugged for screw fixing; for other walls 2½in. cut nails will suffice. If replacing section of rail, take piece with you when buying to check match. Allow extra for mitring corners, and for joining lengths with mitres, too, as shown above

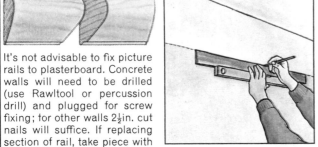

4 Using a straight edge and spirit level, pencil line on walls where rail is to be fitted, having decided on depth of the frieze

5 Cut rail to suitable lengths using mitre block for external and internal angles; cut ends, square for windows and doors

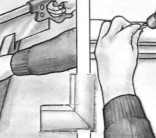

6 Fix to wall using 2½in. cut nails (screws in concrete). Drive home at downward angle so weight goes towards wall

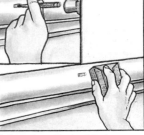

7 Punch nails just below surface of wood; countersink screws. Paint nail or screw heads to prevent rusting

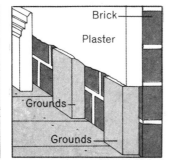

8 Skirting boards are fitted to grounds with cut nails. Don't split board. Punch nails below surface, fill holes with putty

Brick

Plaster

Grounds

Grounds

9 Grounds are nailed to the walls before plastering is completed. This ensures skirting will be flush and have a good fixing

Skirtings vary according to their age, from the older 375mm. (15in.) high with ornamental mouldings to 75mm. (3in.) modern chamfered types. Renewing a section of heavily moulded skirting may be quite expensive; it is almost impossible to buy from stock and would have to be purpose made. Replacing skirting is simple providing one knows that the fixing will be by nails into breeze walls, or to grounds – small pieces of wood fitted to the wall. You'll need: hammer, bolster, saw, punch, mitre block

10 When taking down old skirting start in the corner with board that overlaps. Use hammer and bolster to lever off

11 Replacing damaged section in the middle of a length. Lever away sufficiently to cut a mitre either side of damage, replace

Modernising an old-fashioned skirting and replacing with modern type it will be seen that the grounds are too large and need replacing. Plaster will need to be lowered so that new skirting can cover edge (plaster repairs, p. 18). Fit new grounds and cut lengths of skirting. External angles are mitred. For internal angles mark profile of skirting either on face of next section and cut out or, if curves make this too difficult, reverse board, mark on back at other end, then cut and put into place; nail home

12 Place length of skirting with square cut end against return wall, place skirting at right angle, pencil shape of profile

13 Using coping saw, carefully cut to line. Nail square cut board to wall. Position second board tight to fixed board and nail

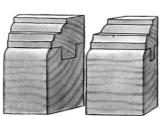

14 Join two lengths of skirting by using a mitred, not a butt, joint. This takes a little longer but will look neater and more professional, and will be stronger. Use a mitre block

15 To fix the skirting first mark position of the timber grounds on the face of the skirting, then place in position, nail home

Drawings by Su Huntley

OLDER OR PERIOD HOMES, AND SOME OF THE PROBLEMS OF UPKEEP

In the past 100 years or so most domestic building has settled into a comfortable rut of brick walls, tile or slate roof; but suppose you plan to buy an older house, a flint cottage, a timber house – or even one of the 1920s 'modern' houses; what problems will you meet? Home We've asked an architect about such houses. His comments are below. We also talked to a 300-year-old building company who deal with many such houses; their comments are in *italics*.

No matter how the inside of a house has been planned, the outside will always reflect the people it was originally built for. A country cottage with mud walls and a thatch roof looks like an extension of the land it was built on. Its garden, an essential part of the livelihood of the original owner, is an integral part of the design. By contrast, the 18th-century town house was designed to represent an ideal of elegant sophistication, man as the gods would

like him to be, not as he was. Victorian affluence is demonstrated by flights of fancy, executed with extravagant craftsmanship and use of materials. At the end of the century even the most humble of houses had a profusion of decoration. But there were some with simpler tastes, looking back on the Georgian and earlier periods with nostalgia. Neo-Georgian (really neo-William-and-Mary) was born. So was neo-Tudor, a picturesque but

economical style, easily applied to simple houses of the period, which had never quite gone out of fashion for estate cottages. Whatever the period, it is essential when redecorating or restoring a house to try to understand the ideas of the original designer. Look at the house from across the street and list any visual improvements – putting back the original window bars, moving the TV aerial, disguising pipes and cables. *Check the condition of roof tim-*

bers; woodworm treatment is almost inevitably necessary. Chimneys may be a cause of internal damp; fireplaces were provided in most rooms but seldom used today, so moisture isn't evaporated. Sealing the top of the flue while maintaining air movement by ventilators top and bottom will help, but you may have to replace old affected plaster. Rising damp isn't so serious as it once was; specialist firms can usually treat it effectively.

20th-century Concrete and Steel After the First World War contemporary engineers were excited with the combination of two old materials, concrete and steel, to make reinforced concrete, and architects felt obliged to explore the new materials for houses that would appear light, airy and labour-saving. Unfortunately, reinforced concrete required skills not easily available to the average builder. Reinforcement was often laid too near the surface, became damp, expanded with rust and broke the surrounding concrete away, allowing more damp to get in. The mouldings of earlier buildings, thought to be purely decorative, were found to have a function – they broke up the force of water flowing down a building. Cement renderings were often not resilient enough and cracked badly. Flat roofs, another symbol of the modern movement, proved disastrous as the structure below expanded and contracted, splitting the waterproof covering. Effective repairs to these houses require considerable expertise.
Parapet walls were usually of 9in. in unsuitable bricks which flaked; usually have to be rebuilt. Metal windows were not galvanised; replacement costly.

18th-century Mud Cottage A late 18th-century thatched cottage at Haddenham, Buckinghamshire, built from wychert – a local chalky clay which, mixed with straw, makes a good mud wall. A similar mix of chalk and clay made artificially is used elsewhere. Few mud houses are seen today because it lasts only as long as it is protected; to survive it must have good waterproof foundations and a roof with a large overhang, such as thatch, so that the rain is thrown clear of the walls. These cottages are warm in winter and cool in summer because both mud walls and thatch have great insulation values. There are several types of mud construction. In Devon they use cob, a mixture of earth, straw, gravel and sand mixed to a glue-like consistency and placed in layers, trodden down, the surplus pared off and holes for windows and doors cut out when it has dried. In East Anglia mud is formed into blocks and laid like bricks. Mud walls should be protected with lime plaster rendering and regularly-applied limewash.
The same decoration problems as stucco; right treatment essential to keep surface sound.

17th-century Stone This stone house near Bath has its main and garden walls, roof and paving all made from the same local limestone which is a glorious colour and can be easily cut to shape or split into slates. With so much richness it is unnecessary to use any other material. Extensions in new stone can be expensive, but it is possible to buy second-hand stone or to use one of the contemporary imitations which, from a sufficient distance, match well. There are many areas where stone is not so amenable. Here the carved stone is limited to small areas, around windows and on corners, the rough stone between being rendered. When these houses were built stone was relatively cheap, but now it has become expensive and thus a prestige symbol. For this reason many of these houses have had their rendering mistakenly stripped, exposing stone which was never meant to be seen. As a result the houses suffer from damp, since the rendering was an essential covering for the coarse material beneath. Cleaning stone should only be undertaken with expert advice and with the greatest care. Many fine stone buildings have been ruined by over-cleaning. Conversely, many grubby stone buildings have been allowed to be demolished because the planners did not realise the quality beneath. Buildings of this age usually had lead rainwater pipes and it is best to paint recent pipes lead grey. Rendered stone should be painted white to highlight exposed stonework.

19th-century Artisan Every prosperous town in Britain has such terraces, minimum houses of the late 19th century, yet well-built, ingeniously designed to use every inch of space and to give an air of solidarity and well-being. They combined a high degree of craftsmanship in their brickwork, plaster mouldings, joinery and the small tiled areas inside the front door. They are usually laid out in identical rows; in these everyone was equal. After 100 years their Welsh slate roofs are failing, usually due to the fixing nails rusting through. These roofs are an essential part of the design, and nothing looks worse than such a house re-roofed with red clay or black cement tiles. The best solution is to strip the roof, line it, and re-slate it with aluminium nails, using all the good slates on the front elevation; the rear roof can have cheaper alternatives. The bay window is often a source of damp (broken damp-proof course, or garden too high) which must be cured before starting on any exterior decoration. Use a stone-coloured masonry paint for the rendered sections, and a colour to blend with the brickwork for the timber. Try to get the council to replace street trees which have been cut down; these terraces usually had a small tree to each house.

19th-century stone This pair of cottages near King's Lynn, Norfolk, is built of local Snettisham sandstone, the only hard building stone in the county. Snettisham stone is difficult to shape and has many of the problems associated with flint, another material locally available. In these two cottages the stone has been treated as flint would have been, with brick surrounds to the windows and doors and at the corners. The design is simple and practical, with a central chimney stack keeping the warmth within the cottages. The delicate wrought-iron fence is typical of East Anglia, designed to keep the rabbits out while still allowing a view across the fields. Repointing, as with any house built before 1900, should be done with a weak mix, using white cement. The pantile roof is a development of the Roman system. Here they are red, but they are often glazed black. They are 's' shaped and were originally imported from Holland during the 17th century. At the beginning of the 18th century they were made at Tilbury and became popular in Somerset and the East and the North. The strong colours of the stone and roof tiles limit the possible choice of colours for the woodwork.
Stone houses have often been spoiled by rendering 'to keep the damp out' when the real cause was condensation.

20th-century Tile Hung The various taxes on bricks between 1784 and 1850 led builders to reduce the number of bricks used, especially in cottages. One method employed was to build only the ground floor in brick, while the upper half of the house was a timber frame clad in weatherboarding or clay tiles. This pair of cottages, built in 1902, long after the tax had been abolished, still reflects pre-1850 tax avoidance. The tiles are carefully made and laid in patterns, and on a simple design such as this they form the only decoration. If any of the tiles need replacing, as many as possible should be preserved and re-used to follow the original design. It is possible to purchase second-hand tiles to match from buildings which have been demolished in the area. (One of the marvellous things about traditional building materials is that they can be used and re-used over the centuries. Too many modern materials inherently have only short lives, and most modern construction methods have no possible reincarnation after demolition.) In redecorating cottages like these, the fences, garden and trees are just as important as the house. The brick ground-floor walls can look very pleasant in colourwash as an alternative to brick, but never paint the tiles.

Regency stucco. Stucco was developed during the 18th century to give a house the appearance of having been built with the finest stone. The texture, colour and mouldings associated with Portland and Bath stone were exactly simulated right down to reproducing the joints. Behind the stucco the real walls could be rough stone, brick or even timber. In many cases the mouldings have dropped off and the delicate window frames have been replaced by large sheets of glass. In restoring these houses try to get the original design copied exactly; if none of the original windows remain it is usually possible to find a similar house in the neighbourhood. The surrounding walls were always part of the architectural design and generally the railings and gate were cast iron, now often in bad repair and expensive to restore. In this house the original ironwork has been replaced by less-expensive timber, carefully designed to conform with the general character of the house.
Originally, stucco would have been decorated with a lime material; later coat after coat of modern cement-based paints may have been built up, imposing a load and tension which the soft lime beneath couldn't stand, and the surface may break away in great flakes. The only final cure is to strip off all the decoration and start again.

Early 19th-century Weatherboard Cottage When the great oak forests of Britain were spent and where there was no good local stone, substitute building materials had to be found. In the South East imported softwoods were used. Houses were built with light timber frames and then clad with weatherboarding, afterwards painted or tarred. It was part of a tradition of building which originated in Scandinavia, was carried by immigrants to North America, spread to the West Indies, and has since been re-imported as American colonial. This simple house at Tenterden, Kent, carries on the traditions of stone and stucco into timber. Such houses are often cold and draughty, because of their construction, but it is very easy to strip off the boarding, fill the framework with insulation such as glass fibre, line the walls with building paper and then re-cover it. It's a good idea to re-coat the woodwork with preservative at the same time. When replacing defective boarding, make sure it is the same size as the original. In Essex and Hertfordshire these houses are often painted black, with the windows and doors picked out in white; in Kent and Sussex, usually white. South London once had many, painted cream with red pantile roofs.

The houses, also often built with oak from demolished properties, are prone to woodworm attack, but people worry too much about woodworm; old houses always show woodworm holes. Provided the timber is treated there's nothing to worry about, though long-term neglect is dangerous, and expensive.

19th-century Flint This pair of flint cottages in Norfolk, one as it was built, the other altered to look like a contemporary council house, is like an antique chest of drawers, half of which has been covered with plastic laminate. Flints are extremely durable and have been used for house building since earliest times. Building with them requires great skill – because of their awkward shapes – and the craft is now almost dead. To help bind a flint wall bricks were often introduced in a random pattern. Bricks were also used for corners and window and door surrounds, all too difficult to make with flints. The Victorians liked to build country cottages in flint, despite the expense involved. Many of these cottages are now being raised in social status with the addition of coach lamps, Spanish pine doors and picture windows, making them sad little misfits; all the decoration they need is a simple colour scheme for the woodwork and a few roses in the garden. These cottages can be damp, because of the loose nature of the walls. The solution is to repoint them carefully with a weak mixture including white cement. The original mortar will have been lime, the whiteness of which shows off the delicate hues of the flints. Grey cement will kill their colours.

Sometimes faint cracks appear between edges of the flints and the pointing, even after repointing; an antidote has never been discovered, and such walls may be rendered as the only way to keep water out. Sometimes a wall improves as it weathers.

15th-century Timber Frame This 15th-century timber-frame house in Essex was built at a time when oak was plentiful; houses were also built from willow, hornbeam, elm and chestnut, but few have survived because those woods do not last as long as oak. Normally the frame was covered with rendering, tiles or boards, since these methods allowed the frame to move about without causing cracks and draughts. When the frame was designed to be exposed, it was always carefully proportioned and often carved. Exposed wood was usually left to weather a silver grey, or sometimes painted in bright colours – the black-and-white tradition is not Tudor but Victorian; black paint was not available before the mid-18th century. Because timber is always moving, and because English oak is impossible to season, timber-frame houses like these were put together after carpenters had studied how individual timbers were moving so that each was chosen and positioned then be restrained. The best material for repairing cracks in the framework is pliable polysulphide plastic.

If framing needs extensive repair there will be problems; each case will need study to find the right method of repair, and the joint skills of builder and a good timber merchant to select the right timbers. Weatherproofing is difficult, especially in exposed positions, and it is usually necessary to form a separate internal skin with a waterproof membrane between that and the outer wall. The original roof would have had cleft laths nailed to rafters and clay tiles hung with oak pegs. Later repairs have replaced the laths with sawn battens, the pegs with nails.

TOOLS OF THE TRADE and SPECIAL PROJECTS

Barry Jackson

Power tools

Power tools save time; they cost money, but because they enable the amateur to tackle jobs he couldn't do without them, they can save money too. With their various attachments they can lend the ordinary householder some of the accuracy it takes months to acquire with hand tools: "We sell saw-attachments so well because the average chap can't cut a straight line with a hand saw," admits one power-tool manufacturer.

Power tools fall into two groups: the purpose-built one-job tool with its motor self-contained, and the power drill with its accessories and attachments. Keen amateurs who want to do a lot of woodwork, for example, may need a purpose-built power saw and a cheap drill for other jobs. For most people a good drill with attachments added as they are needed would be a better buy.

All power tools for the handyman now are double-insulated. This eliminates the possibility of electric shock by using a non-conductive body for the tool: you can't touch anything that might become 'live'. It does away with the need for an earth connection, a source of fatal accidents in the past when amateurs – and even professionals, who should have known better – wired up their drills wrongly.

Most drills are classified by the size of their 'chuck' – the jaws that clasp the twist drill or accessory. The bigger the chuck the bigger the metal drill it can take. (You can drill bigger holes in wood because the business end of a wood drill can be larger than the shank which fits into the drill chuck.) The bigger the chuck the more power it will need and the greater the cost – and the weight – of the tool. Power tools incorporate a fan to keep the electric motor cool, so that a drill operating at full speed won't overheat even if used for long periods without a break. A drop in motor speed – a sign of overloading – can lead to overheating and a burnt-out motor. The more powerful the tool the harder it can work without slowing or overheating. Different materials, however, have different safe cutting speeds. A single-speed drill operates at about 2500 revs a minute. This is fine for sawing, sanding, and drilling up to about $\frac{3}{8}$in. holes in timber, but if you are boring bigger holes, or drilling steel, masonry or concrete, a slower speed is necessary to prevent damage to the twist drill or the material being drilled.

To get this lower speed, all but the cheapest drills are now available with a two-speed gearbox, usually giving 2500 rpm in top gear and about 1000 rpm in low gear. The same basic drill with a gearbox will cost about £5 more than without, and it is worth the extra money. Some tools – both single and two-speed – have a trigger speed control which gives lower speeds by restricting the electricity supply.

A $\frac{5}{16}$ or $\frac{3}{8}$in. *two-speed drill*, 1, is probably best all-round value for the householder; it will cost between £12 and £16 – though look out for bargains because there's a lot of price-cutting, in spite of rising costs.

Drilling bits, 2, vary in price from a few pence according to type and size.

Purpose-built power tools are more convenient than drills with attachments because you don't have to stop in the middle of a job to change accessories. Since they are built specifically for one job they are more efficient, but they cost more than attachments. They are the keen amateur's equipment rather than for the ordinary save-money householder.

Among the attachments for drills are *change-speed gearboxes*, useful if you already have a single-speed drill; they cost about £5. A *hammer attachment*, 3, about £5, is useful if you are going to make holes in hard concrete, and a *screwdriver* attachment (about £5) seems like a luxury until you tackle a piece of woodwork with 20 screws to drive home and your wrist is already aching after the first five.

Portable circular saw attachments, 4, about £7·50, take the hard work out of sawing; *jig saws* can cut intricate shapes in wood, plastics or metal. They are £5 to £8 each. Various bench stands (£5 or so) and drilling stands (£10–£15) enable you to fasten the tool on the bench and free your hands to control the job.

Rubber arbor, 5, is useful for quick sanding and removing old paint. *Wire brushes* will remove dirt and rust from outside ironwork, *grinding wheels* help take care of edged tools – remember to wear goggles to protect your eyes – and rag *buffing wheels* are useful for polishing. You can get a complete sanding-brushing-polishing-grinding outfit for £3–£6. An *orbital sander* attachment, 6, is best for a really smooth finish, leaving no sanding marks behind. It costs £4·50–£7. Don't forget that power tools are potentially dangerous. For their size and weight they pack a lot of power, between a third and half a horsepower, enough to do a lot of damage to the work or the operator.

Never leave them plugged in; switch off at the plug, or better still, unplug them when changing accessories. Check occasionally that accessories are firmly attached – vibration can sometimes loosen them. With circular saws make sure guard drops in place properly. Always use portable saws with both hands and never lock the trigger on. A circular saw can sometimes kick back unexpectedly if it hits a knot in wood, and if it slips out of your hands with the power on it becomes a fearsome weapon.

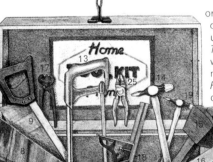

Hand tools

Our team of experts is not suggesting you need all the tools shown here if you are to tackle household jobs – which is just as well considering the current cost of tools. You may not need more than one or two of them for most jobs. Buy the tools as you need them, or hire some of them from your local hire shop. Remember, though, that most tools will earn their keep at some time.

If you are replacing a door, for example, you'll probably need a chisel, a screwdriver, a plane, a bradawl, maybe a saw. The total cost is likely to be no more than a builder might charge to hang the door for you – and he won't leave the tools behind for you to tackle the next job.

This is how the experts list a good tool-kit for the amateur prepared to do his own woodwork repairs:

Smooth plane, 7, steel No. 4; about £5. (You can substitute a Surform or similar plane at about half the price.)

General-purpose saw, 8; about £2. (Some new saws have replaceable or throw-away blades. It seems a waste, but a saw is no good when blunt, and people who sharpen saws are hard to find and expensive.) Or you may be able to use a power saw, less convenient but less hard work, and a *Tenon saw*, 9; (about £2), useful for delicate work and small jobs.

Chisels, 10; 1in., $\frac{1}{2}$in., $\frac{1}{4}$in.; about £4 for three. Ask for *firmer* chisels. They have square, not bevelled, sides, making them tougher and easier for the amateur to sharpen.

Hammer, 12oz., 14; For this our experts suggest a *Warrington* or *cross pein* pattern, where the head is round and the other flat for starting small nails without damaging your fingers. The alternative is a *claw hammer*, where the back of the head is used for clawing out nails. Hammers come with wood or steel handles and cost anything from £1 up to several pounds.

Tack hammer, 19; light weight, easier on small nails and fingers.

Files, 26; one fine, one coarse; you can get them flat or half round – one side rounded, the other flat. Useful for rounding off corners, minor shaping and smoothing. From about 50p. *Pincers*, 17; (about £1), *pliers*, 25; (about £2).

Mallet, 15; about £2 – but we'll show how to make your own.

Oilstone, 16; 2in. medium, about £1. Sharp tools make light work; oilstones keep them sharp.

Combination square, 18; £1 to £3, to get your work square.

Hacksaw, 13; for cutting metal and plastics (useful when you come to plumbing, too), £1 to £4.

Bradawl, 12; holes to start screws; 25p to 50p.

Screwdrivers, 20; large, medium, small. Using wrong-size screwdriver ruins screws, sometimes hands too. Right size makes the job easy. A Philips pattern screwdriver, 11, (for screws and small bolts with a cross instead of a slot) is useful too. From about 20p to about £2 according to size.

Panel push-pin, 21; easier than a hammer if you've a lot of panel-pins to drive home. About 60p.

G-cramps, 22; from about 50p according to size; big ones are expensive.

Quick-acting cramp, 23; also known as veneering or lush cramp. Holds things still while you work on them, glue them. About £3; hard to find, worth finding.

Mitre box, 24; slots saw for cutting angles.

All prices are approximate – shop around for the best.

Tools of the trade, and how to use them

Where possible use nails so any pull on them is sideways, not vertical. Nail bottom of a box, for example, through sides into edges of bottom rather than up through bottom into sides where the weight could easily pull the nails out

Panel pin: for fixing thin wood or ply. Best driven in with push-pin tool, not a hammer

Hardboard pin: when driven into hardboard, tapered head disappears almost completely

Galvanised clout nail: for roofing felt, sashcords, fencing. Galvanising prevents rust

Lost head nail: for quality flooring and work where head needs to be inconspicuous

Cut floor brad: for floorboards where visible head doesn't matter. Shape avoids splitting

Oval wire nail: for general woodwork, especially in thin or short-grain wood

Cut nail: grips very strongly. Blunt point tears wood which cuts risk of splitting

Round wire nail: general purpose nail; head helps grip and won't spoil appearance

Corrugated fastener: for joining battens in rough frames; quick, cheap, can cause splits

Dome head screw: chrome screw-on cover hides slotted head. For mirrors, bath panels

Round head screw: usually black-painted steel, or brass. For fitting ironmongery to timber

Raised head screw: usually brass when needing occasional removal – brass won't stick

Star head, Philips, Pozidriv screws: grip of cross reduces risk of screwdriver slipping

Countersunk head screw: for most uses, e.g. wood-to-wood fixing and fixings to wall plugs

Zinc-coated or sherardised screw: Rust-resistant; stronger than alternative alloy screws

Steel screws rust, so for damp situations use zinc or alloy screws or (more expensive) brass. Avoid using zinc or alloy screws with ironmongery composed of other metals, where corrosion may be set up

Some special fixings

Rawlnut: Flexible cylinder expands to grip hole when bolt is tightened

Gravity toggle: for fixing to skin of vertical cavity (like a flush door).

Spring toggle: arms fold, then spring out

FIXINGS
Nails, screws and pins

Nails and screws look simple, but there's a skill in using them and in knowing which ones to use. That's why shelves put up by an expert stay up, while shelves many amateurs put up fall down; and why the amateur carpenter often splits the wood he is working on (and sometimes his thumb) while the professional carpenter gets away with what looks like the same operation without any damage. Here we show some of the experts' methods

The art of nailing—and how to protect the wood

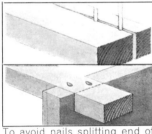

To avoid nails splitting end of wood, keep them at least nine times nail diameter from end, blunt end of nail, or nail first, trim end of wood off afterwards

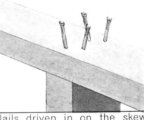

Nails driven in on the skew ('tosh nailing' to the experts) give better resistance to pulling out. One nail driven straight first will prevent wood slipping

Small nails in big fingers mean that fingers get hammered more than nails. Put nail into piece of thin card first, use that to hold it, pull off when secure

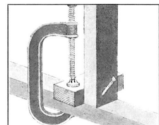

Nailing at angle is difficult – wood moves out of place – unless clamped block is used to give firm grip until the nail has been hammered fully home

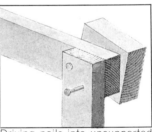

Driving nails into unsupported timber, as in this piece of framing, may strain bouncing wood, so hold heavy block (or a hammer) on the other side

The tightest grip—preparing wood for screws

Timber to be fixed with screws should be pre-bored with a drill the size of the screw shank, countersunk if it is a countersunk head screw. Piece of timber receiving the screw should be drilled with a small drill or a bradawl to make driving easier, lessen risk of splitting. If driving is still difficult rub screw with soap. Brass screws are soft, and rough treatment can break heads off, so drive home a steel screw first, remove and then screw home the brass one. For fastening ironmongery to brickwork drill (slow speed) with masonry drill and use fibre or plastic wall plug. Drill and plug should have same number as screw – 10 drill and 10 plug for No 10 screw, for example. Concrete chews up masonry drills so use Rawlplug chisel instead, turning as you hammer it. If you run out of plugs use strip of paper rolled into tight cylinder and put into hole with spiral anticlockwise. For irregular holes use plastic wall-plugging material, making hole in it when set.

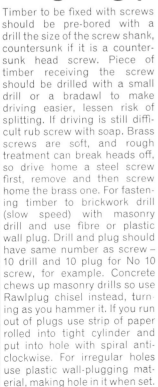

When using wall plugs, plug and masonry drill should be the same number as the screw

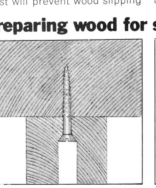

Where thick timber is to be fastened, deep countersunk hole avoids need for long screw

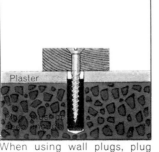

Mark screw positions first, and then use a drill of the same diameter as shank of the screw

Rough-shaped filler

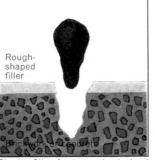

Plastic filler for irregular holes is moistened with water, rough-shaped, pushed into hole. When set, a pilot hole is made for the screw. This kind of fixing is reasonably strong, but not so strong as a

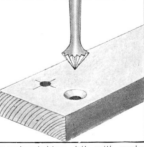

Countersinking bit will make tapered hole so head of screw lies snugly below the surface

Pilot hole for screw

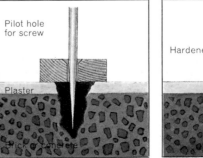

hole drilled into brickwork and plugged. Substitute for light loads: cotton wool mixed with Polyfilla

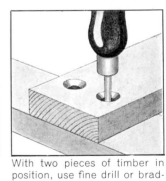

With two pieces of timber in position, use fine drill or bradawl to make pilot hole for screw

Hardened filler

Making your own workbench

Self-sufficient householders need a work-bench: it saves time, trouble, gashed fingers, spoiled work. A stout table will do – most modern kitchen tables aren't tough enough – but making your own workbench is even better. The top is a second-hand panelled door (a few shillings from a demolition site: don't pick a very wide one) or a piece of blockboard. It stands against a solid wall – inside the garage is a good place – and can either be set up permanently if there's room, or be made to fold down flat against the wall until needed

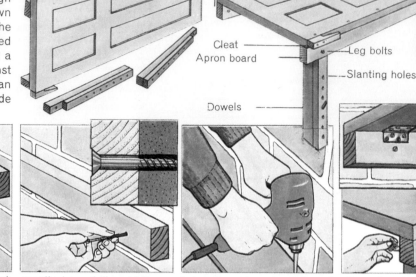

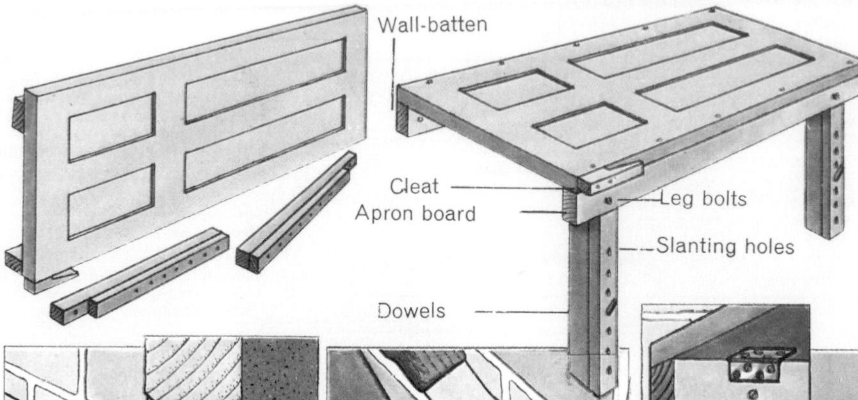

Wall-batten · Cleat · Apron board · Leg bolts · Slanting holes · Dowels

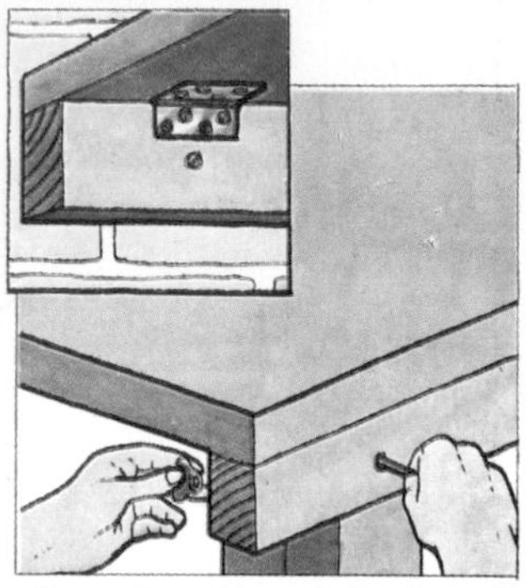

Bench legs are 2in.x2in.; comfortable working height is the length from your knuckles to the ground. (1) Screw and glue each to a 2in.x1¼in. piece, 3¾in. shorter. (2) Prop legs against wall to hold wall batten, a piece

To make the special work bench you'll need these materials: old panelled door or sheet of 19mm. blockboard; 4 metres of 100mm.x30mm., 2 metres 50mm.x50mm., 2 metres 50mm.x30mm., and a piece of 12mm. ply about 12in.x10in.; 3in. No 10 screws, No 10 wall plugs, a short piece of ½in. dowel, two 3in.x⁵⁄₁₆in. bolts with wing nuts, three 3in. backflap hinges (for the folding bench) with screws to fit, and some PVA wood glue.

of 4in.x1¼in., length of bench top. Drill five holes through wood and 2in. into wall with No 10 masonry drill. (Drill brick slowly, with single speed drill use short bursts, press gently, clean out dust fre-

Basic information: joining timber with screws is easy if you remember: clamp pieces to be joined, drill through outer piece with drill same size as shank of screw you plan to use – No 10 drill for No 10 screw, for example. Just touch inner piece of wood to mark position. ●Use countersink bit to start if you're using countersink head screws. ●Start hole in inner piece with awl or gimlet. ●Rub screw on soap to lubricate it. ●Use big enough screwdriver.

quently, keep drill cool.) Power drill makes things easy; if not a geared hand-drill will do, or a brace for the timber, a Rawltool and hammer for brick. (3) Plug bricks with No 10 wall plugs, screw batten to wall. Drill five

To grip material being worked at the bench make this wedging cleat. Then drill ½in. slanting holes 1in. deep and 4in. apart on legs. Short ½in. thick dowels at appropriate height will hold boards to be planed; cleat will steady front edge, a G-clamp grip against apron board if necessary. For bench top jobs make bench hook from ½in. ply and two battens glued and nailed or screwed. You are now equipped to tackle almost anything about the house that

holes through outer edge of bench top, screw another 4in.x 1¼in. piece flush with edge as front apron board, then drill through apron board and leg to take bolt with wing nut on inside. (4) For fixed bench, screw

needs a woodworking bench, and you've saved around £40.

Bench hook

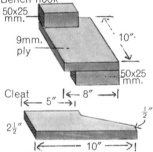
50x25 mm. · 9mm. ply · 10″ · 50x25 mm. · Cleat · 5″ · 8″ · ½″ · 2½″ · 10″

other edge of bench top to wall batten; for folding bench hinge top (5) to batten (to fold just unbolt legs). Drill holes in floor under legs, drive screw halfway into bottom of leg, cut off screwhead for a locating peg

Going Metric

Timber is officially sold in metric sizes, though any timber merchant will take orders in feet and inches and supply the nearest (very close) size. Most still think in inches anyway. Nuts, bolts and ironmongery generally are still usually sold in inches. Quick conversion: 25mm.=1in.; 1 metre=3ft. 3in. approx.; 1ft.=305mm. We have given sizes both ways here.

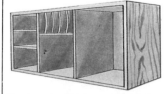

STOWAWAY
storage unit

This useful storage unit, with or without doors, fits on the shelf system (p. 91)

Use template (see page 91) to drill ⁷⁄₁₆in. holes 5in. apart in unit sides

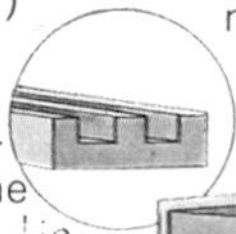

Similar ply dividers with glued and pinned joints can form light shelves or pigeonholes for a desk tidy to fit over the desk unit. Take care shelves don't block holes for hanging dowels. Ply doors (use plastic piano-hinge) can be added if needed

Like the modular shelf unit and desk unit, the storage unit is built from birch ply and hangs on the upright rails by short lengths of ⅜in. dowel for which rails and storage unit sides are pierced. Unit is designed to be 14in. deep, 14in. high, though these measurements are not important; the vital dimension is the width so unit fits snugly between rails. Top and bottom are ¾in. ply 29in. wide, making overall width when the ½in. ply sides are fitted, of 30in., same as the desk.

Easiest doors to make for the whole storage unit are of ⅛in. birch ply sliding in grooved strip – you can buy this, either in wood or in plastic, from most do-it-yourself shops. The strip is glued and pinned into place, then measurements taken from which to cut the doors. Sand the complete storage unit – any supporting shelves and desk – before either priming and painting or finishing with clear or coloured varnish. To hide ply edges, glue and pin ½in. moulding neatly over them.

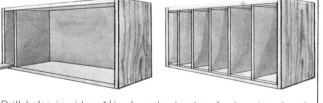

Drill holes in sides, 1⅛in. from back edge, for hanging dowels. Then use No. 6 drill through sides into edges of base and top, fit wall plugs into holes in edges, screw on sides. Add a ⅛in. ply back to unit, glued and pinned. Cut dividers from ⅛in. ply. Glue and pin narrow ply strips inside top and bottom as spacers, starting from left; slide divider into place, glue and pin next strip and so on. (Easier than grooving top and bottom to take dividers.)

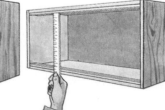

Pin and glue wood track into place. Punch nail heads below track or doors may stick on them. Plastic track is better drilled for nails to avoid splitting; glue may be enough

Top track has deeper groove than bottom so doors can slip into place. Hold ruler right into top track, measure to top edge of bottom track. Cut doors so they slip in, drop into groove

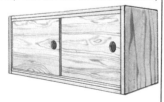

For handles cut circular hole to take circular sunk handle-plates. Wooden handles can be screwed from inside door, or other handles fitted if fastening will clear other door

SHELVES

No house ever has too many shelves, and owners who can put them up will be popular.

A cupboard used to be just that; the board or shelf where cups stood. It was given doors to keep out the dust; now that central heating and clean-air campaigns have cut dust, shelves are coming out into the open again and the introduction of man-made boards, especially standard-sized veneered or plastic-coated chipboards, has made the fitting of shelves easier and cheaper. There are other shelf materials; planed timber, plywood, blockboard (which, unlike all the others, should have the surface grain running from back to front, not lengthways). Thickness depends on the load; try a sample loaded with books if you are not sure. For various kinds of shelf supports look round do-it-yourself shops – there are scores of systems. Most are held up by plugging and screwing into the wall; ensure plugs go through plaster well into bricks or sooner or later the lot will collapse.

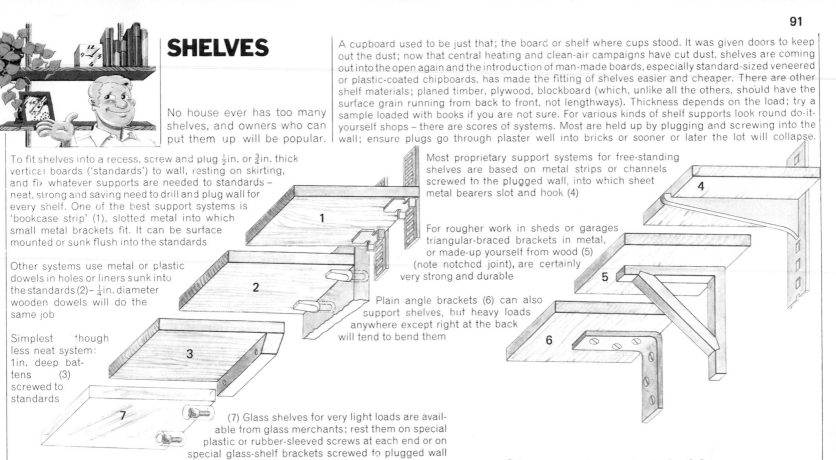

To fit shelves into a recess, screw and plug ½in. or ¾in. thick vertical boards ('standards') to wall, resting on skirting, and fix whatever supports are needed to standards – neat, strong and saving need to drill and plug wall for every shelf. One of the best support systems is 'bookcase strip' (1), slotted metal into which small metal brackets fit. It can be surface mounted or sunk flush into the standards

Other systems use metal or plastic dowels in holes or liners sunk into the standards (2)– ¼in. diameter wooden dowels will do the same job

Simplest though less neat system: 1in. deep battens (3) screwed to standards

(7) Glass shelves for very light loads are available from glass merchants; rest them on special plastic or rubber-sleeved screws at each end or on special glass-shelf brackets screwed to plugged wall

Most proprietary support systems for free-standing shelves are based on metal strips or channels screwed to the plugged wall, into which sheet metal bearers slot and hook (4)

For rougher work in sheds or garages triangular-braced brackets in metal, or made-up yourself from wood (5) (note notched joint), are certainly very strong and durable

Plain angle brackets (6) can also support shelves, but heavy loads anywhere except right at the back will tend to bend them

Secret hold-up: the stopped housing joint

Shelves fitted between standards don't have to have any visible supports. A housing joint – a slot the thickness of the shelf, made by chiselling out between two saw-cuts – will enable the shelf to slip into place. Neater, but more difficult, is a slot which doesn't show at the front, a stopped housing. Don't use these for long shelves which might bend in the middle and slip out of the housing; if in doubt fit a support in the middle and glue and screw the joints.

This modular system, designed for simplicity, will take shelves, storage cabinets and a desk, and the various fittings can be changed or moved about. It can be as large as you like, covering a wall from floor to ceiling, or start small and be extended later. The only precise measurements are between the holes through which dowels support the various parts on the vertical rails, and for this you'll need to make a template. Do this by drilling two holes 5in. apart with a 7/16 inch drill in a strip of half-inch ply.

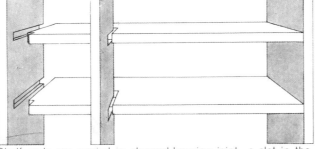

Shelf ends are carried in stopped-housing joint – a slot in the vertical supports which isn't visible from front. If shelves are long and liable to bend when loaded stiffen with a centre support

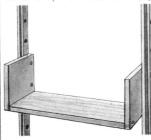

Using shelf as spacer, plug walls and screw rails in place. Use ⅜in. dowels through rail and shelf-ends to hold shelves in place. (With units side by side, one dowel can hold two.)

Clamp two strips of ½in. by 2in. timber together, mark straight line 1¼in. from edge and, using template, drill 7/16in. holes through both strips together

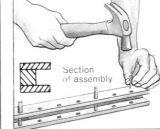

Assemble strips with glue and panel pins to sandwich a 1in. square strip. Put dowels in holes to keep holes in line during assembly; *this is important*

Once you've built one shelf unit, you can go into mass-production of them until you've as many shelves as you want. With the same principle you can build a desk – or his-and-her desks. The top is a piece of half-inch ply 29in. wide and 26in. from back to front, reinforced with 1in. strip all round underneath and supported by ½in. ply sides, one piece 28in. by 21in. To get the curve right, cut it from cardboard first; one cut should make both sides. Draw round cardboard, turn it over to check.

Cut the curve with a jig-saw or padsaw; if you've doubts, it can be straight-cut. Use template to drill holes in sides. Screw and glue 1in. square strip all round underside of top; screw and glue sides to top. A piece of 3in. diameter half-round strip glued and pinned in place will cover the desk edge and its reinforcing strip

Shelves that climb ladders

Dowels and 2in. by 1in. timber make this system of two miniature ladders which can support shelves at any height or distance apart. Clamp all four ladder sides while you drill them to make sure holes are same distance apart on each strip. It can be free-standing (a diagonal brace will keep it square) or frame can be screwed to wall. If you don't like look of dowel ends, drill holes in outer frame only part-way through. Insert the dowels from back.

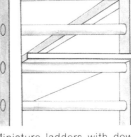

Miniature ladders with dowels for rungs hold shelves; frame joints are glued and screwed

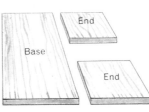

Shelves are ¾in. birch ply, the base 28½in. long, 8in. wide, the ends 8in. square. Clamp two ends and use template to drill 7/16in. holes in them. Panel-pin ends to shelf temporarily while you screw them together

Drill (No. 10 drill) through ends into shelf; insert wall-plugs (to grip end-grain better), countersink and screw ends to shelf using three 2in. No. 10 screws

Desk fits between rails and is held, like the shelves, by ⅜in. dowels tapped through rails into the sides.

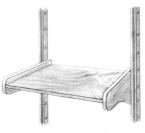

Wall-cupboards are built in precisely the same way, but smaller: we suggest 32in. high, 15in. from back to front. Drill and plug wall to fix them; for extra strength – and a place to hang kitchen tools – rest wall-cupboards on a 1in. by 6in. board screwed and plugged to wall. Before fixing, check with spirit level

kitchen unit

This kitchen unit with its working top is based on sections approximately 25in. wide; but check the space you want to fill and if necessary adjust the measurements to fit. Construction, in ply and softwood, is simple.

Ends and dividers are of $\frac{1}{4}$in. ply reinforced with 1in. or $1\frac{1}{4}$in. square softwood strips (it does not matter which you choose, but stick to the same size throughout) glued and pinned to the plywood. Crosspieces support shelves or drawers

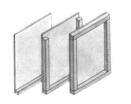

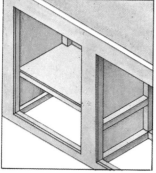

Dividers have framing on both sides; ends on the inside only. Glue framing and panel-pin every roughly 4in. With a lot of panel-pins to fasten buy a pin-push – easier than hammering

Assemble by screwing through reinforcing strips, front and back to ends and dividers, and up through ends, front and back to the top – a sheet of $\frac{3}{4}$in. ply. Half-inch ply doors can be fixed with plastic piano-hinge or ordinary $1\frac{1}{2}$in. brass or steel hinges. Magnetic catches are cheap and easy to fix, or you can use push-release catches – one push shuts the door, another releases it and it springs open. Handles? Buy them, or drill a finger-hole in each door, or file away the inner edge of the door to provide an easy grip

Unit assembled, with shelf in position. Add extra side strips if you want more shelves

The front is cut from one sheet of $\frac{1}{4}$in. ply, in our case 75in. long by 32in. wide (a good working height; alter it if you are extra tall or short). Don't worry about the waste cut out – that will make some of the shelves. Drill hole in corner of each marked-out opening, insert padsaw or (worth getting) blade of jigsaw attachment to power drill. Reinforce with softwood strips. Gap between these strips is width of ply dividers plus each divider's two reinforcing strips; check this because timber measurements can vary slightly. Back is same size cut from $\frac{1}{8}$in. ply similarly reinforced. Doors are of half-inch ply; they will not need any reinforcement

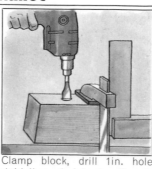

Doors: here with push-release catch and individual hinges; or use magnet catch, piano-hinge

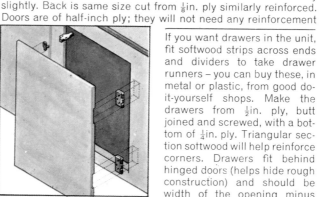

If you want drawers in the unit, fit softwood strips across ends and dividers to take drawer runners – you can buy these, in metal or plastic, from good do-it-yourself shops. Make the drawers from $\frac{1}{2}$in. ply, butt joined and screwed, with a bottom of $\frac{1}{4}$in. ply. Triangular section softwood will help reinforce corners. Drawers fit behind hinged doors (helps hide rough construction) and should be width of the opening minus clearance for drawer runners. These runners screw or pin on framing and sides of drawer.

Cover the raw edge of the $\frac{3}{4}$in. ply top and its covering laminate with a rounded plastic moulding glued and nailed into place. Punch these (and all other) nails below surface, fill holes with wood-filler

All reinforcing strips 1in.–$1\frac{1}{4}$in. square: keep to one size

Shelves are from $\frac{1}{4}$in. ply with reinforcing strip back and front. Cut away back corners and reinforcements to clear upright framing of ends and dividers. Sides of shelves rest on crosspieces of the ends and dividers. Don't fasten them in place – loose ones are easier to clean

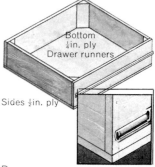

Drawer runners: several kinds are available from good iron-mongers or do-it-yourself shops

Barry Jackson

How to make a hardwood mallet

To wallop wood without damaging it, the amateur carpenter needs a mallet; here's how to make your own. You need a block of beech or other close-grained hardwood about 125mm. by 80mm. by 50mm. (5in. by 3in. by 2in.) for the head; a piece of dowel or broom handle an inch in diameter and about a foot long, and a wedge cut from scrap wood.

Clamp block, drill 1in. hole right through (check with set-square to get a right-angle)

Slot dowel end; shape block with plane, saw ends to angle meeting at bottom of handle

Hammer home wedge until handle is firm; then saw off flush with the top of block

BUILDING TERMS EXPLAINED

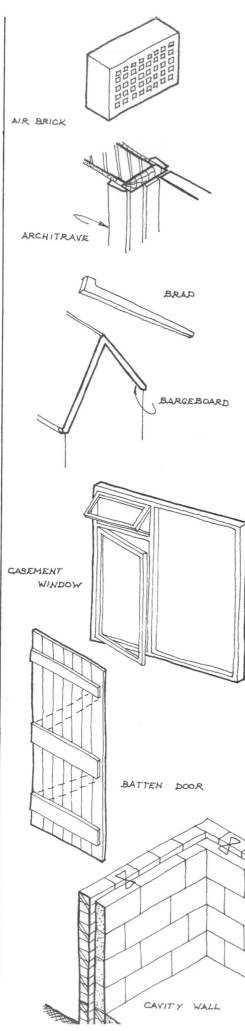

AIR BRICK

ARCHITRAVE

BRAD

BARGEBOARD

CASEMENT WINDOW

BATTEN DOOR

CAVITY WALL

Aggregate
Broken stone, gravel, sand or slag used with cement to form concrete. Aggregates may be coarse or fine and are measured by the size of a screen or mesh through which they will pass.   see also: BALLAST.

Air Brick
A perforated brick for building into a wall to allow the passage of air for ventilation purposes. Used, for instance, to ventilate the underside of a wooden floor.

Architrave
A moulding round a doorway or window opening. It usually covers the joint between the frame and the wall finish, thus hiding any shrinkage gaps which may occur.

Ball Valve or Ball Cock
A valve or cock actuated by a spherical copper or plastic float on the end of a cranked lever. The level of the water on which the ball floats determines whether the valve is open or closed.

Ballast
Unscreened gravel containing sand, grit and stones; excavated material from sea or river deposits in the form of sand and shingle, used as an aggregate in concrete; "all-in ballast" is a combination of stones and sand suitable for use as the only aggregate required in concrete.

Baluster
A post or vertical pillar supporting a handrail or parapet rail.

Balustrade
A collective name for a row of balusters or other infilling below a handrail on a stair, bridge, parapet, etc.

Banister
Term used in Scotland and several other areas for a baluster.

Bargeboard
A gable board or verge board. The inclined board, on a gable of a building, which covers and protects the ends of the roof timbers. Old barge boards were often decoratively carved.

Bat
A part of a brick, cut crosswise, and referred to by size, e.g. ½ bat or ¾ bat.

Batten
1) A length of square-sawn softwood 48 to 102 mm (2 to 4 inches) thick and 102 to 203 mm (4 to 8 inches) wide.
2) Softwood length of small section (50 x 25 mm, or 2 x 1 inch) used as a fixing for roof slates or tiles, or for sheet materials.
3) A vertical board in a batten door.
see also COUNTER BATTEN.

Batten Door or ledged door
A door composed of vertical boards or battens fixed to three or more horizontal ledges at the back, which are often diagonally braced. There is no frame round the edges.
cf FRAMED AND LEDGED DOOR
      FRAMED LEDGED AND BRACED DOOR

Bed
1) A bearing surface of any component in a building, being normal (i.e. at right angles) to the loading pressure.
2) A layer of mortar or other material which forms a bearing surface. e.g. mortar under bricks or stones, concrete under a drain pipe, putty under glass.

Bit
1) An interchangeable cutting point used in a brace, a lathe or a drilling machine.
2) The head of a soldering iron, usually made of copper.

Blockboard
A built-up board, having a core of wooden strips up to 25 mm (1 inch) wide laid with alternating grain and

glued between outer veneers whose grain runs in the opposite direction. This gives the board good rigidity and dimensional stability.
cf CHIPBOARD, HARDBOARD, LAMINBOARD, PLASTERBOARD, PLYWOOD.

Bolster
A bricklayer's cutting chisel, about 120 mm wide.

Bond
The regular arrangement of bricks or stones in a wall so that the units are held together in a solid, stable mass. Recognised patterns or bonds are used, the principal ones being English, Flemish, header, stretcher, garden wall and diagonal.

Bookcase Strip
A metal strip with slots at regular intervals into which nibs or angles may be fitted as required to provide support for a shelf. The strips are fixed vertically on a timber frame or divider.

Brace
1) A cranked tool used for holding and revolving a drilling or boring bit to make holes in wood.
2) That part of a framed structure which crosses a space diagonally and provides extra strength by its resistance to tensional or compressive forces.

Brad
A cut nail, tapering in width but of constant thickness, with a square head projecting on one edge only. Used chiefly for fixing floorboards they vary in length from 50 to 62 mm (2 to 2½ inches). Confusingly, an oval-wire brad is a wire nail formed from oval wire.

Bradawl
A small hand-tool with a narrow chisel point which is pushed into timber to make starter holes for nails or screws.

British Standard, or British Standard Specification, or BS
A description or specification of the qualities of a material and, where applicable, the dimensions of a product. The specification is determined by a specially appointed committee of the British Standards Institution, and issued as a numbered publication. Reference to it is usually by the initials BS followed by the appropriate number.
cf. CODE OF PRACTICE.

Buttering
The spreading of mortar on the vertical face of a brick before laying — difficult for the novice to achieve but an important part of bricklaying if the finished wall is to be well bonded.

Capillary Joint
A joint used in light gauge copper tubing. Several types are available but all are based on the same principle. A pipe is inserted into a fitting which is only slightly larger in diameter, thus creating a capillary space which aids the flow of molten solder round the faces to be joined. In some jointing fittings rings of solder are built in so that once the pipes are placed in position heat applied to the outside of the joint causes the solder to flow, thus completing the joint.
cf COMPRESSION JOINT.

Capstan Head
On a tap, a head with projecting bars as an aid to turning the tap on or off.

Casement
The hinged, pivoted or fixed sash of a window.

Casement Window
A window composed of hinged, pivoted or fixed sashes.

Cavity Wall
Wall constructed of two separate thicknesses or leaves separated by a 50 mm cavity (2 inches). The leaves are connected at intervals by *wall ties,* and may be of equal thicknesses or may have a thicker inner leaf to take the floor loads.
see also: WALL TIES

Ceiling Rose
A decorative plate, boss or trim through which an electric light flex hangs from a ceiling.

Chair Rail
A wooden moulding fixed horizontally on a wall to prevent damage by chair backs. The development of hard plasters made such rails unnecessary.
see also: DADO RAIL.

Chase
A channel or groove formed or cut into walls and floors to receive pipes, cables or conduits.

Chipboard
Waste wood chips compressed into a board, using synthetic resins as binders. The board may be obtained faced with veneers if a decorative finish is required.

Chisel
A steel cutting tool. There is a wide variety of these used by different craftsmen working in wood, metal, brick or stone. Wooden-handled chisels require a mallet but all-steel chisels, known as cold chisels, are used with a hammer.

Circuit-Breaker
A switch or other device for interrupting an electric circuit. It turns off when overloaded by current.

Cleaning Eye
Sometimes known as an access eye or rodding eye. An opening in a drain closed by a bolted-on plate, the removal of which allows the drain to be rodded to clear blockages. It is often provided at pipe bends and in inspection chambers.

Cleat
A small piece of wood (1) used to give positive location to another timber, (2) plugged to a wall to carry a bracket or shelf, (3) used as a cramp when working on timbers, (4) used to give a foothold on a raking board.

Closer
A brick or stone cut to complete the bond at the corner of a wall.
see also: QUEEN CLOSER and KING CLOSER.

Club Hammer
A double-faced hammer with a head weighing 0.7 to 1.8 kg. Used by bricklayers and stone-masons.

Cobbles
Rounded stones used for decorative paving.

Cock
A valve for controlling the flow of water, gas or other fluid in a pipeline.
see also: DRAIN COCK, FULL-WAY VALVE, PLUG COCK and STOP COCK.

Code of Practice, or BSCP, or CP
A statement, issued as a numbered publication by the British Standards Institution, of what is considered to be good practice in the trade or craft described. Reference to a British Standard Code of Practice is usually by the initials CP followed by the appropriate number.
cf. BRITISH STANDARD

Cold Chisel
see CHISEL.

Collar Beam
A horizontal tie-beam of a roof, which is joined to opposing rafters at a level above that of the wall plates.

Compression Joint
A joint used in light gauge copper tubing. It is made by screwing together the ends of the pipes to be joined and the special jointing fitting. Brass nuts are tightened to draw the pipe end into the joint where a wedging action is achieved which makes the connection watertight. Although the finished joint is not as neat as a capillary joint it is simpler to make.

Coping
A finishing to the top of a wall, made of hard bricks, stone, concrete, metal or terra cotta, designed as a protection against the weather. It often has a sloping, or weathered, top surface, projects beyond each face of the wall and has grooves or "drips" on the underside of the projection to help to throw off the rainwater flow clear of the wall face.

Coping Saw
A bow saw, used for cutting tight curves, with a blade about 3mm wide and 150mm long.

Cornice
(1) A large moulding at the junction between an inside wall and the ceiling. see also: COVE.
(2) A moulding at the top of an outside wall which projects and throws rain drips clear of the wall.

Counter Battens
In roofing, battens fixed parallel to the rafters on top of boarding and felt. Slating or tiling battens are then nailed over them. In this way any rain or snow blown under the roofing slates can escape when it flows down the roofing felt instead of being held by the horizontal battens as it might otherwise be. Because of the cost, this type of construction is used only in high quality work.

Countersinking
The conical sinking round the end of a hole drilled for a screw, which enables the screw head to lie flush with the surrounding material. It is made by a countersink bit.

Cove
A concave moulding at the junction between an inside wall and the ceiling or, less frequently, between an inside wall and a floor.
The ceiling cove may be of fibrous plaster, plasterboard or expanded polystyrene in pre-formed sections and is useful in concealing the cracks which often occur in plasterwork at this junction.

Cylinder Lock
A lock for an entrance door, opened by a key from the outside and a knob from the inside. A catch on the inside enables the latch to be fixed in either the shut or the open position. Cylinder locks may be fitted on the inner face of the door (rim type) or within the thickness of the door (mortise type).

Dado
The lower part of a wall, usually from the skirting to about waist-height, which is panelled or decorated differently from the upper part of the wall. Originally designed to avoid the soiling or damage of the wall where people or furniture brushed against it.

Dado Rail
A wooden moulding fixed to the wall or capping panelling and forming the topmost part of a dado.
see also: CHAIR RAIL.

Damp-Proof Course or DPC
A layer of impervious material. Placed in walls, usually at 150mm. above ground level and below any ground floor timbers, to prevent moisture from rising. Also used round door and window openings, in solid ground floors and in parapet walls above the junction with a roof, to prevent moisture penetration to the inside of the building. Vertical damp-proof courses (known as tanking) are used to keep basements dry. The material used for this purpose is asphaltic, but other damp-proof courses may be of flexible sheet metal, vitreous engineering bricks, plastic sheet or other impervious material.
cf. FLASHING.

Dead Shore
A heavy vertical timber, used in pairs to support a needle and thus carry the weight of the wall above.

Double-Hung Sash Window
A window in which the opening lights slide vertically within a cased frame, counterbalanced by weights supported on sash cords which pass over pulleys in the frame (sash pulleys).

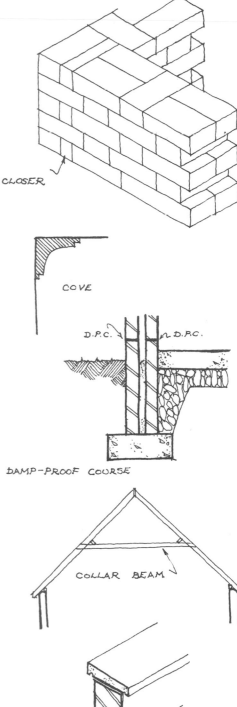

CLOSER

COVE

D.P.C.   D.P.C.

DAMP-PROOF COURSE

COLLAR BEAM

COPING

COUNTER BATTENS

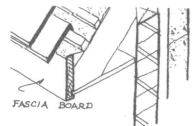

FASCIA BOARD

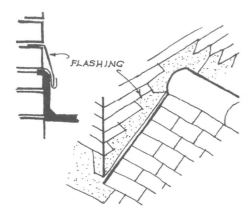

FLASHING

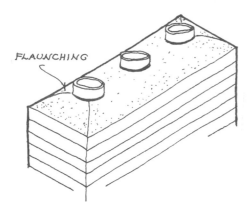

FLAUNCHING

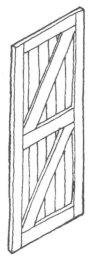

FRAMED, LEDGED
& BRACED DOOR

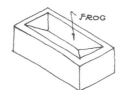

FROG

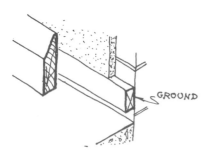

GROUND

Dowel

A short, cylindrical rod of wood or metal used for fixing one piece of material to another (or, for masonry, a rectangular section often made of slate). It fits into holes drilled in both parts or may be cast into, say, a concrete floor to provide a fixing for the bottom of a door post. Wooden dowels are often used in woodwork instead of a mortise and tenon joint, and should be grooved to allow air and excess glue to escape.

Drain Cock

A cock or tap fitted at the lowest point of a water tank or system and used for draining the tank or system when required.

Efflorescence

A powdery white appearance on a wall surface to be seen when the wall dries out, caused by dissolved alkaline salts from the wall crystallising on the surface as evaporation takes place. On an outside wall, although unsightly, the salts will eventually be washed away by rain.

Expanded Polystyrene

A lightweight material used for thermal insulation. Obtainable as a loose fill or in blocks, sheets or tiles.

Fascia Board

A wide board set vertically on edge and fixed to the lower ends of the rafters, to the wall plate or the wall. It carries the fixing brackets for the gutter round the eaves.

Fascia Bracket

A bracket, used to support a gutter, which is fixed to the fascia board.

Fibreboard

Board made up of felted wood or other vegetable fibres. Used for its insulation properties and known as insulating board. (When compressed in manufacture it becomes hardboard and then has different properties). Some types are treated to improve their resistance to flame spread.

Flashing

A strip or sheet of impervious material, often flexible metal, used to prevent water from penetrating the joint between a roof covering and another surface (such as, for instance, a chimney stack). The upper edge of a flashing is usually wedged tightly into a raked out mortar joint.
cf. DAMP-PROOF COURSE.

Flaunching

A cement mortar weathering on the top of a chimney stack and surrounding the chimney pot(s) to throw off the rain and thus prevent it from saturating the stack.

Float

(1) A rectangular wooden tool used for smoothing plaster or cement work.
(2) The ball of a ball valve.

Float Glass

Glass made by floating molten glass on a surface of molten metal, the resultant sheet being perfectly smooth and polished and comparable with plate glass.

Floating Coat

The second coat in three-coat plastering.

Flux

In soldering, a fusible substance used to cover the metals to be joined. It prevents oxidation, aids the flow of the solder and helps in the successful fusion of the metals.

Formwork

Temporary construction of timber or metal within which concrete is cast.
Also known as SHUTTERING.

Framed and Ledged Door

A door composed of stiles, top rail and battens — all

seen on the face side — with horizontal bottom and middle ledges on the back of the door.
cf. BATTEN DOOR and FRAMED, LEDGED AND BRACED DOOR.

Framed, Ledged and Braced Door

A framed and ledged door with the addition of diagonal braces to give greater rigidity and prevent the striking edge of the door from dropping. (The lower corner of the brace, therefore, is always the one nearer the hinge).
cf. BATTEN DOOR and FRAMED AND LEDGED DOOR.

Frenchman

A knife used by the bricklayer together with a jointing rule for trimming the edges of mortar joints when pointing. A kitchen knife with the edge bent over serves the same purpose.

Frog

An indentation, usually V-shaped, in the bedding face of a brick to reduce its weight. 'Frog down' or 'frog up' are the generally accepted ways of describing how the bricks are laid.

Full-Way Valve

A valve which does not obstruct the bore of a pipe and therefore does not impede the flow.

Fuse Box

The cast-iron box, near to the main power switches, in which the fuses or circuit breakers for premises are fixed.

Galvanising

A coating of zinc given to ferrous metals to provide protection from corrosion.

Grommet

A ring edging or lining for a hole to make a tight joint and prevent friction or chafing.

Grounds

Timber fixings, usually unwrought, nailed or plugged to a wall to receive joinery, building boards or other material. Usually fixed flush with the floating coat of plaster.

Gulley

A glazed earthenware trap into which rain and waste water are collected before entering the drain. These are sometimes designed to receive water discharged into them from an open-ended pipe above and sometimes have a built-in socket to receive a pipe connected below ground level.

Gutter

A channel along the eaves of a roof or the edge of a path or road for the removal of rainwater.
see also: PARAPET GUTTER, SECRET GUTTER, VALLEY GUTTER.

Hacksaw

A saw for cutting metal, with a fine, replaceable steel blade stretched tight in a metal frame.

Half Bat

A half of a brick, cut crosswise.
cf. QUEEN CLOSER.

Hardboard

Board of wooden fibres felted and formed under pressure to produce various densities of sheet material, referred to as medium, standard and tempered, usually with one face smooth and the other textured. The smooth face may be veneered with plastics or wood or may be embossed and finished to look like tiles.

Hardcore

Broken bricks or stone which, consolidated, are used as a foundation for paths, drives and solid concrete floors.

Hawk

A square board with a short vertical handle beneath,

used for holding mortar or plaster when pointing or plastering.

Header
A brick so laid that the end shows on the face of the wall. The term is also used to describe the end of the brick.
cf. STRETCHER.

Hip
The outstanding angle formed by the intersection of two inclined roof surfaces.
cf. VALLEY.

Hip Hook
A metal bar fixed to the hip rafter and projecting in a hook at the foot of the hip to prevent the slipping of the lowest hip tile.

Hip Tile
A saddle shaped or angular tile fitting over the intersection of those roofing tiles which meet at a hip.

Hoggin
Coarse sand, sifted gravel or fine ballast.

Horse
(1) Framing used as a temporary support.
(2) A short board on which is mounted a supporting structure to receive a wooden-backed, metal template (usually zinc) which is shaped to the profile of a plaster cornice moulding. The horsed mould is guided when it is moved along the angle between wall and ceiling by a continuous batten nailed to the wall and by nibs nailed to the ceiling. Plaster fed on to the wall is shaped by the scraping action of the mould.

Housing
A shallow sinking in one timber to allow for the insertion of the end of another timber. The joint thus formed is known as a housed joint. Stair treads and risers, for instance, are housed into the string.

In Situ
In position — applied to work done in the position where it is finally required. e.g. concrete may be pre-cast in sections which are later taken to the position where they are required or it may be cast in situ.

Inspection Chamber or Pit
A brick or concrete underground chamber into which several drains are collected and from which one drain emerges. It has a manhole cover which allows access for cleaning purposes.

Intumescent Paint
A type of paint used as a protection against fire. Under the heat of a fire the paint swells into a foam, thus providing an insulating layer which delays or prevents any effect of the fire on the underlying material. The foam can also be effective in sealing gaps round doors, thereby increasing the fire resistance of the door assembly.

Jamb
(1) The vertical side of an opening in a wall, extending the full thickness of a wall.
cf. REVEAL.
(2) The vertical post of framing fixed to the jamb, as door jamb, window jamb.

Joist
A wood or steel beam directly supporting a floor and sometimes alternatively or additionally supporting a ceiling. Steel beams are usually referred to as RSJs (rolled steel joists).

Jumper
(1) A brass part in a water tap which carries the washer. The jumper has a flat disc on the end of a stalk. The stalk points upwards and moves in a guide and the washer is fixed to the lower side of the disc.
(2) A long octagonal or round steel chisel used in quarries or by a mason for making holes in hard stone.

Junction Box
A box which covers the joints between the ends of leads or wires in electrical work.

Key
The roughness of a surface which provides a bond for any application of paint, plaster, rendering, tiles, etc., or the spaces between laths or wire meshes which provide a grip for plaster.
Previously painted surfaces may be roughened by sandpapering to provide a key for new paint.

Kicking Rail
The bottom rail on a door.
see also: RAIL.

King Closer
A brick used as a closer and having one corner cut off along a vertical plane which joins the centre of one side to the centre of one end.
see also: CLOSER and QUEEN CLOSER.

Laminboard
A board resembling blockboard in its construction but with narrower core strips.

Latch
A door fastening, of which the two most common types are:
(1) a bevelled metal tongue controlled by a spring which causes it to engage in a striking plate when the door is closed. It is operated by a knob or lever handle.
(2) the thumb latch, a bar which is pivoted on the door and engages in a catch on the frame. It is operated by a lift — a subsidiary bar, passing through the door, which has a down-turned end on the latch side of the door and a horizontal saucer-shaped flattening or thumb press on the outer side of the door.

Lath
A sawn or split strip of wood of small section for carrying plaster work. Usually about 1m long and up to 10mm x 32mm in cross section the laths are nailed with narrow gaps between them across the underside of joists and provide a key for the plaster.

Ledges
The horizontal timbers on the back of a batten door.

Lintel
A horizontal beam over a door or window opening, usually carrying the load of the wall above. Sometimes a concrete lintel has a shallow projection along its foot to carry the facing brickwork behind which the greater depth of the lintel is concealed. This is known as a boot lintel.

Lock Rail
That rail of a door which carries the lock.
see also: RAIL.

Masking
In painting, the protective cover placed over surfaces adjoining an area which is to be painted. This may be special adhesive tape which is stuck on, and peeled off when the paint is dry, or a piece of card, plastic or metal held over the area as work proceeds.

Mitre
The intersection of two members or mouldings meeting at an angle. The line of the mitre bisects the angle, and is therefore 45° for a right angled corner, so that corresponding shapes in a moulding meet on the mitre and turn the corner. In woodwork, a simple angle joint between two members cut at the same bevel and butted and glued together may be strengthened by the insertion of a glued cross-tongue.

Mitre Block or Box
A square U-shaped or rebated solid block of wood or metal with slots in it at 45° to the main axis of the block. Material to be mitred is held firmly in the block or clamped to it and can then be cut to an exact mitre for a right angle, the slots acting as guides for the saw.

Mortise
A recess or rectangular slot formed in one member to receive a tenon or projection on another member, or for receiving a mortise lock. To avoid undue weakening of a member the thickness of the mortise should not exceed one third that of the wood in which it is cut.

HOUSING

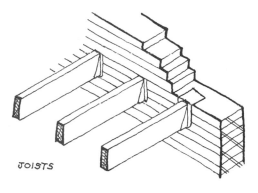

JOISTS

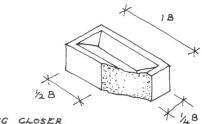

1 B
½ B
¼ B

KING CLOSER

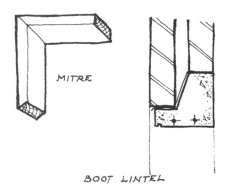

MITRE

BOOT LINTEL

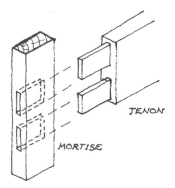

TENON

MORTISE

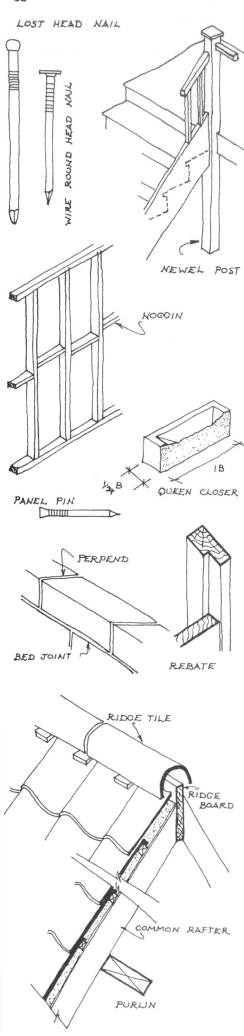

LOST HEAD NAIL

WIRE ROUND HEAD NAIL

NEWEL POST

NOGGIN

PANEL PIN

⅓ B   QUEEN CLOSER   1 B

PERPEND

BED JOINT   REBATE

RIDGE TILE

RIDGE BOARD

COMMON RAFTER

PURLIN

Mortise Lock
A lock set within the door thickness, in a mortise, and thus hidden from view.
cf. RIM LOCK and CYLINDER LOCK.

Mouse
A small, smooth weight which can be tied to a piece of string or fine cord and used to draw other cables, cords or wires through confined and awkward spaces. For example, tied to a new sash cord the mouse and string are slipped over the sash pulley, and then drawn through the pocket, thus feeding the new cord into its correct position for attaching to the sash weight.

Muntin
A subsidiary vertical member in timber framing, framed into the rails and usually of the same thickness as the other members. e.g. the vertical member which separates the panels in a panelled door.

Nails
Nails vary in size from spikes (the largest, and over 130mm long) to pins, tacks and sprigs, and are classified as wire nails, cut nails or wrought nails according to the method of manufacture. The most common are those cold-forged from bright round or oval steel wire, up to 6mm diameter. Cut nails are sheared from steel plate and have a rectangular cross-section and wrought nails have forged heads.
There is great variety in the shapes, metals and finishes used, according to the purposes for which they are required. Galvanised wire nails may be used for work where moisture is not likely to be a problem, otherwise brass, aluminium alloy or copper could be chosen, and where gypsum plasterboard is to be nailed a sherardised finish is called for.

Needle
A short timber or steel beam passed horizontally through a hole in a wall and supported on dead shores, to support the wall above during structural alterations.
see also: SHORE.

Newel Post
A post in a flight of stairs which carries the end of the outer string and the handrail, supporting them at the foot of the flight or at a corner.

Nib
A small projection for fixing purposes, as, for instance, at the upper end of a roofing tile.

Noggin or Nogging Piece
A short horizontal timber placed between studs in a partition for stiffening purposes.

Pad-Saw
A saw used for small circular work, having a narrow blade which passes through the handle from which it is extended and screwed fast for use.

Panel Pin
A slender round wire nail with a small head which is barely visible when driven below the surface of joinery work.

Parapet Gutter, Parallel Gutter or Box Gutter
A wooden gutter of rectangular cross-section with a flexible metal or other impervious lining. Used behind a parapet or sometimes at a valley. The depth varies according to the length and the number of drips or steps used. Occasionally it is constructed with a taper towards the lower end because of the roof slope, in which case it is known as a tapered parapet gutter.

Parquet Flooring
A wooden floor covering formed of hardwood slips or shallow blocks laid in geometrical patterns, glued to the floor and polished. It is now obtainable already fixed to a plywood base for ease and speed of laying.

Penetrating Oil
A light oil with additives to increase its flow and capillary properties.

Perpend
A vertical joint in brickwork. It goes across the wall, the end of the joint appearing on the face of the wall.

Piano Hinge
A continuous length of hinge, as used on a piano lid and other items of furniture. It gives smooth action and is useful in spreading the load and thus preventing, say, a much-used door from pulling away from the stile.

Plasterboard
A building board which has a core of gypsum or anhydrite plaster enclosed, usually, between sheets of heavy fibrous paper. May be used as a base for plasterwork (in which case it needs an application of two coats) or, in cheaper work, as a substitute for a plastered surface. There are insulating plasterboards with a layer of aluminium foil on one side.

Plate Glass
A high quality glass which is formed by casting and subsequent polishing, which gives two smooth surfaces free of blemishes. Available in large sheets and often used for shop windows.

Plug Cock
A simple valve consisting of a tapered plug, a hole through which permits the passage of fluid. Turning the plug through 90° closes the valve.

Plywood
A strong board made up of a number of sheets of veneer glued together, with the grain of adjacent sheets at right angles to each other. Three-ply is frequently used, but five-ply or multi-ply may be required where greater rigidity and strength are necessary. Waterproof glue is used in some qualities of plywood, and a wide range of decorative facings is also available.

Pocket
The hole near the foot of a pulley stile in a double-hung sash window frame. It gives access to the sash weights when new sash cords are to be fitted, but is normally closed by the pocket piece which fits in the hole flush with the rest of the stile.

Primer
A paint used to give the first coat on new or bared metal or wood. On wood it penetrates the surface and forms a good key for the following undercoat and finishing coats of paint. Metal primers contain rust inhibiting additives.

Purlin
A horizontal beam supported by the principal rafters of a truss (and sometimes, additionally, by one or more cross-walls) and itself supporting the common rafters at some point between the wall plate and the ridge.

Queen Closer
A half of a brick, cut vertically lengthwise.
cf. HALF BAT.

Quoin
The external angle of a wall.

Rafter
An inclined timber extending from the eaves to the ridge of a roof. A common rafter carries the roof covering, a principal rafter is part of a truss, and carries the purlin.

Rail
(1) A horizontal member, framed into vertical stiles. In a door the bottom rail is known as a kicking rail and that which carries the lock is known as the lock rail.
(2) A horizontal member of a fence.

Rebate or Rabbet
A long rectangular recess forming a step along the edge of a piece of timber (or other material) to receive another piece of material.

Reinforced Concrete
Concrete made with a number of steel bars, a steel mesh or other reinforcement built into it to provide extra strength against tensional forces. For this reason the position of the reinforcement in the concrete is important and must be carefully designed.

Rendering
Applying stucco, cement mortar or the first and second coats of plaster to the face of a wall. The term is also used to describe the finish thus applied.

Reveal
The vertical side of an opening in a wall, between any frame built in the opening and the outer face of the wall, and usually at right angles to the face of the wall.

Ridge
The highest part or apex of a roof, usually horizontal.

Ridge Board
The horizontal board set on edge to which the top ends of rafters are fixed.

Ridge Tile
Specially shaped tile for covering and making watertight the ridge of a roof. These tiles may have a rounded or angular cross-section.

Rim Latch
A fitting for keeping a door closed, consisting of a spring latch in a metal case screwed on to the inner face of the shutting stile of a door and operated by a spindle and knobs.

Rim Lock
A rim latch which can be locked by means of a key. see also: CYLINDER LOCK and MORTISE LOCK.

Ring Main or Ring Circuit
A system for wiring power circuits in houses, now in wide use and much simpler than the system previously employed. Each socket outlet is connected by two short lengths of cable to the main cable, and each plug contains its own fuse.

Riser
(1) The upright face of a step.
(2) In a snecked rubble wall, a deep stone which builds up the masonry higher than does its adjacent stone on the same bedding plane.

Rising Main
The cold water supply pipe which rises vertically from the principal, external source to supply water to each floor of a building. The term may also be used for the electrical power supply cable or the gas supply pipe which similarly rises vertically within a building.

Roof Ladder or Cat Ladder
A ladder, or long board with cleats nailed on it for foothold, to be laid on a roof slope to give access for repair work and to protect the roof covering by spreading the load. The ladder or board may be fitted with wheels on one side, for ease of movement, and hooks on the end which, when the ladder is turned over, may be engaged over the ridge of the roof for stability.

RSJ
Frequently-used abbreviation for rolled steel joist.

Rubble
(1) Broken bricks, old plaster and similar waste material.
(2) Stones of irregular size and shape used in walling. They are sometimes squared and coursed but are never smoothed.

Sash Window
see DOUBLE-HUNG SASH WINDOW and SLIDING SASH.

Screed
A layer of mortar to give a finish to a jointless floor or other concrete slab to provide a smooth surface which will be suitable to take floor tiles, linoleum, roofing felt, etc.

Screw
A steel or rustproof metal fastening device of a wide range of diameters (or gauge) and lengths. Wood screws have pointed ends, to pierce the timber, and spiral threads. Other screws have blunt ends and helical threads when they are to be fixed in conjunction with

nuts or screwed into metal. Screws are additionally classified by the type of head, e.g. dome head, countersunk head, star head (gives a better bearing for the driver), and finish (sherardised, chrome plated, etc.).

Scrim
A coarse canvas, cotton or other woven fabric for bridging the joint gaps between building boards before plastering and as reinforcement for fibrous plaster work.

Secret Gutter
A valley gutter almost hidden by the mitred slates or tiles adjoining it, or a similar gutter against a gable parapet or alongside a chimney stack. (It is a type of gutter subject to blockage by leaves).

Secret Nailing
Nailing so fixed that the nail holes are concealed in the finished work, as, for instance, in tongued and grooved floorboarding where nails are slant driven through the tongue and subsequently hidden under the next board to be fixed.

Setts
Small square blocks of stone, often granite, used for paving roads or paths.

Sewer
A large, underground pipe or drain used for conveying waste water and sewage. The local authority is usually responsible for the sewers, which collect the effluent from various drains, the drains being the responsibility of the landowners.

Shavehook
A tool used by painters for scraping off burnt paint, or by plumbers when shaving lead pipes prior to soldering.

Sheet Glass
The glass used for most ordinary windows, where the uniform thickness of float or plate glass is not necessary. Referred to by the weight in "oz per sq. foot."

Sherardising
The coating of ferrous metal items such as screws with zinc, as a protection against rusting. Zinc dust is applied in a heated, revolving drum to give a penetration of finish which is more durable than galvanising.

Shoe
(1) The section at the end of a downpipe which is angled to direct rainwater away from the building and into a gulley.
(2) A metal socket enclosing the end of a timber such as a post.

Shore
A temporary support, often made of wood but sometimes of other material. This may be vertical (a dead shore), sloping (a raking shore) or horizontal (a flying shore).

Shuttering
see FORMWORK.

Siphonic Closet
A water closet which has a double seal. This, in conjunction with a small air pipe, creates a siphonic action on flushing which aids the emptying of the bowl or pan.

Size
A liquid sealer applied to wood or plaster so that varnish, paint or paste applied to the surface will not be too much absorbed by the otherwise porous surface.

Slate Ripper
A long narrow tool used by slaters for inserting under broken roofing slates to remove the fixing nails.

Sleeper Wall
A dwarf honeycomb wall supporting ground floor joists in buildings without basements. In addition to being economical in its use of bricks, the wall allows ventilating air currents to pass under the floor.

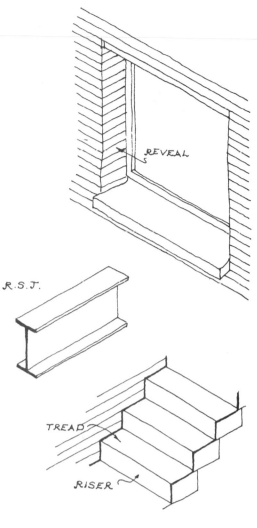

REVEAL

R.S.J.

TREAD

RISER

WOOD SCREW

SELF DRILLING SCREW   MACHINE SCREW

SECRET NAILING

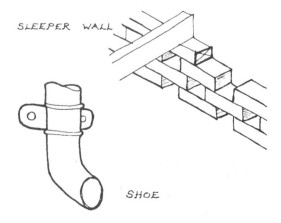
SLEEPER WALL

SHOE

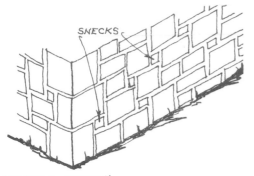

SNECKED RUBBLE

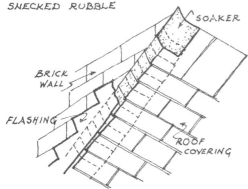

SOAKERS

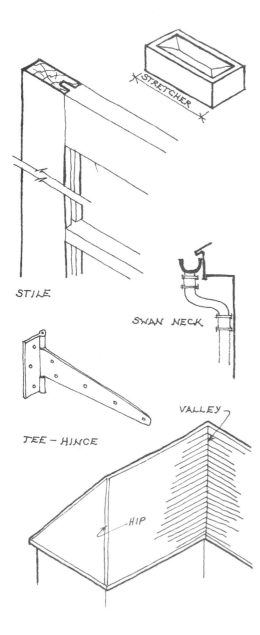

Sleeving
A close-fitting tubular covering for fixing or protective purposes.

Sliding Sash
A sash which opens by a sideways, horizontal movement.

Sneck
In a snecked rubble wall, the small squared stone which has its top surface level with that of an adjoining riser.

Snecked Rubble Wall
A rubble wall, built of uncoursed squared stones of irregular size, in which snecks are used.

Soakaway
A pit, filled with broken stones, clinker, etc., to take the drainage from rainwater pipes or land-drains and allow it to disperse.

Soaker
A piece of flexible metal fitted to interlock with slates or tiles and make a watertight joint between a wall and a roof or at a hip or valley. Stepped flashings are used over the soakers at a joint against a wall.

Socket
(1) The enlarged end of a pipe into which another pipe is fitted. (cf. SPIGOT).
(2) A cavity into which anything is fitted.

Socket Outlet
An electrical fixture on a wall into which the pins of an electrical plug are inserted.

Soffit
The underside of an arch, beam, staircase, cornice, eaves or other feature of a building.

Soil Pipe or Soil Stack
A vertical pipe which conveys sewage to the drains. Its upper end is vented above the eaves.

Solder
An alloy, such as lead-tin or copper-zinc, used for joining metals.

Spandrel
The triangular infilling under the outer string of a staircase or at each side of an arch to the level of the crown. The term is sometimes used to describe the rectangular infilling between the sill of one window and the head of the window below in a multi-storey building, or similar infilling panels.

Spigot
The straight end of a pipe which is inserted in the socket of another pipe to give a socket-and-spigot joint.

Sprig
A small wire nail with no head, or with a very small head. A glazing sprig is used to retain a pane of glass in its frame.

Spur
A socket outlet connection from a ring main, having a single cable which forms a branch off the ring main.

Square
An L-shaped metal or metal and wood tool for testing or setting-out right angles. (Often known as a try-square).
An adjustable square is hinged to enable angles other than right angles to be set as required.

Standard
(1) The upright post of a scaffold, of wood or metal.
(2) A bench end (as the ornamental end of a church pew) or a vertical board to take the ends of shelves, sometimes against a wall.

Stile
The outer vertical members of a frame into which the rails are tenoned.

Stopcock
A valve on a gas or water supply pipe which is used to cut off the supply.

Stretcher
(1) In brickwork, the long face of a brick (which is seen on the face of a built wall).
cf. HEADER.
(2) In furniture, a horizontal cross-bar or tie — as between the legs of a table or chair — to resist tension and prevent the legs from spreading under load.

Striking Plate
A plate with a rectangular slot in it, screwed to a door post, against which the door latch strikes when the door closes and within the slot of which the latch engages when the door is closed.

String
An inclined board supporting the ends of the treads of a staircase.

Strut
An inclined member of a frame, which takes compressional forces.

Stud
A vertical member in a framed partition, to which lathing, wallboards or other materials are nailed.

Swan Neck
An S-bend, as in the topmost section of a rainwater pipe where it joins the eaves gutter.

Tamping Board
A board used for consolidating concrete within its formwork or shuttering, and for levelling the concrete.

Tapered Parapet Gutter
see PARAPET GUTTER.

Tee-Hinge
A long strap-like hinge, with its tapered length fixed on the face of a door, and its cross bar screwed to the door frame. Early types of tee-hinge were made of highly decorative wrought iron for the doors of churches and cathedrals.

Template
A full-size pattern usually made of wood or sheet metal and used as a forming or testing shape when reproducing the pattern in plaster or other materials.

Tenon
The end of a rail or other piece of wood which is cut and stepped to give a reduced area so that it can be inserted into a recess or mortise in another piece of wood. The width of a tenon should be about four times its thickness.

Tenon Saw
A saw having a thin blade stiffened by a fold of steel or brass along its back, and used by a woodworker for sawing tenons.

Terminal
(1) The cable or wire connection where power is led into or out of a piece of electrical equipment.
(2) The end of a gas-flue, etc.

Tread
The horizontal part of a step.

Trestle
A support for scaffold boards, used in pairs to form a working platform, or for a large board to form a work-table. Each trestle consists of two broad, ladder-like structures hinged at the top and often braced with cords to prevent the feet from spreading too wide.

Two-Gang Switch
An electrical switch assembly with two switches mounted side by side in one box.

Valley
The recessed angle in a roof where two roof surfaces meet and towards which rainwater flows. Where the

junction is angular there is a gutter, but the roofing material may be laid in a continuous sweep, (a swept valley) when there is no need for a gutter.

Valley Gutter
A gutter in a roof valley, usually lined with flexible metal though other impervious material may be used.

Veneer
A thin layer of wood used either as a decorative facing to a less attractive wood or for building up into plywood. Or a thin layer of some other material used to provide a decorative facing.

Ventilation Pipe
The pipe which provides ventilation at the top of a soil drain. This may be a continuation of the soil stack, extended above the eaves.

Wall Plate
A horizontal timber laid along a wall to distribute the load from joists or rafters which sit upon it.

Wall Tie
A piece of twisted bronze or galvanised steel plate or a twisted piece of galvanised wire with two loops for building into the bed joints of the two leaves of a cavity wall to strengthen the wall. The twist is intended to prevent any moisture from the outer leaf of the wall from travelling along the tie to the inner leaf.

Waste Pipe
A pipe from a wash-basin, sink or bath to carry away the waste water into the drains. It has a bend or trap in it which always retains a sufficient amount of water to fill the bore of the pipe and thus prevent smells from the drains from penetrating the building.

Water Waste Preventer, or WWP
A flushing cistern that discharges only a given quantity of water at any one time, as for a W.C., incorporating a ball-valve which closes the inlet pipe when the cistern is refilled.

Weatherboard
A moulding or piece of wood planted along the bottom of an external door to keep out driving rain.

Weatherboarding
Horizontal, overlapping boards nailed on the outside of a building to provide the finished wall surface. They are painted, varnished or treated with a preservative stain.

Weathering
(1) A slight slope to throw off rainwater, as on a sill or coping.
(2) The change of colour and possibly, also, of surface texture to be seen in a building material after exposure to the elements.

Washdown Closet
The simplest and most common form of water closet, in which the efficiency depends on the force of water washing the contents of the bowl or pan through the single trap.

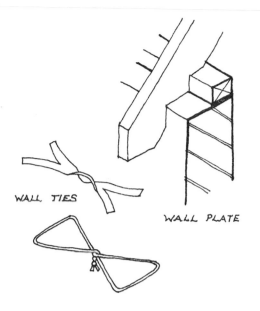

WALL TIES

WALL PLATE

KNOW YOUR MATERIALS

Asbestos Cement Sheets

Use	Cladding of roofs and walls.
British Standards	BS 690. Asbestos cement slates, corrugated sheets and semi-compressed flat sheets. BS 1494. Fixing accessories for building purposes.
Composition	Asbestos fibre and Portland cement.
Method of manufacture	Raw materials mixed with water and formed into sheets which are then cured.
Accessories	Cover strips, hooks, bolts and other fixings available.
Shape	Flat sheets. Corrugated sheets in various profiles.

Dimensions		Length mm	Width mm
	Flat sheets	1220 to 3050	915, 1220
	Corru. sheets	915 to 3050	762, 1090

		Thickness mm
	Flat sheets	4.8, 6.4, 9.5, 12.7
	Corru. sheets	5.6, 6.4

Weight	Thickness mm	4.8	6.4	9.5	12.7
	Weight kg/m²	8.4	11.2	16.8	22.4

Density	1520 kg/m³.
Appearance	Front face has a smooth slightly grained surface, but applied finishes are also available. Reverse face has a textured surface. Grey colour but can be obtained with applied colour finish.
Impact strength	Fairly good when new, but decreases with age.
Combustibility	Non-combustible.
Surface spread of flame	Class O and Grade A.
Change in volume	Shrinks slightly due to carbonation of the cement.
Moisture content	10-20 per cent by weight.
Water absorption	28 per cent maximum, completely immersed in water for 24 hours.
Permeability to water	Very low

Solubility in water	Insoluble
Dimensional changes	Dry to fully saturated, 0.25 per cent.
Effect of chemicals	Acids may attack the Portland cement. Alkalies other than ammonia in damp atmosphere have no effect.
Effect of impurities	Any likely to be present will have no harmful effect.
Effect of micro-organisms etc.	Immune to insect and vermin attack. Does not support mould growth.
Thermal conductivity, k	0.43 W/m °C
Effect of heat	Withstands heat up to 260°C.
Effect of thermal shock	Liable to shatter if exposed to direct flame or temperatures above 260°C.
Thermal expansion	12×10^{-6} per °C.
Effect of frost	Unaffected.
Effect of sunlight	Unaffected.
Health hazard	None in use. Precautions required when material is mechanically cut or worked.
Reaction with other materials	No reaction with other materials.
Durability	The normal minimum life is 40 years by which time the material has become brittle.
Ease of cutting, etc.	Can be cut with an ordinary hand saw. Holes should be drilled and not punched, the size being a little larger than the bolt or hook to be fed through the hole.
Surface treatment	Paints affected by alkali attack should be applied over an alkali-resistant primer. Sheets should not be painted on one face only as this will restrict carbonation to the other face and cause the sheets to warp.

Asbestos Insulating Board

Use	Fire protection of structural steelwork, ceilings, walls, partitions, etc.
British Standards	BS 3536:1962. Asbestos insulating boards and wall boards.
Chemical analysis	Hydrated calcium silicate. Slightly alkaline.

Composition	Asbestos fibre, silica and hydrated lime.
Method of manufacture	Raw materials, together with any pigments, mixed with water and fed into machines which yield a wet sheet which is then autoclaved.
Shape	Flat sheets, usually with square edges.

Asbestos Insulating Board (contd.)

Dimensions	Length mm	Width mm	Thickness mm
	1220 to 3050	510 and 1220	6.4, 9.5, 12.7

Weight	Thickness mm	6.4	9.5	12.7
	Weight kg/m²	4.6	6.9	9.2

Density 500-900 kg/m³.

Appearance One face fairly smooth, reverse face slightly textured. Normal colour is grey-white. Available in natural and sanded surface finish.

Properties in tension 28 MN/m² across grain 93 MN/m² with grain — 30 per cent loss of strength when saturated, recoverable on drying out.

Properties in bending Modulus of rupture 138 x 10 MN/m² across grain. 93 x 10 MN/m² with grain.

Hardness Brinell hardness 1.4 to 1.8 mm, 25 kg load, 10 mm ball.

Combustibility Non-combustible.

Surface spread of flame Class O and Grade A.

Water vapour diffusivity 0.015 - 0.03 g/MNs.

Moisture content 3 - 5 per cent

Water absorption 100 per cent by weight.

Dimensional changes due to moisture 0.15 - 0.20 mm per 1000 mm from normal to saturated state.

Effect of chemicals Affected by acids, but not necessarily by acidic fumes.

Effect of chemicals (contd.) Resistant to other materials likely to come into contact with it.

Effect of impurities None likely

Effect of micro-organisms, etc. Does not nourish mould growth. Immune to insect attack.

Thermal conductivity 0.108 to 0.115 W/m °C.

Thermal expansion 5×10^{-6} per °C up to 200°C. Slight contraction above 200°C.

Light reflection 65 per cent for untreated sanded board.

Sound absorption Sound absorption varies from 0.05 to 0.08 dependent upon thickness and conditions of usage.

Health hazard No effect when in use. Precautions may be required when cut or worked mechanically.

Effect on other materials No effect on other materials likely to be in contact with it.

Durability Very durable when used internally.

Ease of working Can be cut and worked with ordinary wood-working tools.

Surface treatment Various decorative materials can be stuck on the boards, using appropriate adhesives.

Painting treatment Sealing coat may be required prior to decoration with paints, etc.

Ease of cleaning Natural surface is not easily cleaned.

Bitumen Felt

Type 3 main types according to nature of base.
Type 1 - Fibre base, with various finishes.
Type 2 - Asbestos base, with various finishes.
Type 3 - Glass fibre base, with various finishes.

Use Finish for roofs. Material of similar type used for DPC and flashings.

British Standards BS 747. Part 1:1968 (Imp). Part 2:1970 (Metric)
CP 144. Part 1:1968 (M+Imp). Part 3:1970 (Metric)

Chemical analysis Covered in detail in BS 747.

Composition Fibre, asbestos or glass fibre impregnated with bitumen.

Manufacture The fibre mats are passed through a tank containing bitumen in a hot fluid condition, the excess bitumen being removed by passage between rollers, and appropriate finishes applied.

Dimensions Supplied in rolls, length 4.6 and 9.3 m, width 910 mm, thickness up to 3 mm.

Weight (per unit area) Type 1 : 0.9 - 3.6 kg/m² — In all cases the heavier
Type 2 : 0.7 - 3.6 kg/m² — grades are those with
Type 3 : 1.8 - 3.2 kg/m² — mineral surfaced finishes.

Appearance Normal finish is blackish in colour, and fairly smooth, but coloured finishes including light colours are produced and these have a rough texture depending upon the surfacing material used.

Strength properties Not self-supporting.
No tensile strength tests in BS, but tests are given in standards of some other countries.
The significance of any figures depends upon the method of use of the material and the temperature changes to which it may be exposed.
Pliable, though less so when cold.

Resistance to tearing Liable to tear if not handled carefully.

Adhesion Self-adhesion in the roll prevented by use of a

Bitumen Felt (contd.)

Adhesion (contd.)	surfacing material or production with a dry surface. CP 144 describes the material to be used when bonding bitumen felt to concrete and other surfaces and for built-up roofing.	Thermal conductivity	Since the material is relatively thin it provides little contribution to the thermal insulation of a roof.
Effect of fire	The material is inflammable. Types 2 and 3 should be used where fire resistance is important. Softening of the bitumen may cause it to run or drip. The classification for fire resistance depends on a number of factors and reference should be made to the Building Regulations.	Effect of high and low temperatures	Solar heat causes softening of the bitumen. Low temperatures result in stiffening and hardening and tendency to become brittle.
		Effect of frost	Unaffected apart from contraction.
Permeability to air and gases	Very low permeability.	Effect of sunlight	Sunlight causes changes in constitution of the bitumen contributing to its weathering, but the effects are reduced by site-applied surface dressings to minimise solar heat gain. The surface may craze or blister.
Water absorption	Very low indeed. No test in BS.	Reaction with other materials	Direct effects are small, but the hot bonding bitumen may soften expanded polystyrene insulation and some protection may be necessary.
Permeability to water	Very low indeed. No test in BS.	Durability	Built-up roofing consisting of three layers of bitumen felt laid according to CP 144 should require little maintenance to give a life of upwards of 20 years.
Porosity	Mainly non-porous.		
Effect of chemicals	Not affected by materials normally likely to come in contact with built-up roofing.	Changes during preparation and use	Softens on warming. Overheating the bonding bitumen will cause the material to become hard and brittle.

Blocks, Concrete

Types of concrete	*Dense*	*Dense*	*Lightweight aggregate*	*Lightweight aggregate*	*Lightweight aggregate*	*Lightweight aggregate*
Types of aggregate	Gravel	Limestone	Clinker	Pulverised fuel ash	Expanded clay	Foamed slag
Use	Outer leaf of external walls (rendered or other treatment). Inner leaf and partition walls (usually plastered). Internal partition walls, (usually plastered).					
British Standards	BS 2028, 1364:1968 Precast concrete blocks. BS 877 Foamed blastfurnace slag for concrete aggregate. BS 1165:1966 Clinker aggregate for plain and precast concrete. CP 121.201:1951 Masonry. Walls ashlared with natural stone or with cast stone. CP 121:Part 1:1973 Brick and Block Masonry.					
Composition	Portland cement and aggregate in wide range of mix proportions.					
Method of production						
(a) aggregate	Natural sources	Crushed limestone	Furnace residues	Powdered coal ash	Clay heated to bloating temperature	Minimum amount of water on molten slag
(b) block	Semi-dry concrete mixes are moulded in machines, with tamping, vibration and/or pressure, cured naturally or in a steam chamber.					
Shape	Rectangular- or square-sectioned blocks, solid or with core holes.					
Dimensions	Length 448 mm, Height 219 mm. Thickness (mm), 64, 76, 102, 152, 178, 203 and 209 mm					
Weight (kg) 76 mm thick blocks	14-17	14-17	7-11	7-12.5	5.5-12.5	7-14
Bulk density (kg/m^3)	2000-2400	2000-2400	1050-1520	950-1760	720-1760	950-2000
General appearance	Plain, textured or riven faced.	Plain, textured or riven faced.	Rough textured as cast.	As moulded and textured.	Rough textured (cast).	Fairly rough textured.

Blocks, Concrete (contd.)

	Gravel	Limestone	Clinker	Pulverised fuel ash	Expanded clay	Foamed slag
General appearance (contd.)	Natural and limited range of colours.	Natural and limited range of colours.	Dark grey.	Grey.	Grey.	Grey.
Compressive strength (MN/m^2)	13.5-42	13.5-42	2.0-7.0	2.75-55.0	2.0-62.0	2.0-24.0
Resistance to insertion and extraction of nails	Not nailable	Not nailable	Nailable with cut nails	Nailable with cut nails	Not readily nailable	Nailable with cut nails
Fire resistance	Concrete is incombustible. Fire resistance of walls up to 6 hours can be obtained by using blocks of appropriate thickness, plastered if necessary with gypsum plaster.					
Water absorption	7 per cent by wt. 16 per cent by vol.		Varies according to density but generally of little importance under normal conditions of use.			
Drying shrinkage (per cent)	0.03-0.035	0.02-0.035	0.04-0.08	0.04-0.07	0.04-0.07	0.03-0.07
Effect of chemicals	Normally Portland cement is susceptible to attack by sulphates and concrete blocks should not be used in damp situations where sulphates are present. If this is unavoidable the blocks should be made with sulphate resistant Portland cement or high alumina cement.					
Effect of impurities	None usually present	None usually present	Occasionally contains small pieces of lime which subsequently "blow"	None usually present	None usually present	None usually present
Thermal conductivity (W/m $^\circ$C)	1.10-1.75	1.10-1.75	0.35-0.60	0.20-0.50	0.20-0.60	0.20-0.60
Thermal expansion coefficient (per $^\circ$C)	$12\text{-}13 \times 10^{-6}$	$6\text{-}8 \times 10^{-6}$	$8\text{-}10 \times 10^{-6}$	$8\text{-}10 \times 10^{-6}$	$8\text{-}12 \times 10^{-6}$	$10\text{-}12 \times 10^{-6}$
Effect of frost	Frost resistant.					
Acoustic properties	Transmission of air-borne sound increases with decrease in density.					
Reaction with other materials	None	None	Liable to corrode iron and steel	None	None	None
Durability	Excellent					

Bricks, Clay

Type	London stocks, Flettons, Facing bricks, Engineering bricks and Common bricks. (Engineering bricks are used for special purposes and are not dealt with here in detail).
Use	Mainly for walls, including foundations. Engineering bricks are used where high strength, low porosity and high resistance to frost are required. Facing bricks are used for external work where good appearance is required. Common bricks are used where appearance is not important or where they are to be plastered or rendered.
British Standards, etc.	BS 3921:1974, Clay bricks and blocks. CP 121:Part 1:1973, Brick and block masonry.

Bricks, Clay (contd.)

	London Stocks	Facing Bricks	Common Bricks	Flettons	Facing or Common	Facing Bricks	Common Bricks
Composition	Very variable, depending upon the raw material used, but consist essentially of aluminium silicates.						
Chemical analysis (soluble salts)	B	A or B	B	D	D	A or B	D

Because of the variability of the soluble salt content it would be misleading to quote individual figures but the general trend is indicated by letters A, B, C and D.
A. Normally meets the requirements of BS 3921 for *special quality*.
B. Soluble salt content usually moderate, but not normally of special quality.
C. Soluble salt content may be moderate or fairly high but does not normally cause trouble when the bricks are used in normal conditions.
D. Salt content may be relatively high, especially of gypsum (calcium sulphate) and can give rise to troublesome failures if the brickwork remains wet for long periods.

	London Stocks	Facing Bricks	Common Bricks	Flettons	Facing or Common	Facing Bricks	Common Bricks
Method of manufacture	Brick earth. Moulded or pressed wire cut	——— Wealden clays ——— Hand-made, machine-moulded or wire-cut	Stiff plastic-pressed or wire-cut	Oxford clay. Semi-dry pressed	Keuper marl. Wire-cut	Carboniferous clays or shales Hand-moulded, stiff plastic-pressed or wire-cut	Stiff plastic-pressed or wire-cut
Shape and size	The standard size is 225 x 112.5 x 75 mm with relatively large tolerances in view of method of manufacture. Some non-standard sizes are available. Standard specials (closers, squints, bullnoses, etc.) are produced for use at corners, etc. of walls and are illustrated in BS 3921:Part 1:1965.						
Weight (dry) kg	2.0-2.5	2.2-3.0	2.5-3.1	2.3-2.6	2.4-3.0	3.0-3.3	2.5-3.4
Bulk density kg/m³	1400-1750	1550-2100	1750-2200	1600-1800	1650-2050	2050-2300	1750-2350
Colours	Yellow with purplish markings	Red, purple or brown	Reddish brown	Cream to pink. Other colours available	Cream to red. Other colours available	Buff, brown or red. Other colours available	Buff, red or blackish
Compressive strength MN/m²	5-21	7-50	34-50	17-36	20-50	20-110	25-145
Effect of fire	The fire resistance of brickwork is high, with no real differences between bricks from different sources.						
Moisture content	Equilibrium moisture content in contact with moist air is generally less than 1 per cent. When exposed to rain the moisture content may reach two-thirds of the porosity figures temporarily.						
Porosity per cent by vol.	30-50	13-42	17-46	30-40	22-42	2-22	10-38
Permeability	Not usually of practical importance.						
Moisture expansion	Initial moisture expansion of kiln-fresh bricks is variable but may be appreciable, exceeding 0.1 per cent. It decreases rapidly for day-old bricks and approx. 50 per cent of it will have occurred in 1 week, though the remaining 50 per cent will take a much longer time. Subsequent dimensional changes with changes of moisture content are very small.						
Effect of chemicals	Good resistance to acids and chemicals. The more porous bricks may be damaged by salt crystallisation either because of original high salt content or becoming contaminated.						
Effect of impurities	Particles of lime, derived from limestone present as an impurity in the clay, may cause the overlying brick surface to spall off revealing the lime underneath. Soluble sulphates may cause surface disintegration or under wet conditions attack mortars containing Portland cement or semi-hydraulic lime. They may also appear as efflorescence on the surface of the bricks but this effect is generally temporary.						
Thermal conductivity (W/m °C)	0.45	0.5-0.7	0.6-0.8	0.55	Up to 1.0	0.83	0.88
Linear thermal expansion	$5\text{-}8 \times 10^{-6}$ per °C. Usually of little importance except in long walls built in dense mortar.						
Effect of frost	Behaviour in frost depends upon conditions of exposure and the water content at the time of freezing, underfired bricks being more susceptible. Bricks are divided into two classes:— Ordinary quality - normally durable in the external face of a building.						

Bricks, Clay (contd.)

Effect of frost (contd.)	Special quality - durable even when used in situations of extreme exposure, e.g. retaining walls. Engineering bricks normally attain this quality, facing and common bricks may do so, except those produced from Oxford clay and Keuper marl.
Changes in use	Little foundation for statements that bricks harden on exposure except for a limited hardening of bricks of high lime content.
Durability	Very dependent upon the type of brick, degree of firing, soluble salt content and conditions of exposure.

Cement, Portland

Type	*Ordinary and Rapid-hardening*	*Portland-blast furnace*	*Low heat Portland*	*Sulphate resisting*
Uses	Can be used neat, but more usually as a binding agent for sand and other aggregates for making mortars and concrete.	As for ordinary Portland cement.	As for ordinary Portland cement but particularly useful for mass concrete where evolution of heat may be harmful.	As for ordinary Portland cement but particularly useful where sulphates are likely to be present.
British Standards	BS 12:Part 1:1958 (Imperial) Part 2:1971 (Metric)	BS 146:Part 1:1958 (Imp) Part 2:1973 (Metric)	BS 1370:Part 1:1958 (Imp) Part 2:1974 (Metric)	BS 4027:Part 1:1966 (Imp) Part 2:1972 (Metric)
Composition	Mainly calcium silicates and calcium aluminates.	Mixture of Portland cement and granulated blast furnace slag.	As for ordinary Portland cement.	Mainly calcium silicates. Low content of tri-calcium aluminate.
Manufacture	A mixture of chalk or limestone and clay, burnt at high temperature and ground to a fine powder with gypsum to control the rate of set.	Slag may be mixed with PC clinker and ground together or be pre-ground and mixed. Slag content not to exceed 65 per cent.	As for ordinary Portland cement.	As for ordinary Portland cement.
Colour	Grey colour normally, but may be pigmented with pigments conforming to BS 1014. White cement also available.	Normally grey.	Grey	As for ordinary Portland cement.
Compression strength MN/m^2 (1:3 cement:sand)	3 days 15.4 7 days 23.9	15.4 23.9	7.7 14.1	15.4 23.9
Rate of strength development	Medium (ordinary) High (rapid hardening)	Medium	Low	Low to medium
Resistance to cracking	Medium (ordinary) Low (rapid hardening)	Medium	High	Medium
Effect of fire	Behaviour largely depends upon the aggregate. The dehydration of the cement is a slow process.			
Permeability to water	Permeability to water and other liquids of mortars and concretes made with PC depends upon proportion of cement:aggregate. Very low for rich mixes.			
Dimensional changes	Mortars and concretes have an initial drying shrinkage 0.3-0.5 per cent. Subsequent changes in moisture content are accompanied by dimensional changes.			
Effect of chemicals - weak acids - alkalies - sulphates	Poor Good Poor	Fair Good Fair	Poor Good Fair	Poor Good V. Good
Effect of impurities	Any impurities generally have no effect.			
Thermal expansion coefficient	12-13 x 10^{-6} per $^\circ$C (1:6 gravel concrete).			

Cement, Portland (contd.)

	Ordinary and Rapid-hardening	*Portland-blast furnace*	*Low heat Portland*	*Sulphate resisting*
Effect of frost	Unset mortars and concrete liable to frost damage. Frost resistance of hardened material may be very high but depends on mix proportions and water cement ratio.			
Reaction with other materials	Affects materials susceptible to alkalies, e.g. aluminium. Flash set if mixed with high alumina cement.			
Durability	Durability depends upon mix proportions, water/cement ratio and exposure conditions and is generally excellent.			
Setting time - initial - final	min. 45 min max. 10 hours	min. 45 min max. 10 hours	min. 1 hour max. 15 hours	min. 45 min max. 10 hours

Fibre Building Boards

	Hardboards.	Wallboards.	Insulating boards.
Material	Hardboards.	Wallboards.	Insulating boards.
Type	Standard, tempered and medium. Decorative faced.	Homogenous. Laminated. Decorative faced.	Homogenous. Bitumen bonded. Decorative faced.
Use	Linings for walls and ceilings.	Linings for walls and ceilings.	Linings for walls and ceilings
British Standards	BS 1142:Part 2: 1971	BS 1142:Part 2: 1971	BS 1142:Part 3: 1972
Composition	Wood and other vegetable fibres.		
Manufacture	Wood fibre pulp with adhesive additives fed on to endless belt or cylinder, excess water sucked out and wet board rolled, dried and cut to size. These boards may be converted into hardboards, but the latter may also be produced by pressing the wet pulp boards at a high temperature.		
Shape	Rectangular boards.		
Dimensions Width (mm) Length (mm) Thickness (mm)	915, 1220, 1530 Up to 3660 2-12	610, 915, 1220 1220-3660 6-10	610, 915, 1220 1220-3660 12-25
Density (kg/m³)	Standard 880 Medium 480-800	Not over 480	Not over 400
Appearance	Smooth surface on one side. Usually mesh texture on reverse.	Smooth, rough or moulded surfaces. Cream to grey colour.	Smooth, rough or moulded surfaces. Cream to grey colour.
Combustibility	Combustible.	Combustible.	Combustible.
Surface spread of flame	Class 3, undecorated. Can be raised to Class 2 with certain decorative treatments. Can be raised to Class 1 with intumescent paint treatment.	Class 4 undecorated. Can be raised to Class 1 with certain decorative treatments or by impregnation with chemicals.	

Permeability to water vapour (g/MNs)	0.001-0.002	0.02-0.060	0.015-0.070
Moisture content	*RH per cent* / *Moisture Content per cent*		*RH per cent* / *Moisture Content per cent*
	40 4-5 65 5-8 80 7-11		40 7-0 60 10-0 80 13-0
Water absorption (by weight)	3 mm Standard 10-30 per cent 6 mm Medium 15-30 per cent 3 mm Tempered 5-15 per cent.	Maximum 38 per cent.	10-20 per cent.
Moisture expansion per cent increase in thickness	Standard 7-20 Medium 10-20 Tempered 3-11		
Effect of chemicals	Not affected by chemicals normally likely to come into contact with any type of board. Wall-boards and insulating boards suffer loss of strength when wet.		
Fungal attack, etc.	Not affected by fungal growth.		
Thermal conductivity (W/m °C)	Standard 0.1 Medium 0.07	0.06	0.05
Sound absorption	Sound absorption depends on type and method of use.		
Sound transmission dB reduction for single thickness	3 mm 20 6 mm 23 12 mm 27	12 mm 18	12 mm 18
Durability	Long life under all conditions of usage appropriate to the particular type.		
Ease of cutting	Can be readily cut with fine-toothed saws.		
Ease of cleaning	Depends upon the applied surface finish.		

Floor Finishes

Notes:
1. Domestic means houses, flats, etc. Commercial means offices, shops, schools, etc.
2. Where tiles are given as square, this indicates the commonest shape; obviously for linoleum, etc. they could be circular.
3. Under dimensions thickness is given last. Other dimensions are given in ranges but for some only the commonest sizes are given.
4. Colours where given refer to the commonest ones produced.
5. In several cases a wide range is given for a property to timber. This is because it varies with species, hardwood or softwood, etc.
6. Under ease of cleaning any textured surface would be rated Poor so assessments are for smooth surfaces.
7. Resistance to wear is related to the use categories so should not be compared as if all were used in the same way.
8. Means of laying or fixing gives where relevant the BS Code of Practice written as CP 201, etc. BRS Digests are given as BRS 33, etc.

Type	Ceramic Tile	Composition Block	Cork Carpet	Cork Tile	Flexible PVC	Linoleum
Use	Domestic Commercial	Domestic Commercial	Domestic	Domestic Commercial	Domestic Commercial	Domestic Commercial
British Standards	BS 1286:1945		BS 810:1966		BS 3261:——	BS 810:1966
Composition	Ceramic	Portland cement Gypsum Linseed Oil Sawdust	Cork granules Linoleum cement	Cork granules Resin binder	Plasticised PVC and fillers	Linseed oil Resins Cork and Wood flour
Method of manufacture	Pressing Extrusion	Pressing	Calendering	Pressing Heating	Calendering Moulding Coating	Calendering
Shape	Square Tiles	Rectangular Tiles	Sheets	Square Tiles	Sheet Tiles	Sheet Tiles
Dimensions	75mm x 75mm up to 300mm x 300mm 10mm to 50mm thick	150mm x 50mm 10mm & 15mm thick	180mm wide Up to 8mm thick	300mm x 300mm 3.2mm, 4.8mm thick	900mm to 2m wide 2mm and 3mm thick	1800mm wide Up to 4.5mm thick
Appearance & colour	Smooth or textured surface. Red, brown, buff, patterns.	Smooth. Various colours.	Textured. Plain colours.	Smooth. Various natural shades.	Wide range of textures colours and patterns.	Smooth. Wide range of colours and patterns.
Warmth to touch	Poor	Fair	Very Good	Very Good	Fair to Good	Fair to Good
Resistance to impact	Very Good to Fair	Fair	Poor	Poor	Poor	Poor
Hardness	High	Medium	Low	Low	Low	Low
Resistance to wear	Very Good to Good	Good	Fair	Fair	Very Good to Poor	Very Good to Poor
Degree of slipperiness	High, wet Low, dry Low when textured.	Medium	High	High	High to Medium	Medium
Permeability to water vapour	Medium	Medium	High	High	Medium	High
Water absorption	Low	Low	Medium	High	Low	Medium
Permeability to water	Low	Low	Medium	Medium	Low	Medium

Floor Finishes (contd.)

	Ceramic Tile	Composition Block	Cork Carpet	Cork Tile	Flexible PVC	Linoleum
Moisture expansion	Very Low	Low	High	High	Medium	High
Reaction with other materials	None	None	None	None	Plasticiser migration may affect adhesive	None
Resistance to deterioration through action of water	Very Good	Very Good	Poor	Poor	Good	Poor
acids	Very Good to Good	Good	Poor	Poor	Good	Good to Poor
alkalies	Very Good to Fair	Good	Poor	Poor	Good to Poor	Poor
oils, greases (vegetable and animal)	Very Good	Good	Poor	Poor	Good	Good
mineral oils and greases	Very Good	Good	Poor	Poor	Good	Good
Ease of cleaning	Good	Fair	Poor	Fair	Good	Good
Means of Laying or Fixing	CP 202:1972 BRS 79	Set in mortar	CP 203:1969: Part 2:1972	CP 203:1969: Part 2:1972	CP 203:1969: Part 2:1972 BRS 33	CP 203:1969: Part 2:1972

Floor Finishes (Continued)

Type	Thermoplastic Tile	Vinyl Asbestos Tile	Wood
Use	Domestic	Domestic Commercial	Domestic Commercial Industrial
British Standards	BS 2592:1973	BS 3260:1969	BS 1297, BS 1187
Composition	Resins Asbestos Limestone	Plasticised PVC Asbestos Limestone	Wood
Method of manufacture	Calendering	Calendering	Various
Shape	Square Tiles	Square Tiles	Blocks Boards, etc.
Dimensions	300mm square 3mm thick	300mm square 3mm thick	Various
Appearance & colour	Smooth. Various colours	Smooth or textured. Various colours	Smooth. Various shades
Warmth to touch	Fair	Fair	Good to Very Good

	Thermoplastic Tile	Vinyl Asbestos Tile	Wood
Resistance to impact	Poor	Poor	Very Good to Poor
Hardness	Low	Low	High to Low
Resistance to wear	Fair	Good	Very Good to Poor
Degree of slipperiness	High, wet Medium, dry	High, wet Medium, dry	High to Low
Permeability to water vapour	Low	Low	Medium to High
Water absorption	Low	Low	Low to High
Permeability to water	Low	Low	Low to Medium
Moisture expansion	Low	Low	Low to High
Reaction with other materials	None	None	None

Floor Finishes (contd.)

	Thermoplastic Tile	Vinyl Asbestos Tile	Wood		Thermoplastic Tile	Vinyl Asbestos Tile	Wood
Resistance to deterioration through action of water	Good	Good	Good to Fair	mineral oils and greases	Poor	Poor	Good
				Bending strength	Low	Low	High
acids	Poor	Poor	Good to Poor	Ease of cleaning	Good to Poor	Good to Poor	Good to Poor
alkalies	Good	Good	Good to Poor	Means of Laying or Fixing	CP 203 BRS 33	CP 203 BRS 33	CP 201 BRS 18
oils, greases (vegetable and animal)	Poor	Poor	Good				

Glass Sheet

Types	Wide range of clear and figured sheets; wire reinforced.
Use	Glazing of windows, cladding, roof lights (wire reinforced).
British Standards	BS 952:1964. Classification of glass for glazing and terminology for work on glass. CP 152:1972. Glazing and fixing of glass for buildings.
Composition	Mainly alkaline silicates and aluminates.
Manufacture	Sand, soda ash, limestone, alumina, other materials heated in furnaces and drawn or floated into sheets.
Shape	Usually marketed as rectangular sheets.
Size	Length up to 2m Width, up to 1.2m Thickness, up to 6mm.
Weight	Sheet glass is commonly described in terms of "oz", the normal being 24 oz/sq ft. equal to 3mm thick.
Appearance	Clear sheet having smooth surface. Wide range of figured surfaces. Normally almost colourless, but may be tinted (anti-

Appearance (contd.)	glare, heat absorbing glasses) or coloured by fusion treatment.
Effect of fire	Non-combustible but cracks and melts in a fire.
Effect of chemicals	Very resistant, but surface discolouration produced when thin films of water are trapped between sheets of glass.
Effect of impurities	Greenish-tinge produced by iron.
Thermal conductivity	1.05 W/m $^{\circ}$C.
Thermal shock	Normal glazing quality cracks when heated.
Light transmission	Up to 90 per cent.
Durability	Very durable.
Safety	Relative ease of breakage necessitates care in selection of appropriate thickness to reduce liability to breakage. Special glasses are available which do not cause damage when broken.

Plaster, Gypsum

Type	Neat plasters - Classes A, B, C and D. Pre-mixed - Browning, Metal Lathing, Bonding, Multipurpose, Finish.
Use	Internal plastering on bricks, blocks, boards, lathing.
British Standards	BS 1191. Gypsum building plasters. CP 211. Internal plastering.
Composition	Class A - hemihydrate gypsum (Plaster of Paris). Class B - retarded hemihydrate gypsum. Class C and D - anhydrous gypsum. Pre-mixed plasters - retarded hemihydrate gypsum with lightweight aggregate. Browning and metal lathing - Perlite.

Composition (contd.)	Bonding and multipurpose - Exfoliated vermiculite.
Manufacture	Calcination of gypsum to 160°C for hemihydrate gypsum plasters and to 500°C for anhydrous gypsum plasters. Retarder of set added to Class B and pre-mixed plasters, accelerator of set added to Classes C and D.
Bulk density (kg/m^3)	Classes A and B 700-950; Classes C and D 800-900; Browning 500-700; Metal lathing and bonding 500-600; Finish 500-600.
Density set plaster	25 - 30 per cent above bulk density.

Plaster, Gypsum (contd.)

Warmth to touch	Fairly cold for neat plasters, slightly warmer for pre-mixed plasters.
Transverse strength	Unimportant in practice though useful for checking quality. Varies considerably depending upon type of plaster and water/plaster ratio.
Impact strength	Highest for Class D plasters.
Hardness	Depends upon density of set plaster. Plasters containing lightweight aggregates are relatively soft.
Effect of fire	Gypsum plasters increase the fire resistance of building materials, the extent depending upon thickness of coating.
Permeability to air	Permeable, extent decreasing from Class A to Class D.
Water absorption	High (Class A), decreasing with increasing density.
Solubility in water	Gypsum is slightly soluble, so not used externally, 0.2 per cent at 68°F.
Effect of high temperatures	Set plaster commences to dehydrate above 105°F.
Effect of chemicals	Not affected by chemicals normally likely to come into contact with plasters, except that water causes softening and loss of strength.
Effect of impurities	Very occasionally unslaked particles of lime may be present which expand in due course and blow off pieces of the surface.
Growth of micro-organisms	Undecorated surfaces do not usually support mould growth.
Reaction with other materials	May cause corrosion of embedded metals in damp situations.
Durability	Very durable if kept dry.
Changes and behaviour during use: setting time	Setting time varies from 2-5 min for Class A to 3-4 hours for other Classes.
heat evolution	Appreciable amount of heat evolved, noticeable with Class A.
change in volume	Gypsum plasters expand when setting.

Plaster Board, Gypsum

Type	Plain surfaced
Use	Backgrounds for plastered ceilings. Wall linings, plastered or decorated direct.
British Standard	BS 1230: 1970 (and amendment, July 1973) Gypsum plaster board
Composition	Gypsum plaster faced on both sides with heavy paper.
Manufacture	Continuous process, a wet gypsum plaster mix being fed on to a layer of paper with another being fed on top. Plaster sets quickly, board cut into lengths and dried.
Shape	Rectangular sheets.
Size	Length, up to 2.4m normally. Width, up to 1.2m. Thickness, up to 15mm.
Weight	6.5 - 10.0 kg/m^2 (9.5mm thick).
Modulus of rupture	1.5 - 11 MN/m^2 in dry condition. Strength reduced appreciably when wet.
Impact strength	Relatively low but improved by being plastered.
Nailability	Readily nailable, relatively large-headed nails preferred.
Fire resistance	Used to improve fire resistance of various forms of construction.
Surface spread of flame	Class 1.
Combustibility	Paper lining is combustible.
Effect of chemicals	Not affected by chemicals likely to come into contact with it. Softened by water but hardens on drying.
Effect of impurities	None likely to be present.
Effect of micro-organisms, etc.	None, except possibility of mould growth on wet paper surface.
Thermal conductivity	0.16 W/m °C.
Reaction with other materials	None.
Durability	Very good, if kept dry.

Notes. The above data applies to plain plasterboard. The material may also be obtained with an aluminium foil backing to improve the thermal insulation of constructions in which it is used and also with decorative plastics facings.

Plastics, Cellular Sheets, Boards and Slabs

Material	Expanded polystyrene	Expanded polystyrene	Expanded PVC	Foamed polyurethane	Foamed polyurethane
Type	Beaded	Extruded		Rigid	Flexible
Use	Insulation of walls, roofs and floors	Insulation of walls, roofs and floors	Insulation of walls, roofs and floors	Insulation of walls, roofs, ceilings, etc.	Insulation of pipes and floors
British Standards	BS 3837:1965		BS 3869:1965		
Composition	Polystyrene	Polystyrene	Polyvinyl chloride	Polyurethane	Polyurethane
Method of manufacture	Fusion of expanded beads of polystyrene. Large blocks sliced into sheets.	Extrusion of foamed polystyrene.	Chemical foaming of PVC.	Chemical reaction between two liquid components causes foaming and setting.	
Shape	Sheets, slabs and special shapes	Sheets and slabs	Sheets and slabs	Rigid sheets, blocks and sandwich panels. Available for in situ application.	Sheets, blocks and special shapes
Internal structure	Irregular cells	Fairly regular cells	Cells, 1 mm and upwards	Mainly closed cells, irregular	Mainly regular open cells
Dimensions Width (mm) Length (mm) Thickness (mm)	610, 1220 1220, 1830, 2440 Up to 50	610, 1220 1220, 1830, 2440 Up to 50	600, 1220 1220, 1830, 2440 Up to 50	600-1200 600-2400 25	Various sizes to fit pipes
Density (kg/m^3)	16-40	32-40	24-120	32-60	40-80
Appearance	White	White or dyed in pale colours	Yellow to brown rigid material	Colourless to deep brown	White, grey or coloured
Warmth to touch	Feels warm	Feels warm	Feels warm	Feels warm	Feels warm
Compression strength (N/m^2)	7×10^4 (d=16) 12×10^4 (d=24)	27×10^4	$27\text{-}90 \times 10^4$	17×10^4	$2\text{-}8 \times 10^4$
Resistance to damage by impact	Low	Low	Low	Low	Resilient
Combustibility	Combustible. Softens and collapses	Combustible. Softens and collapses	Combustible	Combustible	Combustible
Spread of flame	Flame-retardant grades available. Increased rate if painted with gloss paints.	Flame-retardant grades available. Increased rate if painted with gloss paints.	Collapses but burns with difficulty.	Flame-retardant grades available	Flame-retardant grades available
Water vapour diffusion 25mm board g/m^2 s bar	0.015 (density 16) 0.0095 (density 24)	0.002 (density 72) 0.0038 (density 40)		0.008	> 0.1
Water absorption (7 days) (Vol. per cent)	Normally low, 2.5-3.0 per cent. Can be high if water does not drain away	1.5 per cent but may be higher if water does not drain away	3.0-3.8	2.5	Up to 10, but may be higher if water does not drain away

Plastics, Cellular Sheets, Boards and Slabs (contd.)

	Expanded polystyrene	*Expanded polystyrene*	*Expanded PVC*	*Foamed polyurethane*	*Foamed polyurethane*
Effect of chemicals	Affected by some organic solvents	Affected by some organic solvents	Very resistant to chemical action	Some are affected by alkali	Chemically resistant
Fungal attack	Resistant	Resistant	Resistant	Resistant	Resistant
Thermal conductivity (W/m °C)	0.033-0.035	0.032-0.035	0.035-0.054	0.020-0.025	0.035
Thermal expansion coefficient (per °C)	$5\text{-}7 \times 10^{-5}$	7×10^{-5}	5×10^{-5}	$2\text{-}7 \times 10^{-5}$	$5\text{-}7 \times 10^{-5}$
Softening point (°C)	86-101	86-101	75-165	150-185	150-185
Max. temperature of use (°C)	80°	80°	65°	100°	100°
Sound transmission (impact)	Appreciable reduction	N.A.	N.A.	Low	May give appreciable reduction
Sound absorption	Low	Low	Low	Low	High
Durability	Durable. Full life not known.	Durable. Full life not known.	Durable. Full life not known.	Durable. Full life not known.	Durable
Ease of cleaning	Not easy to clean. May be decorated with emulsion paint	Not easy to clean. May be decorated with emulsion paint	Requires surface covering before decoration	Will accept surface treatment	Surface retains dirt

Notes. (a) N.A. = non-applicable. (b) Durability assessment is based on proper use of the material.

Plastics, Glass Fibre, Reinforced Sheets

Use	Roof and wall cladding providing diffused natural lighting but use restricted by fire hazard.
British Standards	BS 4154:1967. Corrugated plastics translucent sheets.
Composition	Glass fibre impregnated with polyester resin, with the addition of curing agents. Pigments and fillers may also be added.
Shape	Flat sheets. Standard and non-standard profiled sheets.
Size	Lengths from 1060 to 3050 mm, though longer lengths can be supplied. Widths range from 760 to 1140 mm. Thickness 1.6 mm.
Weight	Flat sheet 1.4 - 1.6 kg/m². The weight per unit area of profiled sheets depends on the profile.
Appearance	Smooth surface. Limited range of standard colours, though non-standard colours are available.
Combustibility	Combustible.
Surface spread of flame	Class 3, but may be improved to Class 1 with flame retardant additions.
Permeability to air	Very low.
Water absorption	0.5 per cent by weight when fully immersed for 24 hours.
Effect of chemicals	Unaffected by materials likely to come into contact with the sheets, apart from areas of high industrial pollution.
Impurities	None present
Effect of micro-organisms, algae, etc.	Immune to insect and vermin attack. Does not nourish mould growth.

Plastics, Glass Fibre, Reinforced Sheets (contd.)

Thermal conductivity	0.03-0.04 W/m °C.	Light transmission	Up to 85 per cent.
Thermal expansion coefficient	2×10^{-5} per °C.	Effect of sunlight	Resistance to sunlight depends upon quality. Colours tend to fade.
		Aggressiveness	Does not affect other materials.
Softening point °C	100-120°C.	Durability	Durable, though full length of life not yet known.
Effect of high and low temperatures	Unaffected by temperatures up to 80°C and down to -40°C.	Ease of working	Can be cut with a wood saw or sheet metal saw.
Effect of frost	Becomes brittle in frosty weather.	Means of fixing	Holes must be drilled for fixing purposes. Nails must not be driven into the sheet.

Plastics, PVC Sheet, Rigid

Use	To provide natural lighting in roofs; also wall claddings.	Effect of micro-organisms, algae, etc.	Immune to insect and vermin attack. Does not nourish mould growth.
British Standards	BS 4203:1967. Extruded rigid PVC sheeting. BS 2782:1970. Methods of testing plastics.		
Composition	Unplasticised polyvinyl chloride.	Thermal conductivity	0.13 W/m°C.
Manufacture	Heated material is extruded through a die and polished by calenders.	Thermal expansion coefficient	5×10^{-5} per °C.
Shape	Flat and corrugated sheets.	Melting point	Softens at 70°C.

Size		Length mm	Width mm
	Flat	1220 to 3050	760
	Corrugated	1220 to 3050	1085

		Thickness mm
	Flat	1.6
	Corrugated	1.6

		Effect of high and low temperatures	Unaffected between 70°C and -40°C.
Weight	2.4 kg/m².	Light transmission	Over 85 per cent for transparent grades. No UV light transmission.
Appearance	Transparent and practically colourless. Coloured, semi-transparent and opaque.	Effect of sunlight	Darkens on long exposure.
Tensile strength	50-60 MN/m². Young's Modulus of elasticity 37 000 MN/m².	Reaction with other materials	No effect.
Impact strength	700-800 N/m².	Durability	Life depends upon extent of atmospheric pollution, but could be in excess of 20 years.
Combustibility	Combustible.	Ease of working	Can be sawn with a fine-tooth saw. The material should be drilled and not punched.
Surface spread of flame	Difficult to ignite, self-extinguishing.	Liability to become dirty	Tendency to become dirty, but easily cleaned.
Permeability to air	Very low.		
Water absorption	Less than 0.15 per cent.		
Effect of chemicals	Slowly attacked in heavily polluted districts.		
Effect of impurities	None present.		

Sealants

Type	Acrylic	Bitumen	Bitumen-rubber	Polysulphide	Polyurethane	Silicone
Grade	Gun	Gun (g), knife (k) and preformed strip (ps)	g, k and ps	g and k 1 and 2 part	g 1 and 2 part	g
Use	Provision of weathertight joints between building materials, components and elements, allowing for dimensional changes and other movements.					
British Standards	BS 3712:——	BS 3712:——	BS 3712:——	BS 4254:1967 (2-part)	BS 3712:——	BS 3712:——
Colour	All colours	Black	Black	Various	Black, grey and cream	Various
Tensile properties per cent movement/joint width	10-15	5 g 5-15 (k, ps)	10	15-25 1-part 20-35 2-part	17-20	8-12
Shear properties per cent movement/joint width	30-40	15-40	30	40-75 1-part 50-75 2-part	40-60	20-40
Adhesion	Fair to Good	Good. Primer required for g and k grades	Fair	Primer required on porous surfaces and on glass	Fair	Good
Rheological properties	Elastic/plastic flow	Plastic flow	Plastic flow	Elastic flow	Elastic flow	Elastic flow
Effect of high and low temperatures	Not affected by temperatures experienced in normal use.					
Effect of sunlight	Slight	Moderate	Moderate	Slight	Slight	Slight
Durability expected life (years)	20	2-10	10-20	20	15	20
Setting time (hours)	12	Does not skin or set	Does not skin or set	24 1-part 6-48 2-part	24	2

Stone, Natural

Type	Limestone Portland Stone	Limestone Bath Stone	Sandstone Yorkstones	Granites	Marbles	Slates	Quartzites
Use	Walling and Cladding		Paving, walling, cladding and coping.	Walling, cladding, plinths, window surrounds and steps.	Window surrounds, cladding, floors and stairs.	Cladding, cills, coping, steps and paving.	Cladding, plinths, paving, floors and stairs.
Composition	Largely calcium carbonate		Quartz in all, mica and felspar grains in some. Bonded largely with silica or calcium carbonate.	Mainly felspar, quartz and mica.	Mainly calcium carbonate.	Mainly silica, alumina and iron oxides.	Mainly quartz.
Method of production	Quarried, cut to size (masoning and sawing), finish as required e.g. patterned, rock faced, fair picked, fine axed, rubbed, eggshell or polished.						Finish-Natural riven

Stone, natural (contd.)

	Limestone Portland Stone	*Limestone* Bath Stone	*Sandstone* Yorkstones	*Granites*	*Marbles*	*Slates*	*Quartzites*
Density (kg/m^3)	2100-2350	2100-2250	2400-3000	2400-2900	2725-2900	2400-2900	about 2600
Compressive strength (MN/m^2)	15-30	10-14	42-85	90-146	About 60	75-200	About 100
Effect of fire	All non-combustible						
Water absorption (per cent)	6-11	7-8	3-4	0.1-0.5	0.1-0.5	$<$ 0.1	0.1-0.5
Moisture expansion (per cent)	About 0.01		Negligible	None	Negligible	Negligible	Negligible
Effect of chemicals	Attacked by acids.	Attacked by acids.	Resistant to most acids.	Resistant to most acids.	Attacked by acids.	Mainly resistant to acids.	Resistant to most acids.
Resistance to effect of soluble salts	Poor-Very Good	Poor-Good	Good	Poor-Good	Good	Good	Good
Thermal expansion (coefficient)	About 4 x 10^{-6} per $^\circ$C.			About 11 x 10^{-6}	About 4 x 10^{-6}	About 11 x 10^{-6}	About 11 x 10^{-6}
Thermal conductivity (W/m$^\circ$C)	About 1.5			About 3.0	About 2.5	About 1.9	About 3.0
Resistance to frost	Poor-Very Good	Poor-Good	Good-Excellent	Good-Excellent	Good-Excellent	Good-Excellent	Good-Excellent
Durability	Dependent on temperature, pollution, moisture content, contact with other materials, etc.						
Ease of working	Fairly easy	Easy	Hard	Hard	Fairly hard	Hard	Hard
Liability to become dirty	Become soiled in urban atmosphere		Become soiled in urban atmospheres.	Resistant to soiling.	Fairly resistant to soiling.	Resistant to soiling.	Resistant to soiling.
Ease of cleaning	Fairly easy to clean		Difficult to clean	Difficult to clean.	Difficult to clean.	Difficult to clean.	Difficult to clean.

Tile, Clay Roof

Types	Plain, single lap; Hand made; Machine made.
Uses	Roofing, but also used for wall cladding.
British Standard	BS 402:--
Composition	Fired clay.
Manufacture	Suitably prepared clays are cast into moulds either by hand or machine, dried and fired, the temperature depending upon the clay.
Shape	Normal shape is rectangular, but various patterns available. Special shapes for ridges, valleys, etc.

Dimensions	*Plain*	*Single lap*
Length	265 mm	340-400 mm
Width	165 mm	200-340 mm
Thickness	9-15 mm	9-15 mm

Weight	Plain 60-70 kg/m^2. Single lap 34-40 kg/m^2.
Appearance	Range of smooth, sand-faced and colour glazed. Natural colours include wide range of browns. Glazed colours include green and blue.

Tile, clay roof (contd.)

Transverse strength	BS min. plain 790 N breaking load, tested wet. Both plain and single lap tiles have more than adequate strength if properly burnt.	Algae growth	Algae grow on tiles that keep damp. Excessive growth indicates porous tiles. Drippings of rain from copper wires kills algae.
Water vapour permeability	Permeable.	Effect of frost	Underfired tiles may have low frost resistance. Some machine-made tiles have a life of 25-40 years, while others have a very long life. Well-burnt hand made tiles, though often more permeable, may have a life measured in centuries. Tiles laid on steep pitches are less affected than those laid on shallow pitches.
Water absorption	BS Limit is 10.5 per cent.		
Drying	Absorbed water dries readily.		
Effect of impurities	Small nodules of lime, if present, may cause 'blowing'.	Durability	Lightly-fired tiles may have a relatively high content of soluble salts adversely affecting the durability by causing disintegration of the nibs.

Tile, Concrete Roof

Types	Plain, single-lap.		Range of colours.
Uses	Roofing primarily, but also wall cladding in the form of tile-hanging.	Transverse strength	BS limits min. breaking load 495N (wet), 675N (dry).
British Standards	BS 473 & 550:——	Water vapour permeability	Fairly permeable.
Composition	Portland cement, clean sand or crushed stone and pigments.	Water absorption	Low.
Manufacture	Cement-sand mix cast or extruded, cured sufficiently to handle. Hardening process continues for a long time.	Water permeability	Very low.
		Drying	Absorbed water dries readily.
Shape	Normal shape is rectangular but various patterns available. Specials for ridges, valleys, etc.	Algae growth	Generally free from algae growth, but may occur on relatively porous tiles.

Dimensions	*Plain*	*Others*
Length	270 mm	380 to 460 mm
Width	165 mm	230 to 380 mm
Thickness	Not less than 9 mm	

		Thermal conductivity	0.5 W/m°C.
Weight	Plain 60-80 kg/m^2. The weight on a roof depends upon the amount of overlap. Single lap 34-45 kg/m^2.	Effect of frost	Tiles unaffected.
		Durability	Excellent.
Appearance	Range of fairly smooth and granule faced surfaces.		

Timbers, Hardwood

Type	Afrormosia	Mahogany African	Oak	Opepe	Sapele	Teak
Use	High class joinery.	Joinery	General	General	General	General
British Standards	See Softwoods.					
Density (kg/m^3)	630-800	520	720	730	560-700	640
Appearance	Fine texture. Yellow-brown	Medium texture. Pinkish brown to deep reddish brown.	Coarse texture. Yellowish brown.	Open texture. Yellow or orange-brown.	Fairly fine texture. Dark reddish- or purplish-brown.	Fine texture. Golden brown.

Timbers, hardwood (contd.)

	Afrormosia	Mahogany African	Oak	Opepe	Sapele	Teak
Compressive strength (MN/m^2)*	22	13 (43)	15 (50)	25 (70)	21 (58)	22
Bending strength (MN/m^2)*	26	15 (80)	21 (92)	31 (110)	23 (110)	26
Impact (related to oak)	40 per cent better	30 per cent inferior	Standard	10-20 per cent inferior	Similar to oak	10-20 per cent inferior
Resistance to insertion and extraction of nails and screws	Marked tendency to split when nailed.	Good nailing and screwing properties.	Holds nails and screws firmly.	Slight tendency to split when nailed but takes screws satisfactorily.	Good nailing and screwing properties.	Fairly good nailing and screwing properties.
Hardness (related to oak)	20 per cent harder	40 per cent softer	Standard	20 per cent harder	Similar to oak	10-20 per cent inferior
Adhesion when glued	Satisfactory	Satisfactory	Satisfactory		Satisfactory	Satisfactory on newly machined surfaces.
Effect of fire	All timbers are combustible but production of charred wood reduces rate of combustion and fire resistance of thick sections is relatively good.					
Surface spread of flame	Class 3 or 4 when untreated, but Class 1 with suitable surface or impregnation treatments (mainly applicable to plywoods).					
Moisture content per cent: at 90 per cent RH	15	20	20	17	Not available	15
at 60 per cent RH	11	13.5	12	12		10
Permeability to preservatives	Extremely resistant	Extremely resistant	Extremely resistant	Moderately resistant	Resistant	Extremely resistant
Dimensional changes per cent 90-60 per cent RH†	1.3 T 0.7 R	1.3-1.8 T 0.8-1.3 R	2.5 T 1.5 R	1.8 T 0.9 R	1.8 T 1.3 R	1.2 T 0.7 R
Resistance to insect attack	Attacked by ambrosia (pin-hole borer) beetles.	Attacked by ambrosia and powder-post beetle.	Sapwood readily attacked by powder-post beetles. Attacked by common furniture beetle. Sapwood and heartwood attacked by death watch beetle.	Generally good resistance.	Sapwood attacked by powder-post beetle.	Sapwood attacked by powder-post beetle.
Effect of fungus	Very durable	Moderately durable	Durable	Very durable	Moderately durable.	Very durable
Linear thermal expansion	The coefficient of linear thermal expansion is relatively small, of the order of 4.5 x 10^{-6} per °C, but individual figures are not available.					
Thermal conductivity	Thermal conductivity is relatively low, of the order of 0.14 W/m °C.					

Timbers, hardwood (contd.)

	Afrormosia	Mahogany African	Oak	Opepe	Sapele	Teak
Reaction with other materials	Becomes stained in contact with ferrous metals and accelerates their corrosion in wet conditions.	No effects	Tannin content leads to deterioration when in contact with ferrous metals. Accelerates the corrosion of metals when wet. Very corrosive action on lead.	No effects	No effects	No effects
Durability	The durability depends largely upon the resistance to fungal attack under conditions conducive to such attack.					
Ease of working - cutting	Medium	Medium (variable).	Medium (variable).	Medium	Medium	Medium
- blunting of tools	Moderate	Moderate (variable).	Moderate (variable).	Moderate	Moderate	Fairly severe

Notes. Single figures are the average of a range which may sometimes be appreciable because of the variation in origin and condition of the various species. Sapwoods of all species are either perishable or non-durable.

† T = Tangential. R = Radial.

* The figures given are for the basic grade (i.e. the best) and refer to the working stresses as classified in CP 112; figures in brackets are the maximum test values.

Timber, Resin-Bonded Wood Chipboard

Type	Standard grades	Flooring grades
Use	Partitions, wall and ceiling linings, roof decking.	Flooring and a base for various floor finishes.
British Standards	BS 2604:—— Resin bonded wood chipboard. BS 1811:—— Methods of test for wood chipboard and other particle boards.	
Composition	Wood chips, asbestos fibres or other materials bonded with resin generally urea formaldehyde.	
Manufacture	Either by pressing or by extrusion, the latter process providing a slightly rougher surface.	
Dimensions	Lengths from 1800 mm to 5200 mm. Widths from 600 mm to 1700 mm. Thickness from 9 mm to 31 mm.	
Density	600-650 kg/m³	675-725 kg/m³
Appearance	Relatively smooth surfaced board, but may be supplied prepared for painting and free from surface blemishes. Available with wood veneer and plastics sheeting finishes. Normal colour of untreated board varies from straw to light yellowish brown.	
Resistance to splitting	Not liable to split	Not liable to split
Screw holding	Face 620N Edge 355N	Face 710N Edge 530N
Combustibility	Combustible	Combustible
Surface spread of flame	Class III. Proprietary finishes will provide Class I.	Class III. Proprietary finishes will provide Class I.

Permeability to water vapour	40 - 80 MN s/g m	40 - 80 MN s/g m
Moisture content	9 per cent ex-works	9 per cent ex-works
Water absorption	6 per cent	4 per cent
Moisture expansion 60 per cent to 90 per cent RH at 20°C.	Length and width 0.2 per cent. Thickness 5 per cent.	Length and width 0.2 per cent. Thickness 5 per cent.
Effect of chemicals	Very slight	Very slight
Insect attack	Not attacked by wood destroying insects but is not immune to termite attack.	
Fungal attack	Liable to fungal attack if moisture content is above 20 per cent.	
Thermal conductivity	0.12 W/m °C.	0.14 W/m °C.
Sound reduction	Thickness 18 mm. 25-26 dB reduction. Reduction for double skins depends upon construction.	Appropriate construction will provide Grade 1 Impact Sound insulation.
Reaction with other materials	Virtually none.	
Durability	Very satisfactory if moisture content is maintained below 20 per cent. May suffer damage if moisture content is higher.	

Timbers, Softwood

Type	REDWOOD		WHITEWOOD		
	Scots pine or Scotch fir	Baltic redwood	Baltic whitewood	Douglas fir	Western red cedar
Use	General	General	General	Particularly useful for structural work.	Particularly useful for outdoor work.
British Standards	BS 565:1972. Glossary of terms relating to timber and woodwork. BS 881 and 569: 1955. Nomenclature of commercial timbers including sources of supply. BS 1186:—— Quality of timber and workmanship in joinery. BS 1297:1970. Grading and sizing of softwood flooring. BS 4261:1968. Glossary of terms relating to timber preservation. CP 112:—— The structural use of timber.				
Density (air dry) kg/m^3	500 (Average figs.)	480	400	500 homegrown 560 imported	370
Appearance	Reddish brown heartwood	Reddish brown heartwood	Pinkish brown heartwood	Pinkish brown heartwood	Reddish brown
Compressive strength parallel to grain (MN/m^2)*	11.4 (48)	11.4 (45)	11.4 (36)	13.3 (55)	8.4 (34)
perpendicular to grain (MN/m^2)*	2.1	2.1	2.1	2.5	1.5
Modulus of rupture parallel to grain (MN/m^2)*	14 (90)	14 (84)	14 (74)	17.5 (96)	10 (56)
Modulus of elasticity (MN/m^2)*	8270 (10 150)	8270 (10 150)	8270 (10 000)	9660 (13 200)	6890 (7600)
Shear strength parallel to grain (MN/m^2)*	1.5	1.5	1.5	1.5	1.25
Impact strength	Softwoods are readily indented by impact.		Softwoods are readily indented by impact.		
Nailability	Good	Good	Good	Harder to nail than most softwoods	Good
Effect of fire	Timber is combustible but the charring action tends to retard combustion and large sections last longer in a fire than comparable sized steel sections.				
Spread of flame	Softwoods except western red cedar are Class 3 but the rate can be reduced by applying fire-retardant paint or by impregnation with certain chemicals.				Class 4.
Moisture content	The moisture content of timber as supplied depends on conditions of drying and subsequent storage. Commonly between 10 and 16 per cent. Varies in use according to humidity of the air and to exposure conditions.				
Permeability to preservatives	Moderately resistant	Moderately resistant	Resistant	Resistant	Resistant
Dimensional changes with changes in moisture content (per cent) (90 - 60 per cent RH)	2.2 Tangential 1.0 Radial	2.2 Tangential 1.0 Radial	1.5 T 0.7 R	1.5 T 1.2 R	0.9 T 0.45 R

Timbers, softwood (contd.)

	REDWOOD		WHITEWOOD		
	Scots pine or Scotch fir	*Baltic redwood*	*Baltic whitewood*	*Douglas fir*	*Western red cedar*
Effect of insects	Softwoods are subject to damage by grubs of the common furniture beetle and in some parts of Surrey by the grubs of the house longhorn beetle.				
Effect of fungi †	Non-durable	Non-durable	Non-durable	Non-durable	Durable
Thermal conductivity	Varies according to density and moisture content. Average value 1.4 - 1.5 W/m °C.				
Linear thermal expansion	4-5 x 10^{-6} per °C.				
Durability	The durability of softwoods depends largely upon their moisture content being below the limit conducive to fungal attack.				Some grades become dark in colour and deteriorate in 10 years.
Ease of working - resistance to cutting	Low	Low	Low	Medium	Low
- blunting effect on tools	Mild	Mild	Mild	Medium	Mild

Notes. * The figures given are for the basic grade (i.e. the best) and refer to the working stresses as classified in CP 112; figures in brackets are maximum test values.

† Timbers are classified in five grades to denote their durability *under conditions favourable to decay.* The grades are: Very durable, Durable, Moderately durable, Non-durable, Perishable. This classification refers to heartwood, sapwood being perishable or non-durable.

The Metric System

For those not familiar with the metric system of measurement the following notes and conversions may be useful.

The metric system is completely decimal. All multiples and sub-multiples (decimal fractions) of units are powers of ten and the names given to the various multiples and sub-multiples are applicable to all units (e.g. 1 kilometre equals 1000 metres and 1 kilowatt equals 1000 watts). Commonly used multiples are kilo (1 000), hecto (100), and deca (10); sub-multiples are deci (0.1), centi (0.01) and milli (0.001).

The basic units are as follows:

	Unit	Symbol
1. Length	metre	m
2. Mass	kilogramme	kg
3. Time	second	s
4. Electric current	ampere (amp)	A

1. Length

1 in	=	25.4 mm
1 ft	=	0.304 m
1 yd	=	0.914 m

2. Area

1 in²	=	645.16 mm²
1 ft²	=	0.092 m²
1 yd²	=	0.836 m²

3. Volume

1 in³	=	16.387 X 10^3 mm³
1 ft³	=	0.028 m³
1 yd³	=	0.764 m³
1 pint	=	0.568 X 10^{-3} m³
1 UK gal	=	4.546 X 10^{-3} m³
1 litre	=	10^{-3} m³

(10^{-3} = 0.001)

4. Mass

1 oz	=	0.028 kg
1 lb	=	0.453 kg
1 cwt	=	50.80 kg
1 ton	=	1016.05 kg ≈ 1.016 tonne

5. Cost per unit

£1/ft	=	£3.28/m
£1/yd	=	£1.093/m
£1/ft²	=	£10.763/m²
£1/yd²	=	£1.196/m²
£1/therm	=	£0.034/kW h
£1/ft³	=	£35.314/m³
£1/yd³	=	£1.308/m³
£1/lb	=	£2.204/kg
£1/cwt	=	£19.684/tonne
£1/ton	=	£0.984/tonne

INDEX